Tommy Burns
Canada's Unknown World Heavyweight Champion

Dan McCaffery

James Lorimer & Company Ltd., Publishers
Toronto, 2000

James Lorimer & Company Ltd. acknowledges the support of the Ontario Arts Council. We acknowledge the support of the Government of Canada through the Book Publishing Industry Development Program (BPIDP) for our publishing activities. We acknowledge the support of the Canada Council for the Arts for our publishing program.

Cover illustration: Nick Shinn

Cataloguing in Publication Data

McCaffery, Dan
  Tommy Burns: Canada's Unknown World Heavyweight Champion

Includes index.
ISBN 1-55028-697-8

1. Burns, Tommy, 1881-1955. 2. Boxers (Sports) – Canada – Biography.
I. Title.

GV1132.B87M32 2000   796.83'092   C00-931904-2

James Lorimer & Company Ltd., Publishers
35 Britain Street
Toronto, Ontario
M5A 1R7

Printed and bound in Canada.

Contents

For my siblings,
Steve, Karen, and Ron,
who have always answered the bell
for me.

Acknowledgements

It is with a great deal of pleasure that I acknowledge the many people around the globe who assisted me during the more than two decades I spent researching this book. First and foremost, I would like to thank relatives of Tommy Burns who provided me with stories and pictures, some of which had never been published. They include his namesake, Noah Brusso, Jean Gateman, Audrey Adamson, Barb Forester, Lynne Rusnell and Phyllis Huddart. Others who helped piece together his early life include Ted Huehn, whose father was one of Tommy's boyhood chums, and Verdun Wendorf, whose father gave the future champ a job washing wagons in Hanover, Ontario. Thanks also to Fred Phipps, whose father was one of Burns's sparring partners.

I would also like to thank heavyweight boxing champions Muhammad Ali and the late Joe Louis (both of whom I had the chance to interview in the 1970s when they were head-table guests at sports celebrity dinners in Sarnia, Ontario). Other prizefighters who gave me a feel for what it's like to be in the ring included Canadians Tim Taylor and Ray Sayers.

The staffs of many worldwide institutions were helpful as well. They include the National Archives of Canada, Irish National Library, State Library of New South Wales, Australia, Michigan State University Library, the University of Western Ontario Weldon Library, the International Boxing Hall of Fame, the Tacoma Public Library, in Tacoma, Washington, the Owen Sound–Grey County Museum and the Hanover Public Library. Special thanks to Allen Stewart of the Canadian Sports Hall of Fame and to Ed McArthur of the Canadian Boxing Hall of Fame. In the Yukon, I would like to thank Darrell Hookey, who provided me with material on Billy Woods.

Others who were of great assistance include noted boxing historians Kevin Smith, an expert on black fighters from 1900 to 1930; Tracy Callis, who has meticulously assembled the won-lost records of many obscure fighters from the Burns era; and Rosemarie Pleasant, an expert on Sam Langford. Thanks also to Dave Menary, a former sports writer with the *Cambridge Times*, who interviewed people who knew Burns for a series of stories he wrote in 1996. The late Red Wilson of the *Sarnia Observer* was also a great help. Although Tommy's career ended shortly before Red became a sports writer, he did hear valuable stories about the champ from oldtime journalists who had known Burns in his early days. Larry Roberts, who has put together a splendid Burns web site, was especially generous with photos of Tommy and his opponents.

Others who helped in various ways include *Lansing Journal* reporter Paul Egan, who gave me a place to stay while I was conducting research in Michigan; Barbara Eaton, Mary Craig, Robert and Marion Gilbert, the late Al Rosaasen, Paul Jerome, Marc Haslip, John Tuck and Jim Quantrell.

At James Lorimer and Co. Ltd., I would like to thank Jim Lorimer and Diane Young, who made many helpful suggestions on how to improve the manuscript, and Ward McBurney, who saw the book through production. I would also like to thank Laura Ellis for her thorough copyedit; the book is much better for her efforts. Thanks also to Garth Woolsey of the *Toronto Star* for his insights.

Last but not least, heartfelt thanks to old friend Mary-Jane Egan and my wife, Val, for their encouragement and support.

Introduction

This book is about a Canadian hero whose legend was lynched by racist American reporters.

More specifically, it's the story of Tommy Burns, the trail-blazing World Heavyweight Boxing Champion whose remarkable feats were belittled during his lifetime and ignored after his death because he refused to boycott black fighters.

Burns was one of the most influential athletes of the past hundred years — the man who broke the infamous "colour line" in big-time sports and the father of the mega-money athletic events we know today. Yet he's been discarded by history, the victim of a cruel and unfair smear campaign that has gone unchallenged for almost a century.

Like so many other poor kids of his generation, Burns turned to pugilism as a way to escape a life of grinding poverty. At the tender age of 19 he became a prizefighter, hoping for a career that would bring him wealth and renown. But unlike so many of his peers, he found what he was looking for. Anxious to escape dead-end jobs as a labourer, he entered the professional boxing circuit, where he immediately excelled at the dangerous and brutal game of fistfighting. Driven by ambition, a fiercely competitive spirit and a blustering public persona that hid a life-long inferiority complex, he knocked out opponents at an almost unbelievable pace, quickly becoming one of the most outstanding athletes who ever lived. He stood only 5'7" and seldom weighed more than 172 pounds, but he beat the best boxers from the middleweight division up. In just eight years, from 1901 to 1909, he won five titles, including the World Heavyweight Boxing Championship, the world light-heavyweight crown, the British Empire heavyweight title and both the Michigan and United States Pacific Coast middleweight thrones. If all that wasn't enough, he also narrowly missed becoming World Middleweight Boxing Champion as well.

Despite his success, however, Burns was never very popular with American sports writers. For one thing, he'd taken the most prestigious sporting title of the era — the World Heavyweight Boxing Championship — away from a citizen of the U.S. For another, he kept embarrassing them by winning fight after fight that they'd predicted he'd lose. But worst of all, in the eyes of many American scribes, was the fact that Tommy Burns occasionally fought black boxers. Past champions, including such legendary figures as John L. Sullivan, Gentleman Jim Corbett and James J. Jeffries, had openly drawn what was called the "colour line." The enormously popular Sullivan went so far as to issue a newspaper challenge in which he declared, "In this challenge I include all fighters — first come, first served — who are white. I will not fight a negro. I never have and I never shall."[1] Jeffries was more crude. He publicly declared, "I've got no use for any living nigger."[2] Corbett suggested it wasn't necessary to fight blacks because they were physically and mentally inferior to Caucasians. "I don't think you often get a dead-game nigger," he told one reporter. "Weight for weight and cleverness for cleverness, I back the white man all the time."[3] These men were not censured in any way for their outrageous and cowardly conduct. On the contrary, they were applauded by fans and journalists alike.

But Burns was different. He announced he'd fight all comers, regardless of race or religion. "I draw no colour line, nor bar any man in the world," he said in a public statement issued at the height of his career.[4] Included among the men he battled were seven blacks, a Jew and a North American native Indian. More disturbing than that, in the minds of many of his contemporaries, was the fact that he hired two African-American sparring partners, often socialized with people of colour and even formed a close friendship with a black fighter. Early on in his career, he was derisively dubbed "the nigger lover."[5]

Despite the hostility of the press, Burns soon won the fame he sought. Indeed, it's safe to say that when he captured the world heavyweight title in 1906 he became the first internationally recognized celebrity his young country had ever produced. The *Montreal Star*

Burns demonstrates his punch-blocking technique.

certainly recognized this feat, declaring, "The brawny Canadian who won the pugilistic championship will probably do more to make people learn what particular dot on the top of the map represents Canada than all our poets since Dumonts and Champlain made their first land fall on this side of the Atlantic."

In addition to being famous, Burns was extraordinarily active. During the two years and 10 months he held the heavyweight crown, he defended it a record 14 times. In the past, world champions had tended to rest on their laurels, sometimes going two or three years at a time without entering the ring. The first champ of the modern era, the legendary John L. Sullivan, defended his title just three times in 10 years. His conqueror, Gentleman Jim Corbett, fought only twice in five years. The Canadian also became the first champion to take his show on the road. Before Burns, all the titleholders had been Americans, and all their bouts had been staged in the United States. But Burns changed that, travelling the globe to seek out and defeat the best boxers in North America, Europe, Africa and Australia.

A colourful and flamboyant man, he created headlines wherever he went. Along the way he also amassed a small fortune. In an age when working people made $500 a year if they were lucky, Burns once collected $30,000 for a single fight. By the time he retired in 1920, he was one of the richest professional athletes who had ever lived. And his reign paved the way for the athletes who followed, allowing some of them to make countless millions of dollars. On top of all that, he helped revolutionize training methods, developing techniques that are still in use by athletes around the world.

Despite his accomplishments, Burns received no credit from a public that could not accept his decision to break the colour line. His detractors, who began looking for ways to discredit him the moment he first stepped into the ring with a black athlete, got their chance to destroy his reputation after he agreed to fight a hulking African-American heavyweight named Jack Johnson. Johnson defeated Burns in a closely contested bout, becoming the first black World Heavyweight Boxing Champion in history. The openly racist American press was almost hysterical over this development. In a front-page editorial, the *New York Times* noted there was widespread dissatisfaction with Johnson's win and a general feeling that "there is a need to do something about it at once."

Anxious to see Johnson dethroned, the press launched a crusade to find a "Great White Hope" who could beat him. That was the plan for the long term. In the short term, reporters decided the best way to discredit the new champ was by running down Burns. The Canadian, they wrote, was a "second rater" and a "lemon," who had won the title almost by accident. It was no credit to Johnson, they said, to have beaten such a pathetic excuse for a champion. Some even questioned Burns's courage, claiming Johnson had "chased" him across the planet to secure a title shot. They wrote wildly inaccurate accounts of the Burns-Johnson fight, claiming it had been the most one-sided contest in the history of boxing. Johnson had suffered a bloody mouth and two broken ribs in the fight, but these facts were covered up. And the public was assured by no less an authority than famous novelist Jack London that most of Burns's ring victories had been scored at the expense of mediocre fighters.

The truth was much different. Burns had, in fact, defeated two world champions and the best boxers on four continents. Four of his opponents would eventually be honoured in the International Boxing Hall of Fame. But the smear campaign worked. Johnson refused to give Burns a rematch, and other leading contenders ignored him as well. Within a generation Burns was all but forgotten, even in Canada. When he died in 1955, only four people attended his burial, and he was interred in an unmarked pauper's grave. Canada's sad tradition of ignoring its heroes had been taken to a shameful extreme.

I first heard about Tommy Burns in 1974, shortly after I interviewed Muhammad Ali for a newspaper article. The fabled Ali, who was about to reclaim his title from George Foreman, told me one of the fighters he admired the most was Jack Johnson, the first black heavyweight champion. Looking up Johnson's record, I was astonished to discover he'd won the crown by beating a Canadian named Tommy Burns. Although I made my living as a sports writer and was a boxing fan, I'd been completely unaware of the fact that Canada had ever produced a world heavyweight champion.

At first I could find out very little about Burns. His biography had never been written, and his only published work was a short how-to book called *Scientific Boxing and Self-Defence*. Although interesting in its own right, it tells the reader precious little about Burns the man or the fighter. He is mentioned from time to time in boxing histories, but usually only in the most derogatory of terms. His name is never mentioned when boxing magazines, authors or fight fans discuss the greatest heavyweights in history. At least one author is on record as saying Burns was the worst heavyweight champion who ever lived. Sadly, the unjust criticisms and outright lies written after his defeat at the hands of Jack Johnson have been accepted verbatim by modern ring historians, almost all of whom have virtually ignored him. Nevertheless, I found myself fascinated by Burns, partly because of his small size. At 5'7" he was by far the shortest heavyweight champ in history. How, I wondered, had a man of his stature managed for any time at all to rule the giants who populated the heavyweight division?

Delving further into his story, I was astonished to discover that nearly a century after his career ended, Burns still held some records. Indeed, the greatest legends of the ring have failed time and again to beat some of the standards set by this compact fighter. When Joe Louis defended his title twice in five weeks in the 1940s, some thought he'd established a new benchmark, only to discover Burns had once taken on two challengers in a single night! During Rocky Marciano's reign over the heavyweight division in the 1950s, many assumed the 5'10" fighter was the shortest titleholder in history, not realizing he was three inches taller than Burns. When Muhammad Ali knocked out Sonny Liston just one minute and 42 seconds into their 1965 title fight, many thought it was the fastest KO ever recorded by a heavyweight champ, only to read Burns had once turned the trick in one minute and 28 seconds. As 1980s champion Larry Holmes closed in on Burns's record of eight consecutive knockouts by a heavyweight king, he chortled, "I'm going to make Tommy Burns famous."[6] Unfortunately for Holmes, he failed to break the Canadian's mark, and no one else has since. And when Lennox Lewis defeated Evander Holyfield in November 1999, many thought he'd become the first British Commonwealth resident to win the undisputed heavyweight title, only to find out Burns had beaten him to the mark by 93 years.

Before long it was clear to me that Burns was one of the best *pound for pound* boxers who ever lived. He was a middleweight by today's standards, but he easily handled gigantic men who stood a foot taller than him and outweighed him by as much as 60 pounds. From a saloon in Nome, Alaska, to a 25,000-seat outdoor stadium specially built in

Sydney, Australia, to accommodate all the fans who wanted to see him fight, he took part in 62 bouts, winning all but a handful.

If Burns was so terrible, I thought, why hadn't anyone broken the records he'd set so long ago? I was also curious to find out what motivated him. What was it that drove a small man to take up such a savage occupation? Why would anyone, for that matter, want to spend much of his life doing something that most people would rather avoid entirely — getting into fistfights?

I spent countless hours poring over old newspaper and magazine articles and checked the records of the Canadian Sports Hall of Fame and the International Boxing Hall of Fame to find the answers. Along the way I had the good fortune to locate major excerpts from Burns' unpublished memoirs, which contained the sad details of his failed marriages, his uneven business dealings and other aspects of his tragic personal life.

Slowly but surely the truth began to emerge. Recognized or not, Burns was a great champion who forever changed the face of professional sports. Had he been an American, his story would be legendary. He'd be lionized as the boxer who had demanded fair treatment for people of colour; heralded as the trail-blazer who had insisted professional athletes be allowed to make a decent living; celebrated as the underdog who repeatedly found a way to win. After I'd poked far enough into Burns's story I knew I wanted to right a terrible wrong. I wanted to restore the reputation of a true Canadian hero. This book represents that attempt.

Dan McCaffery
Sarnia, Canada
May 2000

1

A Deeply Troubled Youth

Tommy Burns, one of the most colourful, innovative and tragic sports heroes of the twentieth century, was born in a little log cabin just outside Hanover, Ontario, Canada, on June 17, 1881.

Before he reached 28 years of age he would defeat nearly 50 men in bloody prizefights and become one of the most famous sports figures on the planet. He was the quintessential underdog, a real-life Rocky Balboa who continually overcame the odds to become a world champion.

Yet Burns was a complicated, even paradoxical man. In his youth he was addicted to violence and often filled with hatred. But later in life he became a minister of religion, touring far and wide to deliver sermons about the power of love. As a young boxer he insisted, at great personal cost, that black athletes be given a fair shake. But at the same time he believed people of colour were inferior to whites, realizing only late in life that all human beings are created equal. He was a money-grubber who held out for the highest purse before a fight. But he once gave his last dime to establish a sports program for needy inner-city kids. He could be a modest, shy individual one minute; a boisterous, tiresome braggart the next. In the ring he was a ruthless adversary who showed his opponents no mercy. Yet once his fights were over he heaped praise on his adversaries and often treated them to dinner.

Some saw him as a skilled, courageous fighter, while others dismissed him as a puffed-up paper tiger. Was he a great athlete who forever changed the face of professional sports or a phoney champion who had no business wearing the world heavyweight championship belt? To get to the bottom of the Tommy Burns legend, it is essential to understand

A Hanover-area 19th century log cabin similar to the one Burns was born in, shown here at the Owen Sound–Grey County museum.

just how complex a person he was. And to understand the forces that shaped his personality, we must go back to the beginning.

From the start, Burns, whose real name was Noah Brusso, had a hard life. The twelfth of thirteen children born to a German-Canadian cabinet-maker named Fredrick Brusso and his wife, Sofa Dankert, he was raised in stark poverty in the rural, rolling hill country of western Ontario. The family home, built in 1850, had only four rooms, which meant there was almost no privacy for any of its inhabitants. And because Fredrick earned less than $20 a week, it was difficult for him to put food on the table. On many nights, Noah would recall later, he went to bed hungry.

Even if the Brussos had had money, they would have found little in Hanover to spend it on. It was a small town devoid of entertainment or cultural attractions. Most of the public buildings were churches or blacksmiths' shops. The dusty, unpaved streets did contain a few taverns and a couple of general stores, but they weren't of much interest to young Noah.

Because Fredrick was often unable to pay the rent, the family was forced to move frequently. By the time Noah reached his mid-teens, he had lived in Hanover, Chesley, Hepwarth and Preston, all small Ontario communities. These experiences robbed him of any sense of having a home town. They may also explain why he was willing to lead such a nomadic life as an adult. In an age when few people journeyed more than a hundred kilometres from home during their entire lives, Brusso would live in twenty communities located in four countries on three continents.

In addition, his boyhood was haunted by a nagging fear of death. Child mortality rates were high in late nineteenth century Canada. Five of Noah's siblings would die before reaching adulthood, and neighbouring homes were hit just as hard. For those who survived to adulthood, the average life expectancy of a Canadian was just 47 years. The leading causes of death included typhoid, diptheria and malaria. Even the common cold was feared because it could lead to pneumonia, which was often fatal. Doubtlessly, young Brusso was deeply affected by the loss of so many brothers and sisters. Their deaths are among the very few facts about his personal life that he mentions in his book *Scientific Boxing and Self-Defence.*

Ted Huehn, whose father was one of young Brusso's buddies, recalled that the future prizefighter faced other trials as well. "Dad told me [Noah] used to have to go to school in bare feet. The kids used to all make fun of him. The only time he was allowed to wear shoes was to church. He used to hide his shoes by a corner fence and put them on just before he went into class."[1]

Inside the one-room stone schoolhouse, which still stands today, Noah had to cope with conditions that twenty-first century children could not imagine. Describing the Ontario school system of the era, author Peter C. Newman wrote,

> Students were perhaps crowded in two to a desk, sweltering if they were too close to the enormous stove, or freezing if they were across the room. Grades one to eight were all packed together, and a normal morning might see one grade reciting, another reading at their desks, and a third working at the blackboard.
>
> But the central purpose of the schools was not just the three "R" s. The 1890s still held to a traditional tenet of the school system: that childish enthusiasm had to be dampened and curbed,

Burns with two of his sisters.

and youthful spirit bent to conformity. As Miss Eliza Bolton of the Ottawa Model Normal School noted in an address to the Ontario Educational Association in 1892, if dogs and other domestic animals are trained from birth, should not the young offspring of human beings be so too?[2]

Reared in a Methodist household with strict Victorian standards of responsibility and morality, Noah was expected to perform chores from the time he could walk. And if he failed to pull his weight, he faced harsh discipline. That fact was graphically illustrated in a comical — yet disturbing — story told in his unpublished memoirs. The boy, who was only 12 at the time, was scheduled to play a lacrosse game one fall afternoon when his father ordered him to stay home and chop wood instead. But when the horse-drawn team buggy arrived to pick him up, the other players told Noah his dad had changed his mind and had agreed to let him play.

"I was surprised, but they all insisted that he had told them, so I went into the house and got my lacrosse stick and suit."

His mother, Sofa, speaking in a low tone, expressed doubts that his father had agreed to let him go, but Noah grabbed his gear and took his leave. It was a wild game, with young Brusso scoring the winning goal in the final seconds. After the contest, a wheel fell off the buggy and Noah didn't get home until nightfall. He was so afraid of what his father might do to him that he sneaked into the house through the back door and tiptoed up to his room. "As I was getting into bed my mother came up and told me that Pa had waited up until 1 o'clock to give me a whipping," he recalled. Sofa, who knew how brutal her husband could be, gathered up armfuls of newspapers and stuffed them inside Noah's pants and nightshirt for protection. "I got no sleep that night thinking about the whipping I was to get, and how to avoid it if possible," he admitted.

At first light he heard his father get up. But Fredrick, assuming Noah had failed to come home the night before, didn't bother to check his bedroom before heading off to work. "After he had left I got up and went downstairs, still with my newspapers under my clothes," he recalled. "After breakfast I sawed wood all morning. About 11 o'clock I asked my mother to put some more papers under my pants as I knew that Pa would soon be home for lunch."

As soon as Fredrick came through the door he called his son into the kitchen.

"I thought I told you not to play lacrosse yesterday!"

"Dad, the boys told me they had talked to you and you said I could go."

Fredrick replied that he hadn't talked to any of the players, then ordered Noah to eat lunch. Moments later, he asked, "Was it a good game?"

"Yes."

"Who got the winning goal?"

"Me."

With that, Noah's father reached into his pocket, pulled out a dollar bill and handed it to his son. "My scoring that winning goal saved me from a whipping," Noah wrote. "I learned later that the boys had seen Pa and told him what a great game I had played."[3]

A devout Christian, Fredrick hoped his second youngest child would grow up to become a minister. Sofa was a loving, if overly protective, parent, who worried constantly about Noah's health. Her dream was that the boy, whom she dubbed "Lil Noah," would become a famous painter. It was soon clear, however, that he didn't have the temperament to follow either path. Noah was an aggressive, hyperactive lad who was forever getting into schoolyard tussles. A boyhood friend recalled in a 1907 letter to the *London Free Press* that "Brusso, from his earliest days exhibited strong fighting propensities and would rather fight than eat. He was always ready for a scrap and any arguments he became involved in were usually settled with his fists. I attended the same school and even fought with him, getting rather the worst of the argument."[4]

Brusso admitted he loved fighting, but insisted there wasn't a mean bone in his body. "Even as a child, I enjoyed boxing, more for self-defence than to hurt anyone," he wrote in his unpublished memoirs. "We children did not have very much in the way of organized athletics or supervised recreation, so the natural result was plenty of free-for-all fighting during recess and after school."[5]

Unfortunately, his high-strung nature made him a mediocre student. He found it difficult to concentrate for any length of time and, as a consequence, both his grades and his self-esteem suffered. His superiors tried to channel his aggression into sports, entering him in a bare-knuckle boxing tournament for boys aged 10 to 12. Noah trounced three opponents to win first place. His description of this barbarous event — written a half century later — is a revealing commentary on the primitive society he was raised in:

> I shall never forget the fight I had with Sam Hill, to settle the school championship. We met after a series of elimination bouts, which left us — logical opponents — to settle, once and for all, who was really the 'boss man' at that little school.
>
> At last the prearranged day arrived and we met in a big vacant lot at the rear of the school. At least a hundred children were there, in addition to people from town who wanted to see the fun. The news had leaked out, and Sam was favoured in the betting, as he outweighed me and had a slightly longer reach.
>
> I figured I was in for plenty of trouble, so I kept away from Sam, boxing, dancing and skipping around. The crowd surged in and out around us, enjoying the scrap immensely. I finally ran into one of Sam's blows, which floored me. After a good rest, we went

The School where Burns won a boxing tournament at age 10.

at it again and I knew then that I had his number. His punches had lost their original force, so I began to box freely. The going got hard, but we were at it about an hour before he was finally played out. Too tired to properly defend himself, he allowed me to slip through his guard and land a solid punch in the solar plexus. The blow did not seem so hard to me, but he gave me an odd glazed look and slowly collapsed, like a deflating balloon. At 10, I was champion of the school. [6]

The youngster was thrilled with his achievement — and the attention it got him. His parents, however, were almost beside themselves with anger — an entirely understandable reaction. To encourage small boys to fight with bare fists for over an hour, until one collapsed, while adults stood by cheering and laying bets, was shocking behaviour even for those times.

For Sofa, the boxing contest was the last straw. She had never approved of the brutal discipline used at the school. And no wonder. The *Hanover Post* weekly newspaper had reported punishments ranging from the strap to being locked in a dark closet. Nor did she like the fact that the pupil-teacher ratio was a staggering 75–1. After hearing about Noah's pugilistic triumph she was so distaught that she yanked him out of class and put him to work as a finisher in a nearby furniture factory. Thus, at age 10, Noah joined the army of two million children who toiled in the North American workforce of the period. Their average wage was just 25¢ a day. Proving he wasn't afraid of hard work, Noah took a second job washing freight wagons at Hanover's train station. Later, Sofa got him a job at the sawmill owned by her brother, Ben Dankert, where Noah piled lumber for a dollar a day. He hated the work, quit after a week and never went near his uncle again.

During off-hours Sofa helped him polish his limited reading and writing skills. Years later, Noah proved she'd done a good job by writing two books, one of which was published. But try as she might, his mother couldn't curb his restlessness. Once, along with his cousin, George Brusso, he horrified the family by scaling the outside of a tall Hanover church spire. This time, Fredrick did take the boy out to the woodshed. No amount of discipline, however, seemed to help. As he entered his teens young Brusso was in real danger of becoming a juvenile delinquent. On at least two occasions a police constable brought him home after he was caught fighting in public. It was one thing to get into schoolyard scraps as a small child, he was told, but it was quite another to brawl in the streets as a young adult.

One of his relatives, Phyllis Huddart, described how Noah was considered such a bad egg that some family members would have nothing to do with him. "My mother wouldn't allow his name to be mentioned because she didn't think too much of him," she recalled in a 1999 interview. "She thought he was a bad influence on my father, who was his first cousin."[7]

In many ways Brusso was a product of his time and place. It was an age in which children learned from adults that violence was an acceptable way of achieving goals. Almost from the time he was old enough to walk Noah was beaten by his father, strapped by his teachers and challenged to fights by his peers. Fistfighting was an everyday fact of life for young Canadian males in those days. It was how they settled even their most minor differences. And anyone who refused to accept a fight would be shunned as a coward.

Sofa, hoping female companionship would smooth out her son's rough edges, encouraged Noah to find a girlfriend. He was a handsome youth,

The teenaged Burns in his first suit.

with sparkling blue eyes, dark hair, a full mouth and a straight nose. More than a few people commented that he resembled a young Napoleon. Before long, females were clamouring for his attention, and he was not shy about asking them out. Long after he died, a Mrs. Bert Peters told reporters that a teenaged Brusso had proposed to her. She found him a little too pugnacious for her liking, however, and ended up marrying the leader of a band instead. "I made a mistake," she joked. "I married a musician instead of the millionaire."[8]

Around the same time that he discovered dating, Noah also developed a keen interest in sports that likely saved him from becoming just another hooligan. He played baseball and lacrosse all summer, football and soccer in the autumn and hockey throughout the winter. He broke his right arm in a football game, but the injury barely slowed him down. At one point he was starring for three different hockey clubs at the same time. He even found time for diving, swimming and speed-skating competitions. By his fourteenth birthday, Noah, who was endowed with exceptionally powerful legs, was one of the fastest skaters in the country, finishing third at the 1895 Ontario skating championships.

In an extraordinary display of audacity, he then challenged world speed-skating champion J. R. McCullough to a three-mile race. McCullough took his youthful opponent too lightly and was trailing with only half a mile to go. The champion barely won with the help of a late surge, beating the teenager to the finish line by a single second. He'd come within an eyelash of a humiliating defeat. It was the first time a world-class athlete had underestimated young Brusso, but it would not be the last. Later, Noah got a glimpse of the money that could be made in sports when Canadian speed-skating champion Whit Hammond rented the local arena and challenged him to three races, with the winner to receive a silver cup filled with silver dollars. A sell-out crowd turned up, with most of the spectators betting their money on Brusso. To make sure he'd win, they went so far as to knock corner barrels into Hammond's path. But the champion leapt right over them and won all three races.

Driven from home

Around this time Noah was hit with a terrible personal shock. His father died in 1896, and the family moved to Preston, near Berlin (now Kitchener), Ontario. Sofa ran a boarding house, and Noah took a job in a moulding foundry to help keep the family afloat. He made just 40¢ a day, and the work was hot, dirty and dangerous. Once, a co-worker named Henry Wagner was horribly burned in an accident. "He was carrying a ladle of molten metal and in some manner stumbled," the *Galt Weekly Reporter* noted the next day. "The foot was terribly burned, the toes being fairly carbonized, and it is likely that part of the foot will have to be amputated."

Life for the 16-year-old Brusso was hard, and it was about to get worse. In 1897 Sofa married a brutish fellow named Hans Kuhlman. It was a loveless match, entered into primarily to relieve the family's financial woes. Noah found himself living with an alcoholic stepfather who openly disliked him. Kuhlman constantly ridiculed the teenager, telling him he'd never amount to anything. His sporting activities, which were so crucial to his self-esteem, were dismissed as a "foolish waste of time and energy."[9] He should, his stepfather added, be doing more to help support the family.

On one occasion, after Noah committed the sin of sleeping in past 7 A.M., Kuhlman marched into his bedroom and clubbed the boy over the head with a baseball bat, inflicting a deep scalp wound. He then punched and kicked him several times, leaving Noah with a scar on the bridge of his nose for the rest of his life. After he had regained his senses,

Noah could likely have beaten the older man within an inch of his life. But, unsure of what to do, the humilitated youngster kept silent. Embarrassed by what had happened, he told friends the cut on his nose had been caused by a dog bite.

The attack would have a profound influence on Noah's future. It may even explain why he eventually took up prizefighting. As amateur boxer and novelist George Garrett once noted, "People went into this brutal and often self-destructive activity for a rich variety of motivations, most of them bitterly anti-social and verging on the psychotic. Most of the fighters I knew of were wounded people who felt a deep, powerful urge to wound others at real risk to themselves."[10]

Kuhlman kept after the boy relentlessly, finally driving him out of the house. The end came after Noah used one of his pay cheques, which was for $40, to buy his first suit. It was a smart-looking garment, and the 17-year-old beamed with pride as he came through the door to show it off to his mother. His stepfather exploded in rage when he saw Noah dressed in such fancy attire.

"You selfish, useless bastard! You spent every cent you have! Not a penny for the family. Get out, and don't come back."[11]

Sofa never forgave her second husband for driving away "Lil Noah," and after Kuhlman died she wouldn't use his first name. "She called him Kuhlman," her granddaughter, Audrey Adamson, recalled. "He wasn't too popular with the family."[12]

Noah moved to the nearby village of Hespeler, where he took a job in a woollen mill, spinning yarn and weaving cloth. During his spare time he played soccer for the village squad. Once, in a game at Drumbo, he was challenged to a fight by the home team's biggest player, a muscle-bound blacksmith. Recalling the incident in 1980, local historian Stan Markarian wrote, "Brusso left-hooked him in the stomach and followed with a right uppercut to the jaw. The blacksmith crumpled to the ground, his ego deflated and his reputation as the town strong man gone with the wind."[13] After the fight Noah was invited to join the Hespeler boxing club, which was run by C. M. Schultz, the local postmaster. He enjoyed the workouts but gave no thought to becoming a professional fighter.

One day as he was playing catch at lunch-hour, the manager of the Galt lacrosse team approached and invited him to join the club. Noah Brusso was about to be introduced to the blood sport of big-time lacrosse.

The fighting goalie

If ever there was a good training ground for boxing it was the brand of field lacrosse played in Canada in the last years of the nineteenth century. It was a violent, rough-and-tumble game in which players routinely clubbed one another over the head, back and shoulders with their sticks. Fistfights were almost as common as goals. The game was so vicious that one Toronto team purchased a sewing kit so its trainer could stitch up any players who suffered facial cuts on road trips. "The move is a wise one, as the physicians' bill for stitching up the boys at Cornwall aggregated $12," the Toronto *Globe* reported in the fall of 1899. The newspaper added, "Some of the members have suggested an ambulance corps should accompany the team."

During one particularly savage game at St. Catharines, Ontario, the home team openly declared it would disable any Orangeville player who dared to even touch the ball. The first visitor to do so was kicked so viciously that one of his kidneys ruptured. Before the match was over, a second Orangeville man had suffered a fractured kneecap, a third sustained a punctured lung and a fourth required seven stitches to close a scalp wound. When the Orangeville players attempted to leave the field early, they were hemmed in by hundreds of hostile St. Catharines fans. The frightened athletes protested to the referee but, possibly fearing for his own safety, he allowed the game to continue. Afterwards, two members of the home team were jailed for assault causing bodily harm. Such incidents caused the *Canadian Sportsman* magazine to declare, "Lacrosse is killing itself, it is too savage."

In spite of the brutality, or perhaps because of it, the game was enormously popular with the public. Spectator sports were just coming into fashion at this time, and Canadians couldn't get enough of them. The pioneer era was ending, and people had more time — and money — for recreational pursuits. Although it's hard to believe now, lacrosse was the most popular game in the country. Major-league baseball was just getting off the ground, basketball had yet to be invented and the National Hockey League didn't exist. So whenever a lacrosse game was staged, huge crowds turned out. Championship matches were so popular that mayors of the opposing communities would declare civic holidays so everyone could attend.

Because he was so much smaller than the other players, Noah was soon inserted into the net, where he quickly developed into a top-notch goalie. His cat-like reflexes caught the attention of reporters. After Galt upset Toronto 7–1 in a crucial match, the *Globe* informed shocked readers, "The contest was much closer than the result would show. The work of Brusso, the Galt goalkeeper, was magnificent, he proving invulnerable."

Noah, however, was doing more than just blocking shots. He was right in the thick of the nasty fights that were commonplace at every lacrosse match. The *London Free Press* reported,

Brusso has a defence all his own. The ordinary goaltender relies upon his stick to protect the net, but Brusso has never lost sight of the fact that hands were known long before lacrosse sticks. Accordingly, when an aggressive person approaches Brusso's net in a way that implies familiarity, Brusso not infrequently meets the intruder with what is technically known as a "stiff punch."

In the ruthless world of lacrosse, players had to fight to survive. Nevertheless, Noah's conduct made him the most hated player in the league. Inevitably, his antics got him into trouble with referees, who began tossing him out of games on a regular basis. Desperate to keep him in the line-up, Galt's coach began bribing Noah to stay out of trouble. The team, which paid its players $25 per week, offered him a $50 bonus for each match he completed without receiving a game misconduct. With that incentive, he managed to control his hot temper for the rest of the season.

With Noah behaving himself, Galt won the Canadian junior lacrosse championship, losing just 3 of 20 games. Along the way, Brusso posted an astonishing total of five shutouts. As far as the *Galt Weekly Reporter* was concerned, the only way the opposition could beat him was by luck. After he narrowly missed his sixth shutout in a game against St. Marys, the newspaper noted, "The fact that they did score was because Brusso was for the moment out of his goal and the ball shot through unhindered." In a league in which teams routinely scored 10 to 12 goals per contest, Noah seldom surrendered more than one or two. Time and again he was the difference between victory and defeat. In one particularly memorable game, Guelph dominated Galt throughout the early going, only to find itself trailing 6–0. As Noah continued to slam the door with one dazzling save after another, his opponents became increasingly frustrated. At half-time they simply gave up, walked off the field and went home.

Brusso's remarkable skill also led his junior team to victories over much older and bigger players from the Brampton intermediates and the Fergus seniors. Brampton scored just twice before going down to an embarrassing 7–2 defeat. Against the vaunted Fergus Thistles he was even more impressive, giving up only one goal — and a disputed one at that — in backstopping Galt to an unlikely 3–1 triumph. His work in that contest again gained him national attention. A Toronto writer reported Noah had "turned back one charge after another." What made the victory all the more remarkable was the difference in the sizes of the clubs. Brusso and his buddies had vanquished "as fine an athletic body of men as Ontario can produce, averaging easily 155 pounds a man. Their speed, agility and strength were marvellous, and their endurance correspondingly great. The local players will not tip the scales at more than an average of 130 pounds, yet they scored three goals to their opponents' one. The solitary goal was disallowed by the umpire, but the referee [who was from Fergus] over-ruled his decision and the one stood."

Taking a stand against racism

It was also at Galt that Brusso first defied the racism that prevailed in sports at the time. The team's management lined up an exhibition match with a native club known as the Seneca Indians. When the players were informed of the decision 48 hours prior to game time, there was open rebellion, with several threatening not to participate. White men, they said, shouldn't be competing with "redskins." Brusso argued passionately for the contest, pointing out that aboriginals had invented lacrosse and that some of them were among the game's best players. If Galt was to be considered the top team in Canada, it would have to take on all comers, regardless of race, he said. But his motives were not entirely altruistic. He also wanted to improve his own skills by pitting himself against the native team.

Grudgingly, the rest of the players agreed to follow his lead. But when Seneca showed up brandishing lacrosse sticks that were considerably bigger and heavier than those carried by the white players, more trouble ensued. Galt complained bitterly, fearing the players would use their larger sticks as weapons. When the referee dismissed the complaint, the whole team stomped off the field, ignoring the pleas of its own horrified coach. The whole team, that is, except for Noah Brusso. He stood in his net, lined up alone against the entire Seneca squad. The referee was about to forfeit the game to the visitors when Galt's captain and leading scorer, "Dad" Stewart, looked back and saw Brusso still standing in his cage. Stewart, a close friend who roomed with Brusso when the team was on the road, turned back and took his place on the field. Moments later the rest of the players returned and the match got under way. According to the *Galt Weekly Reporter*, the game turned out to be one of the best of the season, with the home side winning 8–4. There were no fights, possibly because the normally scrappy Brusso seemed to go out of his way to avoid trouble. He went so far as to give each of the four men who scored on him a friendly nod of recognition. When it was all over, the *Reporter* couldn't say enough good things about the contest: "The Indians were gentlemanly through their visit and we will welcome them again."

For Noah these were among the happiest days of his life. Years later, when he was wearing the World Heavyweight Boxing Championship belt, he still boasted about his exploits in the Galt lacrosse net. "I played with the team that won the championship of Canada in 1898, against the best men in the world," he recalled in a newspaper article. "They had the pick of the Toronto team and others, and still we beat them. There were thousands and thousands [of spectators] there that day in a little village."[14] He loved the sport so much that, after becoming heavyweight champ, he sometimes donned false whiskers so he could play pick-up games without being recognized.

Noah appeared to have a bright future as a professional lacrosse goalie when he joined the intermediate Woodstock Beavers at the beginning of the 1899 season. But he got off to a slow start. "Brusso's work was a disappointment," the *Woodstock Weekly Sentinel* declared after he gave up two quick goals in the home opener. The coach apparently agreed, because he gave Noah the hook before half-time, putting him on a forward line. The teenager responded with a goal of his own before the game ended. After that, he never played between the pipes again.

Performing up front gave him more opportunities than ever to engage in rough play, and he seemed to relish every chance to mix it up. The *Weekly Sentinel's* account of a game between the Beavers and the Brighton Stars gives a clear indication of just how tough Noah could be — and of the excitement he generated every time he stepped on the field:

Some of the spectators had doubts whether they were witnessing a lacrosse match or a series of prizefights. Those who enjoy exhibitions of the noble art of self-defense were treated to four or five fistic combats, those who revel in battlefield scenes saw several men wounded and several others sent to the fence for rough play. Brusso and Hunter got into an argument and started to settle their dispute with their fists. The whole crowd rushed on the field and in a minute or two there were a couple of other scraps going on. All the combatants were stopped, the field cleared, Brusso and Hunter relegated to the fence and the game proceeded with. Brusso tried a trick in this game. When he was ruled off he was wearing a red jersey. He slipped around behind the grandstand, put on a black one, and rushed out to play again. He had only handled the ball a couple of times before the Bright boys noticed him and the referee sent him to the fence again.

Brusso and Hunter proceeded to settle their difficulties after the game but they were stopped again. Brusso was the favourite of the crowd for he was not much more than half the size of his opponent.

This incident was in fact much more serious than the newspaper account suggests. Noah was very nearly attacked by an angry mob. Recalling the game in his unpublished autobiography, he said, "That year a big blacksmith by the name of Jack Hunter knocked me down with a tremendous blow on the jaw. We had been opponents in a game all that afternoon and hot words — not fit for Sunday school — had been exchanged. I jumped to my feet and, after a ten-minute whirlwind of a street fight, I knocked Hunter out. I then ran into a nearby hotel and some of my teammates slipped me out of town to get me away from a crowd that had gathered to see the conqueror of their friend Hunter."[15]

According to the *London Free Press*, three drunken fans attacked Brusso inside the hotel. Within seconds, it reported, he had knocked out all three.

In some ways Brusso was like the 'name' gunfighter in old western movies who is continually challenged by upstarts out to make themselves known. One after another, the biggest players on the opposing teams came after him, most assuming they could easily handle such a little fellow. And one after another, he knocked them out. Before his lacrosse career was over, the situation had spiralled out of control. James Cranston, a sports writer of the era, recalled in his 1951 memoirs that Noah became so wild he sometimes hit game officials. "Brusso never used his stick but he was free with his fists on opponent and referee alike," Cranston wrote.[16]

The fighting took its toll on Noah's personality, and may have begun to dehumanize him. Cranston suspected he enjoyed the violence and may even have been hooked on it. The *Halifax Herald* suggested much the same thing years later. In reporting a prizefight in which he had bloodied an opponent, it said Brusso, "seemed wild at the sight of blood. He sprang in like a demon. An expression of vicious hate was on his face." But despite all the brawling, he still displayed some redeeming qualities. He was known as a player who would never pick a fight with a smaller opponent. Fred "Cyclone" Taylor, who later went on to become professional hockey's first superstar, testified to that fact in 1972. Recalling his days as a lacrosse player, Taylor told an interviewer he had once collided with Brusso while going for a loose ball at mid-field. Both went down in a heap and were momentarily stunned. Noah popped up first and his fists were raised. But when he saw the opposing player was the 14-year-old Taylor, who was considerably smaller than he was, Brusso gave the younger boy a friendly nod and took off down the field.

In 1900 Noah, who was still only 18, moved to Mount Forest, where he obtained a job painting houses. He also landed a spot on the town's senior lacrosse team. Once again he found himself the target of every tough guy in the league. His coach, George Allen, recalled years later that one opposing player even went after Brusso with his stick. "The ball had been thrown behind the net and Brusso and the goalkeeper followed it, the former leading. The goalkeeper kept tapping Brusso on the arm until they reached the ball, when Noah could stand it no longer and, dropping his stick, as was his custom, he landed his tormentor one on the face." The goalie was knocked out and Brusso was given a game misconduct.

Allen considered fighting such an intregal part of the sport that he supplied the team with boxing gloves during workouts. "Brusso had some heavy rounds with the boys," he said. Throughout all of this Noah proved he was more than just a "goon." He scored plenty of goals, showing an amazing ability to deke opposing players out of position before darting smartly around them for a shot on net. As far as Allen was concerned, he was a model player. "He was temperate in his habits, and not a bit lazy. He played for the love of the game, as he got nothing on the side but what he earned."[17]

Lacrosse players in those days didn't earn much. With most teams, they received only enough money to pay for meals and hotel bills when they were on the road. If there was any money left over at the end of the season, it was split equally among all the players. Noah, however, likely would have played for free because he thrived on the excitement and praise.

With Brusso scoring on a regular basis, Mount Forest made it to the 1900 league championship game against Shelburne. The final match was a classic contest. "With two teams eager to land the championship, hundreds of rabid rooters to egg them on, a referee who was not disposed to see everything — and a band — it was not to be wondered that the game was replete with exciting features," the Toronto *Globe* reported. "It was no namby pamby, mother's meeting contest, but a rapid, torrid struggle from start to finish. Brusso and Scott were the most conspicuous of the Mount Forest players, but they marred their good work by indiscriminate slashing. Scott was ruled off a couple of times for roughing it, and Brusso was penalized on one occasion for the same offence."

Shelburne surged into an 8–4 lead but then wilted in the 38°C heat of the scorching August day. Noah, who was in remarkably good condition, brought his teammates tottering back from the brink by scoring one goal and setting up three others with crisp passes. The game was deadlocked 8–8, but Shelburne rallied after that, winning the title 13–10. Still, the drama wasn't over. "At the conclusion of the match Madill, the husky cover point of the Shelburne team, and Brusso, the player who wore a boxing glove to protect his left hand, started a little free-for-all," the *Globe* reported. Once again Noah had tangled with a man considerably bigger than himself and this time he got the worst of the exchange. "Brusso was rather roughly handled," the newspaper said. "Besides stopping a couple of punches hurled in his direction by Madill, he also intercepted a wicked pass with his ear made by a Shelburne man. At one time it looked as if everybody would take a hand in the fray, but the officers of the clubs succeeded in quieting the tumult without any serious damage resulting."

Brusso becomes a drifter

With the lacrosse season over, Noah left Mount Forest and headed for the border city of Sarnia, Ontario, where he took a job as a bouncer in a riverfront tavern. He was destined to earn his money because Sarnia was a boomtown with a frontier atmosphere. Imperial Oil had just built Canada's biggest oil refinery in what was to become known as the "Chemical Valley" and scores of unemployed drifters flooded into the community, looking for work. The news columns of the *Sarnia Ob-*

server were filled with stories about bar fights on Friday and Saturday nights. In a typical story, which appeared under the headline "Breaches of Public Morality," the newspaper reported one man had been shot in the face during an altercation in a downtown tavern. Outside, meanwhile, police had arrested the bar's owner and a prostitute for fighting on the main street. The story concluded by saying,

> Only two or three Sundays ago a scene of drunken carousal took place in one of our hotels which would have been disgraceful in any well-regulated inn on any day, but was certainly far more so on the Sabbath. It is no secret that some left the hotel on the day in question in such a state of intoxication that they were unable to go to their homes without assistance.

Observer reporter Red Wilson described Noah decades later as "a fleeting visitor racking up pool balls in the old Normandy Hotel. His abilities were used mainly to keep belligerent pool players under control."[18] He wasn't a very imposing bouncer and that got him into some tight spots. Standing just 5'7" and weighing only about 130 pounds, the teenager looked like 'easy meat' to the ruffians who frequented the Normandy. But he didn't have much trouble keeping order after word spread that he'd knocked out a pair of burly drunks who came at him armed with pool cues.

Noah left Sarnia soon after that, taking a job on a Great Lakes steamer that plied the waters between Buffalo and Cleveland. On board, he and his mates were constantly bullied by the ship's steward, a massive man who prided himself on his tough-guy reputation. One afternoon, as the ship lay docked at Detroit, he shoved Noah, calling him a "stupid loafer."

"Touch me again and you'll regret it," the teenaged baggage handler replied, his face turning beet red.

Without batting an eye the older man slapped him in the face with a wet towel. "Put up your dukes, Brusso, I'm going to teach you some manners."[19]

Noah froze for one awful moment, fear welling up in his stomach. In the next instant he spun around and caught the bigger man with an overhand right to the mouth. The steward went down like a bag of wet cement, hitting his head hard against the deck. Enraged, he came at Noah again and again, swinging wildly with both arms. The boy, showing remarkable agility for such a stocky individual, managed to elude every rush. Counter-attacking, he knocked the bully down half a dozen more times before the brute finally collapsed in a soggy heap. When he regained consciousness, he locked himself in his cabin and refused to come out until Brusso was off the ship.

It had been a justified assault, a clear-cut case of self-defense. Nevertheless, Noah was fired. He jumped ship at Detroit and got work as a dockhand. A few weeks later he joined the local painters' union and landed a job that paid him $3. 50 a day. It was good money (the average worker made just 22¢ an hour), so he decided to stay in Michigan. In so doing he became one of only 396 Canadians to immigrate to the United States that year. Had he remained in Canada, he speculated later, he might well have become one of the greatest professional lacrosse or hockey players who ever lived. Now, however, it looked as if the sporting world had seen the last of Noah Brusso.

The accidental prizefighter

Brusso would have been hard pressed to find a place more foreign to him than Detroit in the fall of 1900. After spending his entire life in tiny Ontario towns with their quaint, nineteenth century rural settings, he had moved to a modern, industrialized metropolis with a population of 285,000 people. Despite the initial shock, he fit in well, probably because at the turn of the twentieth century Detroit was a vibrant, wealthy city on the move. There was a sense of optimism in the air, fuelled by the development of a number of state-of-the-art industries. They included a factory, established the year before Noah arrived, that produced the new horseless carriage known as the automobile. Most people still relied on Detroit's streetcars, but they realized it was only a matter of time before the automobile took over. The only obstacle in its way was a city statute that probibited motorists from driving more than 12 kilometres per hour.

As he strolled through the downtown area, Brusso found the streets clean, safe and full of life. Describing 1900 Detroit, one Michigan historian wrote, "Confectioneries and bakeries were numerous. An outstanding feature of the downtown was the presence of many artisan shops. The increase in the number during the decade of the 1890s was phenomenal. Furriers, jewelers and gentlemen tailors were numerous and rendered services that reflected an increase in wealth."[20] There were seven theatres, scores of elegant public buildings, highrise hotels and shops that sold everything under the sun. There was also plenty of free entertainment, with bands playing in city parks every night, weather permitting.

Brusso also found a cultural diversity unknown to rural Ontario. Fully one third of Detroit's residents were immigrants, many of them from such places as Poland, Russia and Italy.

In such a setting the last thing on Brusso's mind was prizefighting. Many years later Noah would admit he got into boxing almost by accident. Soon after jumping ship, the 18-year-old joined the Detroit Athletic Club to get a little exercise. Before long he'd signed on with the local lacrosse team. Just as he had done in Ontario, he soon gained a reputation as a hard-nosed player who was not afraid to mix it up with the opposing team's toughest members. One day, as he sat in the office of legendary Detroit sports writer Joe Jackson, the scribe asked him, "Ever think of fighting for a living, Noah?"[21]

Brusso admitted the idea had never crossed his mind.

"Well, you should give it some thought. You've got the build for it, you know? And if you don't mind me saying so, you're mean enough, too. A fighter has to have the killer instinct and you've got it in spades. I think with the right training you could be a top middleweight contender."[22]

Jackson soon introduced Noah to fight promoter and former boxer Sam Biddle, who agreed to take the young man under his wing.

Biddle! The name alone was enough to send shivers down the spines of pugilism's oldtimers. The former Canadian lightweight champion had a reputation as a nasty brute with a ruthless disposition. He'd become an almost mythical figure in the boxing world in the summer of 1886 by knocking out Harry Gilmore in what one reporter called "probably the fiercest ring encounter in the history of the game." The journalist told his readers, "Biddle fought for 26 rounds before getting in on Gilmore. And they fought with bare knuckles until both faces looked like the hamburg steaks prepared by a conscientious cook. At one point Biddle's seconds ran a piece of whalebone up his nose to break clots of blood that kept forming there."

Clearly, Noah had thrown his lot in with a tough customer. An indication of Biddle's expectations can be gleaned from an interview he granted to a Detroit newspaper shortly after the turn of the century. He admired boxers, he said, who "fought on round after round, bleeding and blind, and only asking for another chance to get at the other fellow." A good fighter, he added, should "cut and stab, working slowly but cruelly."

By the time Noah met Biddle, the promoter was a grizzled, toothless, white-haired saloonkeeper who weighed more than 200 pounds. Still, there was something about him that commanded respect. He referred to the modern battles in which fighters wore gloves as "six round pillow affairs that are nothing at all. They talk of blood and gore in the prize ring today; there isn't any."[23]

The old warrior put Noah to work in the gym, frankly telling him he wouldn't be going anywhere near the ring for several months. Despite his public disdain for modern boxers, the crafty old pro wasn't about to throw a teenager into action without plenty of training under his belt. Brusso had handled himself well on the lacrosse pitch and in tavern brawls, but he'd never gone toe-to-toe with a professional boxer. If he wasn't properly prepared he could be badly injured and Biddle knew it.

Sports writer Hary Roxborough, who knew Brusso personally, has left behind the best description of Noah's early days in Biddle's stable. "At first the training quarters were shabby and the equipment crude," he wrote in 1957. "Biddle's gymnasium was but a back room in a Detroit saloon; and for months Noah not only never faced an opponent, but never did he have a glove laced on those big, hamlike hands. Instead, he just punched, punched, punched at a heavy bag that could hurt your knuckles but couldn't hit back. However, ex-pug Biddle knew what he was doing, for he planned to make a puncher rather than a boxer out of his protégé."[24]

Noah was impressed with Biddle's strategy. He was, he said later, determined to become "the best damn puncher on the planet."[25]

Brusso's first bout

Brusso got his chance to prove himself at an unexpected moment. Early in December 1900, he went to a Detroit boxing match with a group of friends. Dressed in their Sunday best, the young men excitedly occupied ringside seats. The fight promised to be a good one, pitting Canadian light-heavyweight star Freddie "Thunderbolt" Thornton against an up-and-coming American fighter named Jack "Tiger" Cowan. Thornton, a black man from Windsor, Ontario, with two dozen victories to his credit, was the betting favourite. Besides his impressive record of wins, he had gone six rounds two years earlier with nationally ranked boxer "Young" Peter Jackson.

There was a buzz of excitement in the air because this was a rare inter-racial bout. Fights between black and white boxers were not illegal, but they were extremely uncommon, mainly because most Caucasian athletes had drawn the colour line very tightly. In this instance, Cowan likely accepted the fight because he knew a victory over a 'name' black boxer would help him move up the ladder. But before the bout could begin, disaster struck. Cowan slipped and fell while climbing through the ropes and suffered a sprained ankle. A collective groan went up from the crowd of six hundred spectators. Fight promoter Mike Dolan was frantic. If a replacement couldn't be found, the entire gate would have to be refunded. Standing on a stool in the middle of the ring, he motioned for silence.

"Tiger Cowan can't fight tonight," he shouted into a megaphone. "Is there anyone in the house man enough to fill in for him?"[26]

Noah's pals, who knew he'd been training for months, urged him on. At first he refused to get off his seat, but they wouldn't take no for an answer, assuring him he could win. Brusso wasn't nearly as confident as the rest of them. Thornton was a well-known fighter, at least in southwestern Ontario and southeastern Michigan. Some thought the Windsor pugilist had the potential to become the next state champion. And he was a lot bigger than Brusso, standing six feet tall and weighing

170 pounds. Noah, who tipped the scales at just 140, was frankly scared. But by now the whole crowd was egging him on. Thornton even called out a taunt from the ring.

"Come ahead, boy. I won't hurt you — much."

Stung by Thornton's patronizing attitude, Noah jumped to his feet and yelled, "Fellah, do you want to fight me right now?"[27]

The roar of the crowd drowned out Thornton's reply, but Brusso thought he'd heard the word "yellow."

Mike Dolan approached Noah, excitedly jabbering about the need "not to let the crowd down." He led Noah into a nearby dressing-room and outfitted him with a pair of oversized boxing shoes and bright red trunks. Brusso, who was by now almost in a state of frenzy, jumped to his feet, bounded up the steps and climbed through the ropes. Dolan suddenly shoved a waiver into his face and demanded he sign it. As Noah glanced at the document its contents gave him a start. The piece of paper absolved the promoter of any liability, should Brusso be killed or maimed.

Thornton was oozing with confidence. The fans expected him to put Brusso away in the first round, and he was determined not to disappoint them. Noah, too, was anxious to get the fight over with quickly. He doubted he could outpoint a professional boxer over the scheduled six rounds. That meant he'd have to score a knockout or lose the fight. He knew, too, that Thornton didn't take him seriously. If he played his cards right, he could probably catch the bigger man off guard.

GONG! Round One!

Mike Dolan shoved Brusso out of his corner, propelling the startled teenager into the centre of the ring. In the next instant the shaven-skulled, muscle-bound Thornton was right on top of him. He came darting through the haze of blue tobacco smoke that hung heavily over the arena, a murderous look flashing in his eyes. Noah glimpsed a tattoo of a jagged lightning bolt on his opponent's left shoulder. There was no time to observe anything else, as Thornton uncorked a bomb. Brusso ducked out of harm's way, then tried to ward the bigger man off by flicking out his left jab. But Thornton kept coming, unleashing a stinging right hand that landed on the side of the rookie's head. It was only a glancing blow, but Noah's ears were ringing and he could still smell the leather from the other man's glove as he back-pedalled for all he was worth into the ropes.

"He gave me a much needed boxing lesson for the first two rounds, a lesson I remember to this day," Brusso admitted half a century later.[28]

Sensing an easy kill, Thornton went to work in the third round with his guard down. At that moment Brusso tagged him. A booming overhand right caught Thornton flush on the jaw and he went down as if he'd been poleaxed. He was up by the count of five and fighting mad. Again and again he crowded Brusso, raining punches at him from every direction. But the teenager was proving surprisingly difficult to hit. His powerful legs, developed through years of lacrosse and speed-skating, allowed him to dance quickly out of the line of fire. And he was an unexpectedly small target. Crouching low, he didn't leave Thornton a lot of body to aim for. Peering over his raised gloves like a groundhog peeking out of its hole, Noah covered up well and launched swift counter-attacks. His unusually long arms continuously caught Thornton by surprise. Standing several feet away, the veteran would be certain he was safely out of range, when the novice would suddenly rock him with a shot to the head. One such salvo, delivered in the fourth round, gave Noah another knockdown.

By now he was clearly in command of the fight. The all-white crowd, wild with excitement, was on its feet, roaring, "Kill the nigger! Kill the nigger!" In the fifth it was all over. Brusso caught Thornton with a right cross to the jaw that sent him staggering backwards. For a second or two he stood still, his great physical conditioning keeping him upright. But it was obvious from the glazed look in his eyes that he was out on his feet. Before Noah could throw another punch, Thornton tumbled forward, landing flat on his face. He was out like a light long before the referee reached the count of 10. The whole building erupted in cheers, and the victor was mobbed as he climbed out of the ring.

"How much do you want for that?" Dolan asked.

"Enough to buy the boys a cigar or two," Noah replied.[29]

He was paid a grand total of $1.25 for his troubles. It wasn't a lot of money, but it was more than some people made toiling for an entire day in a factory. For the first time, Noah began to believe he might be able to make his living full-time as a prizefighter.

2

The Outcast

Noah Brusso unexpectedly found himself something of an pariah after his ring debut, and for the life of him he didn't know why. His conquest of the formidable Thornton, after all, had been an impressive sporting achievement. Even his harshest critics were willing to admit that much. But from a social point of view it was nothing less than a disaster. For days afterwards, he found himself being shunned on the street by people who had previously been friendly with him.

The problem, he soon discovered, was simple enough. Thornton was black, and whites weren't supposed to fight black boxers. At least not those who hoped to go somewhere in the world of prizefighting.

Brusso found out what was wrong when he approached his trainer, Sam Biddle, and asked why everyone was giving him the cold shoulder. Biddle told him, then added reassuringly, "It's OK this time, kid. You didn't know any better. If I'd been there, I'd never have let you into the ring with a coon."

"Why not?" Brusso asked.

"They're animals," the old man replied. "Some whites fight 'em, but not the self-respecting ones. They do it for the spectacle, to get the crowd worked up. But a gentleman would no more fight a nigger than he would an alligator or a grizzly bear."

"I don't want to duck any man," Brusso said.[1]

Biddle insisted blacks were dirty fighters who specialized in low blows. When Noah protested, pointing out that Thornton fought cleanly all the way, the older man just shrugged his shoulders and shook his head in disgust.

As vile as Biddle's opinions were, they were shared by the overwhelming majority of whites in those days. Indeed, just a few years before the Brusso-Thornton scrap, a bout between a black and a white fighter in New Orleans had been broken up by a police officer. "The idea of niggers fighting white men," the cop growled. "Why if that darned scoundrel would beat that white boy the niggers would never stop gloating over it, and, as it is, we have enough trouble with them."[2]

As a result of such attitudes, most black boxers were forced to battle one another again and again. Sam Langford, the great Nova Scotia fighter, for example, fought five fellow blacks a total of 72 times. Unable to find many whites who would face him, he squared off against Harry Wills no less than 18 times, put the gloves on against Sam McVey 15 times, fought Joe Jeanette on 14 occasions, met Jeff Clark 13 times and Jim Barry 12. Many ring historians think he could have been a world champion, had he been allowed to fight any of the white titleholders of his era.

Fight promoter Harry Wyle has left for posterity the best description of what it was like for black boxers of the early twentieth century. He took African-Americans around the United States, trying to land fights with whites. They usually slept in cars or train stations because hotels wouldn't accept them. When they needed to eat, a white associate would be sent into restaurants to buy food because no eatery would serve them. They worked out in church basements and when they entered arenas to fight they had to cover their water buckets to prevent enraged fans from spitting into them. Crowds would routinely cry out, "Kill the coon!" or "Kill the nigger" whenever a black pugilist came into view.

The situation was worst in the South, but it was no picnic in the West or the Northeast either. In fact, when a black boxer named Deacon "Tiger" Flowers journeyed to Ohio to meet a white fighter, police warned him that if he won, he'd be shot. "He knocked his man cold in the third and walked to his dressing room with the fans booing and the deputies following him," Wyle said later. "But the Deacon, a real Baptist deacon in church on Sunday, climbed out of a washroom window, made a freight train and got away, still in his boxing trunks."[3]

Nor was Flowers the only black to face violence from non-boxers. Trainer Dick Sadler said, "In one place I had to cover my fighter's head from beer cans and bottles thrown when he was winning over a white boy. It was hard for an athlete to make a dollar in those days. We were totally barred from big, popular sports like baseball or football or basketball. Boxing was all."[4]

It would be tempting to dismiss such blatant racism as the conduct of the mostly uneducated people who populated the often-seedy world of professional boxing. The sport, then as now, was frowned upon by a great many people. Unfortunately, however, the fighters and their fans were in agreement with the rest of early twentieth century white society. Best-selling novels by famed author Thomas Dixon, including *Leopard's Spot*, written in 1902, and *The Clansman*, penned three years later, make that perfectly clear. These enormously popular books depicted black males as "monsters" and "cunning animals" looking for opportunities to rape white women. And just four years before Brusso stepped into the ring with Thornton, the United States Supreme Court had upheld states' rights to impose segregation in public places. Four years after the Brusso-Thornton fight, the American Automobile Association would suspend championship race-car driver Barney Oldfield for two years for competing against a black man.

Newspaper reporters were as bad as any other group. When Brusso talked publicly about fighting black boxers Joe Jeanette and Sam McVey, the *Winnipeg Tribune* dismissed them as "coons."

Brusso himself harboured some racist feelings, although they were not deeply felt. In that regard he was no different from most Canadians of his generation. He'd never even seen a black person until he moved to Detroit, so his attitudes did not spring from personal experience. But, as historian Brian Reid has noted, "most Canadians of the time considered anyone who was not a white, male citizen of the British Empire as an inferior being and that probably was among their more progressive opinions."[5]

The difference between Brusso and the average American white of the time was that, while he mistakenly thought blacks were "a little slower" than Caucasians, he didn't dislike them.[6] He didn't believe the races were equal, but he was rather ambivalent about the whole subject. No doubt his Canadian roots made him a little more tolerant than his peers. He had been raised in a country that did not have the United States' tortured history of race relations. It should be remembered that slavery had been legal in some parts of the U. S. only 16 years before

Noah was born. The parents of some of his black opponents had been slaves, and the parents of some of his white adversaries had been slave owners. Although white Canadians were far from perfect when it came to the treatment of minorities, they had not been exposed to the same racial atmosphere as that found south of the border.

In any case, Brusso did not believe blacks should be denied an equal opportunity to get ahead in the world. Always a bit of an underdog himself, he did not approve of the bullying of African-Americans that he saw going on all around him. And despite great pressure from his peers, he refused to draw the colour line in the ring.

Despite his relative tolerance towards inter-racial bouts, Brusso was not above hurling racial slurs at black fighters while in the ring. About the best that can be said in his defense is that he did it to 'get their goat.' In his book *Scientific Boxing*, he admitted he taunted and laughed at all of his adversaries, regardless of their colour, hoping to get them so angry that they would make mistakes that might cost them the fight. It was a tactic that cost him some fans. "He went in for glaring balefully at his opponents, stamping on the floor to inspire terror, and worst, 'mouth fighting,' pouring vituperation upon his man and telling him exactly what he was going to do to him," a boxing writer of the era wrote.[7] At one pre-fight weigh-in, Brusso taunted a white adversary with such infuriating effect that several trainers had to restrain the man from starting the fight right then and there. Interestingly, after a hard-fought battle with the African-American fighter Billy Woods, Brusso apologized to Woods for the racial insults he'd directed at him during the bout. The two became good friends and, after he became world heavyweight champion, the Canadian hired the out-of-work Woods as one of his sparring partners. Woods was, in fact, one of two black sparring partners he would employ as champion. Most white boxers of the era wouldn't have dared to include a black man in their camp.

The well-known British boxing writer Bohum Lynch once wrote that Brusso "despised" blacks, but that isn't true.[8] Joe Louis, the great African-American heavyweight champion of the 1930s, said in a 1978 interview that the Canadian was anything but a frothing-at-the-mouth bigot. "He didn't hate Negroes, he hated Jack Johnson [the black fighter who defeated him for the heavyweight crown]. There's a big difference.

A rather youthful looking Burns attempts to strike a menacing pose.

A lot of people, black and white, hated Johnson. I knew a lot of old-time [black] fighters back in the '30s and they all liked Burns. They said he was one of the few whites who wouldn't draw the colour line. He'd even go drinking with them once the fights were over."[9]

Still, it would be a mistake to think of Brusso as some sort of anti-racist crusader. His reasons for fighting blacks were varied and complex. He probably acted at least partly out of stubbornness. He was, after all, a rebel who didn't like to be told what to do. So when the establishment told him it was opposed to inter-racial bouts, he got his back up. His experience of poverty as a child may also have made him a little more sympathetic towards underprivileged blacks. Perhaps he also saw inter-racial bouts as attention-grabbers that would set him apart from his peers. And as was the case with the native lacrosse players he had insisted on competing against at Galt, he wanted to meet good black fighters in order to improve his own skills.

Overcoming a dirty trick

Encouraged by his relatively easy victory over Thornton, Noah quit his painting job and plunged full-time into the brutal, racist world of professional boxing. It was a bold decision, as he was entering a dangerous profession in which a man's career — and his health — could be ruined in an instant. But Brusso accepted the risks, later explaining, "I wanted to be more than just an average person. I wanted to be a somebody."[10]

He also likely wanted to make more money so he could enjoy some of the new inventions that were being introduced on an almost daily basis in those days. Although times were tough, this was an age of surprising optimism. New devices such as the telephone, typewriter, sewing machine, motion-picture camera and automobile were coming onto the scene and people — including Brusso — were anxious to obtain them. Unfortunately, such items tended to cost a lot of money. Only 18 of every 1,000 households had a telephone in 1900, and even fewer had cars. The average automobile went for $1,550, which was the equivalent of about three years' pay for a painter.

By early 1901 Noah's extra work in the gym started to pay dividends in the ring. It happened when he was pitted against Billy "Battleship" Walsh. Like Thornton, Walsh was one of the better-known pugilists in the region, with a long list of wins behind his name. At 6'1" he was a full six inches taller than Brusso and he had a slight weight advantage as well. Moreover, Walsh would do anything to win. He was notorious for hitting below the belt, head butting and — 90 years before Mike Tyson thought of it — biting his opponents. Nor were his dirty tricks confined to the ring. One of his favourite tactics was to send his adversary a telegram just before fight time, telling him his mother had died. Noah received just such a message in his dressing-room only half an hour before the contest was slated to begin. Allegedly sent by his oldest sister, it was, in fact, wired by Walsh. The young fighter was sitting on a stool, sobbing quietly, when Sam Biddle walked in.

"What's wrong?" the old trainer asked. "There's no need to fear the Battleship that much. He ain't that tough, you know. It's all just news-paper talk. You can trim him, otherwise I wouldn't let you fight him."

"It's not that," Brusso replied, waving the telegram. "It's my mother, she's dead."

"For God's sake man, that's just a ploy," Biddle reassured him. "The Battleship sends that very same message to all his first-time opponents."

Noah's grief was replaced in the next instant by white-hot rage. The moment the bell rang he charged out of his corner like a hungry lion released from its cage. He pressed home the attack with such blistering ferocity that by the end of the fourth round Walsh was barely able to make it back to his corner. Before the fifth round was over he was stretched out on the canvas.

When Walsh woke up on his dressing-room table half an hour later, he had no idea what had happened. Looking up at the ceiling, he saw that a chunk of plaster was missing.

"Did I lose?" he asked his trainer.

Not having the heart to tell him the truth, the man replied, "No, you won, but the ceiling fell on you once you got in the dressing-room."

"I thought so," the groggy boxer replied.[11]

Brusso took grim satisfaction from the win, but it did little to ease his fury. He was still fuming about the dirty trick years later when he related its details to sports writer Red Wilson. A week after the bout, he took his anger out on a journeyman boxer named Archie Steele. Steele, a slow, plodding fighter with an indifferent record, was so bland he didn't even have a nickname. He lasted only two rounds before the young Canadian's ceaseless attacks left him spread-eagled on the mat.

Brusso falls in love

Noah Brusso was enjoying good fortune in the ring, but he was not so lucky in affairs of the heart. Around this time he met a beautiful young redhead and fell madly in love. Sadly, the relationship did not last. In a poignant passage from his unpublished autobiography, he wrote,

> It was my unfortunate lot to fall in love at a time when my finances were very low. I used to frequent a confectionery shop owned by Capper and Capper, on Michigan Avenue in Detroit. The attraction was not so much the delicious bonbons and chocolates sold there, but a lovely young girl by the name of Nellie Sweitzer, the cashier. Many were the evenings that I would wander down there and find an excuse to loiter until closing time, so that I could escort her home or take in a show. Our love ripened over the period of a year. While we never disagreed in any way, we began drifting apart as I gradually came to realize that my calling was that of a professional boxer. I held the entirely mistaken thought that marriage with this beautiful girl would hinder me, and I was determined to climb to the top of the boxing profession. What this unfortunate decision cost me was secreted in my heart for 43 years, safe from the scrutiny of anyone. How different my life might have been had I yielded to my true instincts. It was one of those regrettable decisions which sometimes change the entire course of one's life for, of course, I eventually got married anyway — and to the wrong girls!"[12]

Brusso had ended his relationship with Nellie for two reasons. First, he feared the responsibilities of marriage might force him to quit boxing and find a more reliable source of income. Second, Sam

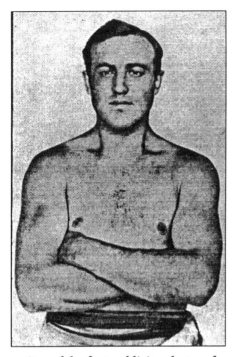

One of the first publicity photos of Burns shows his chest, shoulder and arm development.

Biddle disapproved of her, telling Noah sexual intercourse would sap his strength and take away his will to fight. Several generations later famed boxing trainer Angelo Dundee said much the same thing to Muhammad Ali. Without sex, "a fighter gets mean, angry, willing, anxious to fight," he said. "With it he purrs like a pussycat. It's psychological, maybe, more than physical. You keep a fighter away from women, keep him in camp pounding bags, punching fighters day in and day out, and when he gets in the ring he's ready to take it all out on his opponent. Who wants to fight after good love making? All wars are brought about by leaders who never had good loving."[13]

Becoming Michigan champion

With Nellie out of his life and three straight knockout wins under his belt, Brusso decided he was ready to challenge for the Michigan middleweight championship. To complicate matters, however, two fighters were currently claiming the title. The old champ, whose name has been lost to history, had retired undefeated, and his crown was being claimed by both a Saginaw fighter named Eddie "The Bay City Brawler" Sholtreau and a strapping Polish-American who went by the name of Tom McCune. Most observers thought Sholtreau had the better claim, so Brusso laid down the gauntlet in front of him. Sam Biddle tried to talk him out of it, pointing out that Sholtreau was an experienced fighter with 20 victories behind his name, several of which had come by way of knockout.

"You take care of the training," Noah said with confidence, "and I'll handle the managing of my career."[14]

Biddle was right about one thing — the fight was a mismatch from the start. But it was the champ and not the challenger who was in over his head. Brusso cornered the slow-moving Sholtreau early in the bout, lowering his defenses with several thunderous body blows. The moment his arms dropped, the Canadian knocked him out with a concussive head punch that travelled no more than a foot. Sholtreau had been disposed of in one minute and 35 seconds, and Michigan had a new middleweight champion.

Betraying an almost charming innocence that belied his growing tough-guy image, Noah clipped out a newspaper article about his new status and carried it with him everywhere he went. He was thrilled when reporters started referring to him in print as "Brusso the Bruiser." Years later, he confided that that first title, however humble it may have been compared to what he would later win, made him feel like a somebody for the first time in his life. Despite his obvious athletic abilities, he suffered from a sense of inferiority that would drive him to seek the approval of others throughout his life. This trait was evident in interviews he gave later in his career. While other athletes tended to let their accomplishments speak for themselves, Brusso often appeared to be trying too hard to impress reporters.

Noah ended 1901 in fine style, knocking out Battleship Walsh again, this time in six rounds. During the year he'd fought four times, winning all four fights, by knockout. Overall, he had a perfect 5–0 won-lost record with five consecutive KO's. On the financial front, he'd raised his ring earnings from the $1.25 he made in 1900 to $460 in 1901. The sum, which seems parltry today, represented a decent annual salary at that time. The average teacher of the era, after all, made only $330 a year. Even the typical industrial worker earned only $490, and he was expected to work six 10-hour days a week. At the start of Noah's career, eggs sold for 12¢ a dozen, sirloin steak went for 24¢ per pound and a turkey dinner could be purchased for just 20¢. It should be remembered, too, that there was no income tax in those days, which made his earnings all the more impressive. Still, he wasn't getting rich by any standard.

The Thornton rematch

Thunderbolt Thornton was demanding a rematch. The veteran boxer was telling anyone who would listen that Brusso had laid him low with a lucky punch. He didn't really expect the youngster to oblige him, but, amazingly, Noah accepted, agreeing to go into the ring with a black man for the second time in just six fights.

Sam Biddle argued against the contest, again warning that good fighters didn't fight blacks. He pointed out that former heavyweight champion John L. Sullivan had gone through his entire 45-fight career without facing a single black man. But Noah stood his ground, insisting he'd take on all comers, regardless of race or religion. "You're not a real contender if you duck a man because of his colour," he said.[15] However, he wasn't going to fight Thornton for $1.25 this time around. He knew that despite the disapproval he'd face from some quarters, there would be a lot of interest in the bout. Thornton was an excellent boxer and was seen as such by most fight fans. Besides that, the race factor was a big drawing card to some of the sport's more boorish followers. Pulitzer-prize winning writer David Remnick explained best why this should be so in his 1998 biography of Muhammad Ali: "For decades boxing has been a central spectacle in America, and because it is so stripped down, one-on-one, a battle with hands and not balls or pads or racquets, the metaphors of struggle, of racial struggle most of all, come easily."[16]

Brusso sensed the value of the proposed bout, and when promoter Mike Dolan offered him $50 for the rematch, he turned it down. Demonstrating some of the managerial savvy that would soon be one of his trademarks, he held out for $100 and got it. Keeping in mind that living expenses at the beginning of the twentieth century were only about five per cent of what they are today, Brusso made the equivalent of about $2,500 tax-free that night.

The fight, held January 16, 1902, in Detroit's posh Windmere Hotel, attracted a sell-out crowd. Also on hand were half a dozen police officers. Brusso took one look at the police presence and assumed they were going to stop the bout on the grounds that it could lead to racial tensions. But such was not the case. The chief of police stepped into the ring just before fight time to warn the referee that no knockouts would be tolerated. Prize-fighting was becoming too brutal and too many boxers were being killed in the ring, he said. At all future contests, he added, the action was to be stopped the moment one of the participants was in danger of being KO'd. The controversial ruling came into play in the fifth round, as Brusso and Thornton traded punches at mid-ring. "Brusso had landed right and left on the chin, sending Thornton down for the count of nine," the *Detroit Free Press*

African-American contender Harry Peppers was an early Burns victim.

reported the next day. "The coloured lad got to his feet in time and was ready to continue, but the authorities, who ruled against knockouts, would not allow this, and the bout was awarded to Brusso. The latter had done most of the leading throughout, and had his man practically at the end of his rope."

The fight had been a success all round. Brusso had won fair and square and, as a result of the police edict, Thornton was not seriously hurt. But there was a disturbing end to the night's proceedings. After he'd left the ring and showered, an older woman confronted Brusso in the hotel lobby with a furious look in her eyes. Marching straight up to the prizefighter, she slapped him in the face and shouted out at the top of her voice, "Nigger lover!"[17]

If Brusso was intimidated by such treatment he certainly didn't show it less than three weeks later, when he stepped into the ring with a black boxer from Chicago named Harry Peppers. He was openly thumbing his nose at the boxing establishment by giving African-Americans a chance to fight for the Michigan middleweight crown. He knew he'd lose some fans if he fought Peppers, but he also realized the black man was a good fighter. Brusso was still only 19, but he was smart enough to know the only way he could keep improving was by pitting himself against other skilled boxers. That Peppers was good there can be no doubt. He punched so hard that one of his opponents, a poor fellow named Dutch Neil, had been killed by one of his blows. In all, the six-foot-tall Peppers had scored a dozen victories, almost all of them against black opponents, with nine of them coming via the knockout route. It was small wonder, then, that newspaper accounts of his clash with Brusso referred to it as "the main bout of the evening."

Once again a large contingent of police officers was on hand. This time, the chief and seven of his constables were in attendance, and the referee was again warned not to permit a knockout. One has to suspect that it didn't take eight officers to deliver the message. More likely, the police were there in force because they feared a bout between a white and a black could lead to a racial incident outside the ring, perhaps maybe even a full-blown race riot. To keep the lid on things, they decided on a strong show of force. Despite their concerns, there was no trouble, possibly because Brusso won so easily. He ran circles around his flat-footed opponent, opening a severe gash over his left eye before the fight was a minute old. Peppers was so badly mauled he simply quit at the end of the second round, refusing to come out of his corner. The *Detroit Free Press* was indignant. Under the screaming headline "Colored Man Deliberately Laid Down Against Brusso," the newspaper told its readers, "Peppers is the same pugilist who flunked out against Fred Wellsman and the quicker he is tabooed by the local promoters the better it will be for the game."

Peppers, for his part, shrugged off the criticism. Showing a delightful sense of humour, he said, "I'd rather have people claim I chickened out than have them looking into my coffin and saying 'boy, he sure looks natural.'" [18]

After the fight Brusso sought Peppers out, inviting him to dinner. He wanted to talk to the American about the Chicago fight scene and find out what he knew about world middleweight champion Tommy Ryan. When a Detroit restaurant refused to serve Peppers, Brusso made a scene. Police were called and the two boxers were escorted off the premises. Fortunately, no charges were laid and they spent the evening having dinner in Noah's apartment.

Just two days after the fight with Peppers, on March 5, 1902, Brusso was back in action, this time against a boxer named George Steele. Whether he was related to Archie Steele, whom Noah had beaten a few weeks earlier, isn't known for sure. What is certain is that he didn't fare any better, lasting exactly two rounds. After the battle, a ringside reporter made it plain the Canadian's power-punching reputation was becoming a weapon almost as important as his fists: "It was evident that Noah Brusso has every local boxer of his weight frightened, and it was hard to find a better pleased man than George Steele when referee Eddie Ryan disqualified him for deliberately fouling," the scribe wrote. "In the first round Brusso went after his man in a furious fashion and Steele realized he had little chance to win, preferring to use foul tactics every time they clinched. In the second round Steele was taking punishment but continued hitting below the belt, and the referee met the wishes of the spectators when he stopped the bout and awarded the decision to Brusso."

With yet another easy victory to his name, Brusso was becoming downright cocky. "I fancied myself no end of a hurricane fighter," he admitted in *Scientific Boxing*.[19] But his confidence would soon be put to a severe test.

Learning a hard lesson

If there was one fighter who wasn't intimidated by Brusso's hitting power it was Eddie Sholtreau. The Bay City Brawler was convinced his loss to the teenager was a fluke. Given a rematch, he promised to lick Brusso before the Canadian lost the title to a black man.

The two men met for the disputed middleweight championship of Michigan (Tom McCune still insisted he was the real champ) on May 16, 1902, with an overflow crowd on hand at the Detroit Athletic Club. Brusso, brimming with overconfidence, was about to be taught a lesson he wouldn't soon forget.

He started strongly but was unable to score a knockout and soon began to run out of steam. In the fourth round Sholtreau mounted a comeback, knocking the tired Canadian off his feet with a terrific wallop to the head. Noah had been sent to the floor for the first time in his career and, although he wasn't badly hurt, he was momentarily stunned. Fortunately, he had the presence of mind to stay down until the count of nine. Some downed boxers like to jump to their feet at once, as if to deny that their adversaries inflicted any pain. But Brusso later admitted he was more interested in clearing the cobwebs from his head than he was in engaging in any sort of psychological warfare.

Smelling blood, Sholtreau "almost put Brusso through the ropes" with a sledgehammer blow to the stomach, the *Detroit Free Press* reported. At the end of the sixth, Noah admitted later, "I was far and away worse off than he was. I had a long list of points in my favour, but he was still able to come up fairly briskly at the call of time, while I was feeling as though I wanted horses to pull me out of my chair. How I managed to last out the remainder of the 10 rounds I don't know, but I can tell you it was only by a big effort."[20]

Most likely Brusso got through those final rounds out of sheer fear. Not fear of injury, but of defeat. He knew a loss at this stage of his career would have been a major setback. So he dug deep and somehow found the strength for a final rally that won him the decision. Later, the clearly chastened boxer said, "I got the verdict on points — but I don't think I deserved it, for I certainly couldn't have gone on any longer, while he would, I think, have lasted another two rounds. I had learnt my lesson. I couldn't always expect to knock my opponents out quick and early, so had to calculate on a long, drawn out affair, and lay my plans so that I should be on hand and going strong at the finish."[21] In other words, Brusso the Bruiser was going to have to become a better-conditioned, more scientific boxer if he was going to keep rising through the ranks.

Brusso gets married

There was one more consequence of Noah's gruelling bout with Sholtreau — he met his second love. Her name was Irene Peppers and boxing historian Larry Roberts believes she was the sister of black fighter Harry Peppers. "She was a very light-skinned mulatto and was very likely Harry's sister," he wrote in a July 4, 2000 letter to the author.

In any case, she had sneaked into the match wearing men's clothing, her long dark hair tucked under a straw hat. Women were not legally barred from prizefights, but it was almost unheard of for one of them to be in attendance. This was an age in which women were banned from saloons, clubs, restaurants, tobacco shops and even the voting booth. In 1904, one young woman was arrested and jailed in New York City for smoking a cigarette in public. But Irene, an 18-year-old beauty from Detroit, was a free-spirited girl who had a reputation for doing what she liked, when she liked. While her contemporaries wore skirts that extended to the floor, she braved stares in a daring outfit that bared her ankles. After reading a newspaper story about Brusso, she decided she wanted to see him in action. Despite the fact that he'd nearly lost the match, she felt herself deeply attracted to him. Perhaps it was precisely *because* he had taken such a beating that she found him so alluring. As writer Joyce Carol Oates noted in her classic book *On Boxing*,

> Women, watching a boxing match, are likely to identify with the losing, or hurt, boxer; men are likely to identify with the winning boxer. There is a point at which male spectators are able to identify with the fight itself as, it might be said, a Platonic experience abstracted from its particulars; if they have favoured one boxer over another, and that boxer is losing, they can shift their loyalty to the winner.[22]

Noah hadn't lost, of course, but he had been hurt. Irene was waiting for him outside his dressing-room when he emerged, holding an ice-pack to the left side of his face. Despite the bruises, she could see that while he certainly wasn't very tall, Brusso *was* dark and handsome. In addition to his blue eyes and curly hair he still had a straight nose and, amazingly, most of his own teeth. There were no mouth guards then, but boxers found some protection by placing orange peels between their teeth and lips.

She boldly introduced herself and, Noah admitted later, it was love at first sight. Besides her beauty, Irene was fun-loving and affectionate. Their romance quickly blossomed, giving Brusso a much-needed escape from the boredom of training and the brutality of fighting. Sam

Biddle disapproved of her, once again warning Noah a girlfriend would turn him into a pussycat. One suspects Brusso's early ring victories had been won at least partly because he fought out of pain and anger, but Irene seems to have had no negative impact on his fighting skills. For a time she attended all his bouts, dressed in a man's suit and tie, and he kept winning. Once, she was discovered by an usher just minutes before the gong signalled the start of the fight. Although it was not illegal for her to be there, an overzealous arena employee escorted Irene to the exit. When Noah saw what was happening, he dashed to the scene and threatened to do bodily harm to the man unless he let his girlfriend return to her seat. Needless to say, she was quickly released.

Unfortunately, however, their relationship was headed for failure. Other than physical attraction, the two had little in common. Besides that, Irene's parents couldn't stand Noah. When she brought him home to meet them, the welcome he received was decidedly cool. Noah showed up sporting two black eyes he'd picked up in a particularly rough sparring session, and when Irene's father asked him where he'd got the shiners, he replied, "Oh, I'm a prizefighter."[23] His candour could not have made a more unfavourable impression. Possibly the Peppers figured one prizefighter in the family was more than enough. Whatever the case, Irene's parents were horrified at the thought of this uneducated Canadian ruffian marrying their daughter. There was no way her parents would ever welcome a boxer into the fold and he knew it.

The more her parents disapproved of him, the more determined Irene became to be with Noah. She even followed him in the fall of 1903 when he travelled to northern Michigan for a series of prizefights. There, almost on an impulse, the two got married. One of Brusso's buddies was getting married and suggested he and Irene make it a double wedding. They agreed, tying the knot on November 2, 1903. But they lived together for only six months before getting a divorce.

Nevertheless, the split was embarrassing. This was, after all, an age in which divorce was deeply frowned upon. Indeed, there were only 56,000 divorced people living in all of the United States in 1900. Couples were expected to stay together, no matter how incompatible they might be. Noah Brusso now had to face public disapproval on yet another score.

Brusso the underdog

Noah's relatively poor showing against Eddie Sholtreau had damaged his reputation with fans and sports writers alike. He was still undefeated, with nine straight wins under his belt, but he had lost his aura of invincibility. He was no longer the murdering monster who knocked his man out every time he put on the gloves. For the first time a fighter had gone the distance with him. As a result, when he entered the ring against Dick "Bull" Smith on June 27, 1902, 10 days after his twenty-first birthday, he was considered the underdog. "Both men have trained diligently for the contest, which should be a good one while it lasts," the *Detroit Free Press* predicted, adding, "Smith is the favourite in the betting."

Unfortunately for those who had placed money on Smith, Brusso was by no means washed up. Writer Joe Jackson captured the action best, telling readers,

> The Brusso-Smith bout came to a very sudden ending when the second period was about half fought. Brusso got to Smith when he was a trifle off his guard, and sent over what appeared to be a not very stiff blow. It reached Smith's jaw and sent him backwards. His head hit the boards and the count was almost superflous, Smith being unable to rise for a time after its completion. He claimed later, the force with which his head hit the floor, which was not padded, was the real cause of his defeat. Smith challenged Brusso to a rematch at any time, and Jake Bair, one of his handlers, also expressed a desire to meet the young man who has been putting away local boxers with almost monotonous regularity.

Ever obliging, Noah agreed to a second fight, which came a scant 12 days later in Mount Clemens, a suburb of Detroit. Smith should never have been permitted to fight so soon after suffering what was obviously a serious concussion. But there were few rules at the time to protect boxers, and the bout was allowed to proceed. Brusso dominated throughout, knocking his man out in the tenth round.

Noah had run his record to an even dozen victories without loss by September 19, 1902, when he left Michigan for the first time to battle Cleveland fighter Jack "Torpedo" O'Donnell in Butler, Indiana. "Brusso knocked O'Donnell out in 11 rounds," a Detroit newspaper reported the next day. "It was a hard fight and the Indiana papers speak highly of the work of the local boy."

Although Brusso's fame was spreading, Biddle told him he couldn't expect to get many major fights outside the state until he defeated Tom McCune. Sharing the state middleweight title just wasn't good enough. He would have to become undisputed Michigan champ if he wanted to attract national attention.

3

King of the Middleweights

Who was this talented new boxer who refused to boycott black fighters?

That was the question on the lips of sports fans in late 1902, as Noah Brusso began moving up the ladder in the middleweight division. It was a legitimate query because there had never been a prizefighter anything like him.

Outside the ring, he craved diversion and had difficulty relaxing. Throughout his life, Brusso would wage a private battle against boredom, and any spare time he had usually drove him to distraction. His favourite hobby seems to have been playing poker, probably because he enjoyed the rush of adrenalin caused by risking his hard-earned money so frivolously. Before long, he had earned a reputation as a card shark, and it was said he often made as much money gambling as he did fighting. The theatre didn't interest him much, although he was fond of musicals. He enjoyed singing so much that he occasionally burst into song while riding the train to one of his fights. The tune he loved best was "Wait Till the Sun Shines, Nellie," possibly because it reminded him of his lost love, Nellie Sweitzer. And he liked to stand around a piano, singing late into the night with friends. He even stayed up late before some big bouts, singing chorus after chorus of "Danny Boy," "Where the River Shannon Flows" and other popular ballads of the day. Such gatherings usually took place in private homes. He avoided Detroit's bars because he feared a loud-mouthed drunk would try to make a name for himself by challenging a professional boxer to a fistfight. Brusso knew he could thrash any number of such men blindfolded, but he feared he might seriously injure one of his hands in a bar-room brawl. Moreover, he had a terrible temper that he was forever trying to

Burns dressed to the nines, complete with top hat.

keep under control. One of the best ways to keep it in check, he found, was by avoiding places where he might be challenged.

His niece, Audrey Adamson, said Brusso retained his love of music throughout his life. "He used to enjoy taking his wife and mother to the opera," she said in a 2000 interview.[1] Apart from gambling and singing, Brusso's pleasures were modest ones. He played some pool, enjoyed excursions to the beach, indulged in the occasional cigar and developed a fondness for whiskey, although he was seldom drunk. As for women, other than Nellie and Irene, he seems to have avoided female company during his stay in Michigan. No doubt he believed the stories that sex would sap a fighter's strength were true.

Dressing up in the finest suits money could buy also appealed to him, and much of his discretionary income went into clothing. Pictures taken of him around this time show him in pinstriped suits with starched white collars, wide, patterned neckties, a silk top hat and even a walking stick! On more than one occasion he showed up for a bout wearing his boxing trunks under a tuxedo. His conduct in this regard would no doubt be of interest to modern psychologists. Raised in poverty by an overly protective mother, mingling mostly with rough-necks as a boy, he plunged headlong into a profession that the upper classes saw as ungentlemanly in the extreme. Then, whenever he went out in public, he dressed to the nines. The most likely explanation for his behaviour is that he was raised in an era in which people were judged more rigorously by their appearance then they are today. In Brusso's time, most adult males were not considered gentlemen. Today, we use the term to describe total strangers. We even put it on the doors of our public washrooms. But in 1902 you were a gentleman only if you were a man of means. And one of the ways to signal to the world that you had money was to wear expensive clothes. Brusso was so anxious to be accepted as a "somebody" that he deprived himself of other pleasures in order to dress well.

Although he was belligerent and foul-mouthed during his fights, most reporters found him to be a modest, well-spoken individual outside the ring. Indeed, he was becoming the stereotypical polite Canadian, at least when talking with journalists. After spending a week with him, one scribe noted the boxer had not spoken "a word that would have shamed the saintliest of Sunday-schools. He is like a freshly-scrubbed child. He looks clean, talks clean and (one is open to swear) thinks clean all the time. He is the adult human animal in its most regenerate and highly-bred form."[2] No doubt Noah was on his best behaviour that week, knowing full well that a reporter was writing a feature about him. But there's also little doubt that, after years of antisocial behaviour, he was finally maturing.

As for food, he was a meat-and-potatoes man with a huge appetite. He liked to eat so much that despite the rigours of his workouts, it wasn't long before he was leaning towards fatness. Strangely, considering what he did for a living, the sight of blood on his plate made him sick, and he always insisted that his meat be well cooked. Trainer Sam Biddle, who took Noah deer hunting in the fall of 1902, noticed his aversion to blood. Biddle, a veteran hunter, spotted a large buck and pointed it out to Brusso, offering him the chance for the kill. The younger man raised his rifle, got the deer in his sights, then found he couldn't pull the trigger. Biddle waited several seconds, then shot the animal himself. As they walked up to the carcass, Noah became violently ill. The deer's eyes were wide open and one of its eyeballs had a piece of dirt on it. The sight, Brusso said later, saddened him because the deer had been so defenseless. In his mind, it was acceptable to batter a man around the ring in a fair fight, but it was wrong to shoot a helpless animal.

This concern for the underdog resurfaced when he used his own money to start up a boxing club for boys in one of Detroit's poorer neighbourhoods. For a time it was a popular hangout for lads in their early teens. But all that changed suddenly after Noah allowed a young black fighter to join the group. Parents of the white boys threatened to pull their sons out of the club unless Brusso sent the newcomer packing. When he flatly refused to do so, the adults lived up to their threats and the organization was forced to close. Despite this incident, Noah continued to spend a lot of time helping neighbourhood children. He could be seen umpiring baseball games, coaching lacrosse matches or simply shadow boxing with youngsters in city parks. All the days of his life, in fact, he seemed to enjoy the company of children more than adults.

He was also an incurable practical joker. His sparring partners quickly discovered they had to check their shorts for itching powder before pulling them on. Noah even used the powder on ladies on the dance floor. And one of his favourite possessions was a novelty book that exploded — much like a trick cigar — when you opened it. His niece Audrey said he was the class clown from day one. "He was quite a cutup. He took my mother [his sister Viola] skating on a pond one time and, when she wasn't looking, he stole her shoes."[3]

One of his sparring partners, Joe Phipps, also remembered Brusso as a natural showman. During workouts,

Burns, right, with Joe Phipps.

which were sometimes open to the public, he'd ask Phipps to wear trunks that had been outfitted with special padding. As they traded punches, Noah would suddenly hit Phipps with a low blow that would lift him off the canvas. The crowd would let out a horrified gasp, only to break into applause when Phipps landed on his feet and went right to the attack.

Religion also played an important part in Brusso's life. He went to church regularly and often sought out older parishioners to discuss "the whole purpose of existence" and "why there is such a thing as man." These were deep subjects, which few expected to hear broached by a young boxer. "These questions," he would later admit, "puzzled me all my life."[4] In an age when Protestants and Catholics were barely on speaking terms, the Methodist Brusso occasionally went to Mass, hoping to find answers there.

But his religious beliefs didn't stop him from leading a lifestyle that would have been frowned on by many Christians. Shortly after his boxing career ended he would be arrested for drug possession. Nor did his strong belief in God stop his obsession with money. Phipps, in fact, considered him "as crooked as a dog's hind leg."[5] Throughout his career he would be criticized for demanding much bigger purses for his fights than boxers had received in the past. But it would be a mistake to condemn him out of hand for this. His desire to live on a grand scale was a reaction to the poverty of his youth. Until he arrived in Detroit he had never enjoyed indoor toilets, central heating or electric lights. Like many others, he wanted money so he could afford those new luxuries. It should also be remembered that he lived at a time when there was no social safety net. People had good reason to be anxious about money because they had no health insurance, no unemployment insurance and no access to welfare. Those who fell on hard times could — and often did — starve to death. As one historian of the era has noted, "One citizen of eight lived in dire poverty in festering slums and perished of diseases at about twice the rate of modest-income people."[6] In such a society, Brusso could hardly be blamed if he seized every opportunity to get ahead.

As for intelligence, he seems to have come equipped with more than his share of grey matter. He was a good writer, a shrewd businessman and a quick-witted individual. Throughout his career a number of reporters expressed surprise at his intellectual prowess. Writing in his memoirs, famous boxing referee Eugene Corri said Brusso "would have succeeded in any line of life. He is endowed with wonderful business ability."[7]

The fight with Gentleman Jim

In the fall of 1902 a man who would dramatically alter Noah Brusso's career arrived in Detroit. His name was Gentleman Jim Corbett. Born in San Francisco in 1866, the 36-year-old prizefighter was a living legend. An educated, thoughtful man, he wasn't anything like other pugilists of the era. While most boxers simply tore into their opponents, standing ramrod straight in the centre of the ring while they traded punches, Corbett was the first to rely on speed, fancy footwork and the accuracy of his jabs. A former bank clerk, he'd come to international prominence in 1889 by beating well-known fighter Joe Choynski during a 27-round fight staged on a barge in the middle of San Francisco Bay. The battle had been held offshore to escape the detection of police officers who had vowed to put a halt to it. He later earned a shot at the World Heavyweight Championship by defeating top-ranked contender Jake Kilrain and by fighting the formidable Peter Jackson to a draw over a gruelling 61 rounds.

All of those contests had taken place in the bloody, bare-knuckle era of boxing, but Corbett also made history by becoming the first gloved champion. He seized

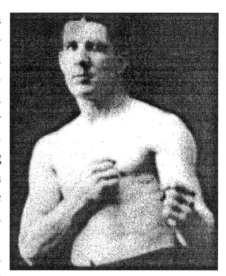

Former heavyweight champion Gentleman Jim Corbett fought Burns early in his career.

the title on September 7, 1892, by knocking out the immortal John L. Sullivan in the seventy-first round. Corbett was so fleet of foot that Sullivan barely laid a glove on him throughout the more than two hundred minutes of fighting.

After his victory, the new champion rested on his laurels, defending his title only once over the next four years. When he finally ventured into the ring again, in March 1897, he lost the crown in an upset to Bob Fitzsimmons. Since then he'd been mostly inactive, but by the time Brusso met him, he was getting ready for a 1903 title fight with new heavyweight champion, Jim Jeffries.

Corbett hadn't been a popular champion, not only because he so seldom defended his title, but also because the public never forgave him for beating the much-loved Sullivan. Nor did most fight fans appreciate his artistry in the ring. They preferred the rock-em-sock-em fighters who used their brawn instead of their brains. Indeed, his nickname, "Gentleman," was occasionally spat out derisively by loutish fans.

But Brusso liked Corbett straight away. For one thing, the former champion was a well-mannered, impeccably dressed individual, and Noah had always appreciated fine clothing. For another, as an artful boxer himself, the Canadian admired Corbett's fighting style. Trainer Sam Biddle, who was from the old school, was forever telling Brusso that he held his hands too low, that he was too reluctant to stand his ground and mix it up. But Corbett liked Noah's relaxed and easy style. He urged him to utilize his speed and reflexes on both defense and offense. Fighters who did "nothing but slug" often ended up "punch drunk" at the end of their careers, he warned.

The pair even staged a three-round exhibition bout at the Detroit Athletic Club that drew a huge crowd. Although Corbett was six inches taller and 50 pounds heavier, Noah held his own all the way. Going into his trademark gorilla crouch, he managed to get inside and score several hits to the body. He even tagged the former champion with a left hook to the head that momentarily stunned him. He could have followed up with a knockout blow, but such a move would have been considered unsporting in an exhibition match. So Brusso simply danced around for several seconds, flicking harmless jabs at Corbett's raised gloves while he waited for the old hero's head to clear. His good showing in this bout convinced him that in addition to the middleweight division, he might have a future as a light heavyweight, or possibly as a heavyweight. For the first time he began to dream that he might even become World Heavyweight Boxing Champion one day.

Following the match, as Brusso and Corbett had drinks together in a downtown hotel, the older man brought up the touchy subject of inter-racial bouts. He made his own views clear, telling the Canadian it was important to "uphold the honour of the white race."[8] That, he added, meant Brusso should stop fighting blacks.

When Noah pointed out Corbett had once fought the great East Indian boxer, Peter Jackson, the former champ would only say it was a youthful mistake that he would never repeat. Corbett would keep his pledge. A check of his record shows Jackson was the only fighter of colour he faced in 19 professional bouts. And that fight had come before he won the title from John L. Sullivan. After capturing the championship, Corbett had followed Sullivan's lead and drawn the colour line.

Noah was not persuaded to duck black fighters, but as a result of Corbett's visit, he was more determined than ever to become a finesse boxer.

Brusso's finest hour

Brusso was anxious for a crack at Tom McCune, but first he had to dispose of a tough middleweight contender named John "Reddy" Phillips, who was considered one of the best young pugilists in Michigan. The fight, which took place in Phillips's home town of Lansing on November 6, 1902, showed just how bush-league professional boxing could be. The *Lansing Daily Journal* reported, "The main bout was late in starting. When the gloves were handed to the fighters, it was found that the box contained three right-handed mitts and one left. A messenger was sent to obtain a left-hand glove, it being nearly half an hour later when he returned."

Once the action got under way, neither fighter seemed anxious to mix it up. Each, no doubt, had a healthy respect for the other. The action was so tame, the *Journal*'s bloodthirsty correspondent complained, that neither fighter was hit with anything harder than a "love tap" for several rounds. But when the referee threatened to call the bout a draw "unless there was a waking up," Brusso went to work, forcing a battered Phillips to quit at the end of the ninth round.

Noah had his thirteenth victory, but the achievement paled in comparison to what he accomplished later that night. A few hours after the fight, as he headed for his hotel room, he noticed yellow flames shooting out of a broken-down apartment building. It was nearly midnight and there was no sign of Lansing's volunteer fire department. On a balcony he could clearly make out through smoke an elderly black lady holding two small girls. It was only two floors up but that was about 20 feet — much too high to jump with a pair of babies in your arms. Running to the scene, the prizefighter called to the woman to drop the children so he could catch them. She hesitated for a moment, as if she wasn't sure she should trust a white man. In the next instant she lowered one of the girls as far as her arms would reach. Then, in a supreme act of faith, she let her fall. The one sport Noah had never dominated as a youth was football, but he caught the girl with ease. After safely lowering the second child to Noah, the woman began to climb over the rail herself, but Noah shouted to her to stay where she was. She looked to weigh a good 175 pounds, and he feared he'd break both his arms if he tried to

catch her. Dashing into the smoke-filled building, he raced up a stair-
case, kicked in a door, found the grandmother and led her to safety.
There was still no sign of the fire department, so he took the woman
and the two babies to his hotel and gave them his room for the night.
With that, he went to the train station, where he spent the evening
sleeping on a wooden bench.

Becoming undisputed Michigan champ

The time had come to settle the issue. Who was the real middleweight
champion of Michigan, Noah Brusso or Tom McCune? McCune, whom
newspaper reporters sometimes referred to as the "Champion of Poland," was an immigrant who had changed his name because he
thought an Irish moniker would make him a more marketable com-
modity. Many of the world's best boxers were Irish, or Irish-Americans,
including Sullivan, Corbett, Fitzsimmons and Jeffries, so the public
almost assumed you *had* to be Irish to be any good. McCune, who
owned his own gym, *was* good. Besides that, he was older, more
experienced and a little bigger than Brusso. "The show will settle the
question of superiority that has long been a mooted point between the
followers of Brusso and McCune," the *Detroit Free Press* declared. "It is
up to Brusso to beat McCune decisively, and establish a reputation for
himself on his first appearance before a big club."

   The fight, held at Detroit's Light Guard Armoury on Boxing Day,
December 26, 1902, was a minor classic. "Brusso and McCune put up
a bout that was surprisingly speedy and free from simple slug," a
ringside reporter wrote.

   As they tapped gloves at centre ring to start the first round, McCune's
supporters chanted, "Kill the nigger lover!"[9] The men started out cautiously, feeling each other out for the first three rounds. In the fourth
Brusso started to gain the upper hand, scoring the first clean knockdown of the fight. In the next round they went at each other
tooth-and-nail, with Brusso scoring two knockdowns and McCune
one. The fighters took the sixth round off, dangling all over each other
in prolonged clinches that were little more than unofficial truces de-

signed to give them both a little rest. Impatient fans became so incensed they started booing and throwing garbage at the combatants.

The end came with unexpected suddenness in the seventh. "Brusso started after McCune when the bell sounded for the seventh, rushing him about the ring and working his left to the jaw," the reporter wrote. "With the round a little more than half gone, he got McCune near the ropes and swung a hard left hook to the point of the jaw, grogging the east-side champion. He followed this with another, but lighter blow of the same order. McCune backed away to the centre of the ring, and Brusso feinted with the left again and shot over a straight right, solid on the point. McCune went down, all gone. He came up inside the count but was easily dropped again and as it was apparent McCune could not finish the round, the referee stopped it and declared Brusso the winner. There were 20 seconds to go."

The writer concluded with an interesting analysis that shows just how far Noah had come as a prizefighter in such a short time:

> McCune boxed as cleverly as he ever did but was outmatched at any time that it became a mixing contest because of Brusso's strength and hitting powers. Brusso has improved immensely since last winter, especially in his defensive work, formerly his weak point. He got away from and covered up for McCune's long left very cleverly. On his offensive work he showed increased speed, though he was carrying more weight than he should have to be at his best. The two blows with which he won, the left hook that started it and the straight right that finished things, showed that he had the hitting powers that count.

Brusso was also doing better financially, at least partly because he was so active. He fought an astonishing nine times in 1902 (not counting three exhibition bouts). Figures from eight of his nine official battles are known, and they show he made $885, or the modern equivalent of about $22,000, tax-free. Assuming he made another $100 or so for the remaining fight, he earned close to the modern equivalent of $25,000 take-home-pay that year. It was a modest but respectable total.

Brusso's chances to make big money were improving with his victo-ries. At the end of the year he had a perfect 14–0 won-lost record, with a dozen knockouts behind his name. It was an impressive tally of wins that was beginning to attract national attention.

The bitter taste of defeat

Noah Brusso's relentless drive towards the top took an abrupt detour on January 16, 1903, when he squared off with a bigger, more experienced fighter named Mike Schreck. Schreck, a burly German-American heavy-weight who outweighed the Canadian by 30 pounds, was a world-class boxer. A newspaper headline written the day before the bout declared, "Schreck best boy that Brusso has yet clashed with." That may well have been the understatement of the year in the sporting world. As the accompanying story pointed out, the Cincinnati boxer had beaten all the best fighters in Chicago, which was a hotbed of prizefighting.

Although the story made it plain Schreck was good, it didn't begin to do him justice. He had demolished former light-heavyweight cham-pion George Gardner before moving up to the heavyweight division. Newspaper accounts described him as "cool and aggressive." One reporter said he'd put an opponent away under "a rain of hammer-like blows." By the time he signed to fight Brusso, no less of an authority than Gentleman Jim Corbett was saying Schreck had the tools to win the World Heavyweight Boxing Championship. "I really believe Mike Schreck could beat any heavyweight living, not barring Jim Jeffries (the reigning champ)," he said. "Take my word for it, he is sure enough coming world's champion."[10]

Brusso was unperturbed, at least on the surface. He had trained diligently for the battle and felt confident his punching power would more than compensate for Schreck's size and experience. What he wasn't counting on was the fact that Mike Schreck, on top of everything else, was a southpaw. And Noah had never been in the ring with a left-handed fighter.

The bout, staged before a sell-out crowd at Detroit's Light Guard Armoury, started out slowly, with an unusually nervous Brusso grimly holding on to his adversary at every opportunity. "The first minute looked like a pursuit race," one reporter wrote, "with Schreck chasing Brusso. Brusso went for the jaw once, but couldn't reach. Schreck gave him ample opportunity, and when he found that the Canadian could not reach, showed no hesitancy in getting in close."

Leading heavyweight contender Mike Schreck was the first boxer to defeat Burns.

As the fight wore on, Brusso became increasingly frustrated. "He found it difficult to map out a plan of campaign against Schreck, who is one of the most awkward boxers in the ring. He is so awkward he puts a clever man at a disadvantage. He is left-handed and he comes in side-on, so to speak, making it hard for a boxer who sees him in action for the first time to get to him. Brusso tried at least a hundred times to put his right hand punch — the bread winner for him — on the jaw. Each time that he tried it in the first eight rounds he was short, or was glancing with it." Schreck, meanwhile, was continuing to pepper Noah's body almost at will. The sustained assault took its toll, and an exhausted Brusso was knocked off his feet in the eighth round. He was up by the count of nine, but it was clear he was losing the fight.

In the ninth a desperate Brusso charged out of his corner, throwing bombs. Twice he connected on Schreck's jaw, staggering the bigger man. Noah was so tired and battered himself, however, that he couldn't finish off his foe. In the tenth and final round Brusso again pressed frantically, but it was too little, too late, and Schreck was given the decision on points.

On the comeback trail

Brusso's first defeat caused a sensation among fight fans in Michigan. The *Detroit Times* speculated that the 21-year-old was washed up, that he had no prospects of becoming a world champion in any weight division. The *Detroit Free Press* was more sympathetic. "The defeat does not discredit Brusso," sports editor Joe Jackson said. "He was naturally nervous, in his first meeting with a man of reputation."

On the positive side, he had lasted the whole 10 rounds with one of the top heavyweights in the world. And he hadn't lost his Michigan middleweight title because Schreck, as a heavyweight, wasn't allowed to claim it. A small man could move up to a higher weight category and win the title, but a big fighter could not take a step down and claim a championship. He could only improve his won-lost record by beating someone in a lower weight class.

Most defeated fighters, then as now, are full of excuses whenever they lose a bout. Many blame the referee, or the judges, claiming they were "robbed." But Brusso made no excuses for his loss to Schreck. In fact, he was magnanimous enough to admit he didn't deserve to win after each of his defeats. Strangely, he complained only about the officiating in bouts that were declared a draw. Asked what had gone wrong during the fight with Schreck, he said simply, "I beat myself."[11]

He was equally gracious when he won, offering words of praise and encouragement to defeated opponents. To understand why Brusso was so philosophical in defeat and generous in victory, we need look no further than to his childhood. In the late nineteenth century, Canadian children learned that heroes were people who believed in honour and fair play above all else. As one historian has pointed out, "Virtually every subject taught in the public schools had some patriotic or moral tone."[12] Even spelling texts of the period used uplifting homilies about the need to be honourable. A hero, Brusso came to believe, was not someone who complained about adversity or kicked a man when he was down.

Brusso took a few days off after the loss, going back to Ontario to visit old friends and relatives. He spent time in Woodstock, travelling with the local hockey team, then visited his mother in Preston. But he found little peace there, mainly because she nagged him to give up boxing before he got seriously hurt. Retirement was the last thing on his mind, however, and when he got back to Detroit a few weeks later he immediately started down the comeback trail by defeating Boston light heavyweight Jim "Elbows" O'Brien on February 13, 1903.

His conquest of O'Brien did little to convince critics that Brusso was a top contender, but his next moved gained him attention across the United States and Canada. On March 25, 1903, he took on two fighters in one night! His opposition included two men he'd bested before — Dick "Bull" Smith and Jim "Reddy" Phillips — but it was a major gamble nevertheless. Smith had gone the distance with Brusso the previous July, lasting the full 10 rounds before losing on points, and Phillips had taken him through nine tough rounds in Lansing just three months earlier. If his first opponent was able to prolong the fight for any length of time, Brusso might not have enough power left to defend his Michigan middleweight crown against the second boxer.

As fight time approached, Smith and Phillips agreed to a coin toss to determine who would go first. Each, of course, was hoping the other man would be first up, but Phillips won and took a seat at ringside. He wore a smug smile as Smith climbed through the ropes to meet Brusso.

At first it looked as if Noah was in for a long night. "Smith went in confident he could stay the limit and for the first round he held his own," a reporter wrote afterwards. In the second round Smith pressed the action, although he found Brusso to be "a willing mixer." In one exchange, "Smith worked in a heavy body punch that shook Brusso but the latter retaliated by bringing his right across and sending the big Delray boxer to the mat. The gong was all that saved Smith. In the third round Brusso went after Smith and scored two knockdowns in succession and finished the work by using the right again to the jaw, which won for him the decision. The referee stopped the bout as Smith was all in."

As Phillips came into the ring, Noah looked ripe for the taking. It had taken him three of the scheduled six rounds to dispose of Smith, and he'd been hurt by at least one of his opponent's blows. If Phillips played his cards right, he'd have an excellent chance of winning. Instead, the obviously frightened boxer committed perhaps the most outrageous foul ever seen in the prize ring. He started out fighting dirty, then got worse. "Reddy Phillips adopted tactics that got him in disfavour right from the start," the reporter said. "In the clinches, instead of breaking clean, he continued to mix it, despite the cautions of the referee. Brusso easily had the better of it in the first round, although

Phillips worked in a few hard blows. The second round was a repetition of the first, in regards to foul work. Phillips continued to hit in the clinches and, when Brusso cut in to finish him, he deliberately kicked Brusso in the groin. Amid the hisses of the crowd he was disqualified and the verdict given to Brusso."

Just 24 days later, Noah followed up his double victory with a third-round knockout of black heavyweight Earl "Hercules" Thompson. Noah had four wins in a row, but he was rapidly running out of local opponents who were willing to fight him.

Defying the colour line — again

Brusso would have to leave Detroit if he was going to improve. Although he'd fought 19 professional bouts, he'd faced only 13 men. He'd beaten Dick Smith three times and had scored double victories over Fred Thornton, Billy Walsh, Eddie Sholtreau and Reddy Phillips. A few of his opponents had come from out of town, including boxers from Chicago, Boston and Cincinnati, but most were from the Detroit area. Obviously he needed to go further afield to find new adversaries. It wasn't a prospect he looked forward to. Travel was exceptionally wearisome in those days. Buses and airplanes were not yet available and there were only 8,000 cars in the entire United States, with less than 200 miles of paved roads in the country. The train was the only option for most people, and locomotives of the era chugged along at about 50 or 60 kilometres per hour.

Nevertheless, Brusso headed north, breezing into the rough-and-tumble copper mining town of Houghton, Michigan, in the fall of 1903. Houghton was a lively little place located about as far north as you could go in the state without ending up in Lake Superior. It had a population of only five thousand, but the local mines were booming and there was plenty of money floating around. The miners worked hard and played hard. On Friday nights they poured into the downtown, looking for entertainment. The community had a professional hockey team, led by Noah's old lacrosse opponent, Fred "Cyclone" Taylor, but boxing was the main attraction. Whenever a fight card was put together, which was often, the town hall was filled to capacity.

Burns in battle formation.

Brusso arrived in Houghton on September 25, 1903, just in time for a bout with a local favourite named Jimmy "Bearcat" Duggan. Duggan had a reputation as a powerful slugger, but like so many fighters from the north, he knew nothing about defense. Noah was able to thwart his maniacal charges with lethal body blows that lowered his guard, exposing Duggan's head to a knockout punch that came in the ninth round.

After the fight Noah spent two weeks in Hougton's saloons, playing poker with miners. He raked in several hundred dollars at the card tables, then travelled to Sault Ste Marie, Michigan, for a fight with a fearsome Detroit boxer named Jack "Spider" Hammond. Hammond was one of the better light heavyweights in the state, with a record of 19 wins, 6 losses and 9 draws to his credit. No less than a dozen of his victims had been KO'd. In one of his fights he'd gone the distance before losing on points to world light heavyweight champion Jack Root. Needless to say, he was not afraid of Noah Brusso. In fact, he spent much of the bout pressing the action before the Canadian tagged him in the third round with an upper-cut that exploded onto his jaw with concussive force. He sagged to the floor and was counted out.

Brusso, realizing he'd landed a knockout blow, retired to his corner and put on his coat before the referee reached the count of 10. The next day, the *Sault Ste. Marie Evening News* described Noah as the fastest boxer the city had ever seen. "He is a wonderfully quick man with both his hands and feet. He was in and out and around, ducking, dodging and hitting with right and left so fast it was impossible to follow his blows."

The victory, Noah's twentieth, paved the way for a confrontation with a formidable African-American middleweight named Billy Moore. Moore, another southpaw, had gained a strong following by going the distance with famed world welterweight champion Mike "Twin" Sullivan before losing a disputed decision on points. Like most blacks of the era, Moore had trouble getting fights with whites. In fact, Brusso and Sullivan were among only a handful of white boxers he would face in a lengthy and distinguished career. The *Houghton Daily Mining Gazette* held out little hope for a Brusso win, telling readings Moore was "a very clever boxer who has far more ring experience." Nevertheless, miners flocked to the October 25, 1903 match, expecting a good show. Brusso and the Chicago fighter gave it to them, battling to a rousing 10-round draw.

Staying in the north, Noah took on a pair of burly boxers who had learned to fight in saloons and hobo camps around the United States. They were tough as nails on offense but basically unskilled in the art of self-defense. Taking advantage of his fast footwork and spear-like jab, Brusso cut them both to pieces. Jack "Big Boy" Butler, an imposing African-American fighter from Brooklyn, was the first to go, collapsing in the second round of a bout staged in Sault Ste Marie. The fight went into the books as Brusso's sixth with a black man. Hopping across the state line, Brusso ended his triumphant northern tour by punching Jack O'Donnell's lights out in the eleventh round of a contest held in Evanston, Illinois.

Noah closed out 1903 in Detroit with a New Year's Eve victory over Tom McCune. In many ways it had been a year of mixed blessings for him. He'd won nine fights but he'd suffered his first loss and had also been held to a draw. On the financial side, the picture was a little brighter. Figures for 10 of his 11 bouts have been accounted for, and they show he made $1,670, or the modern equivalent of almost $42,000. Assuming he made $100 for the other fight, it appears he earned today's equivalent of $45,000, tax-free. Clearly he was making a decent living as a prizefighter. But boxing careers are short, and Noah knew he would have to make his move soon if he was to become a big-name, big-money fighter.

4

The Birth of Tommy Burns

The fight that would change Noah Brusso's life — and his identity — took place on January 28, 1904, in Detroit.

Just back from his successful swing through the north country, Brusso accepted a bout with Ben "Gorilla" O'Grady, a tenacious boxer who'd come to Michigan after beating all the best middleweight fighters in New York state.

"One of my stiffest fights in Detroit was with Ben O'Grady of Buffalo," Brusso wrote in *Scientific Boxing*. "He was a pretty tough customer, and had a great trick of trying to frighten his opponents at the outset. As soon as he got into the ring he started off with his seconds with 'shall I kill him? Which round shall I knock him out in?' And so on. When we met in the middle of the ring he started off to me 'well, you're here, are you?'"

Undaunted, Brusso replied, "Yes, I'm here."

"Well," O'Grady snarled, "you won't be here in a while."[1]

What followed was a bloody slug-fest that landed one man in hospital and the other in jail. "What a gory scrap it was," the *Detroit Times* said later. "O'Grady knew nothing but slug, and Brusso had no chance to fight clever."

The Canadian stung his man with several quick shots to the head, knocking him off his feet twice in the first round. But the fight wasn't over yet. O'Grady was a gladiator who would happily absorb two or three blows to get in one good punch of his own. He went down three times in the second round before he hit Brusso with a terrific overhand left, sending him to the mat for the count of nine. Walking straight through a barrage of punches in the third round, O'Grady continued to pound away at Noah's head and face.

Then it happened. "They were mixing at close quarters when an awful punch, a right cross to the jaw, dropped O'Grady," the *Times* reported. The *Detroit Free Press* was less colourful but offered more details. "It was O'Grady's lack of boxing ability that did him in," it reported. "He came up for the third round, weakened by his previous beating, but aggressive. The period was but half a minute gone when he led his left and missed, Brusso ducking the blow. As the Detroit boy straightened up he drove his own right straight on the point of the jaw. O'Grady went down on his back, his head hit the mat and the count was a mere formality."

For a moment it looked like just another Noah Brusso knockout win, the twentieth of his career. But this time it was different. O'Grady stayed down long after he should have been revived. His seconds got into the ring and dragged him to his corner, but they were unable to bring him around with either smelling salts or water. Looking panic stricken, they carried him gently into his dressing-room. A few minutes later, one of them emerged and cried out, "Is there a doctor in the house?"[2] A physician named Gurney rushed to O'Grady's side and, after a brief examination, concluded the boxer had suffered a brain concussion. O'Grady, who by now had slipped into a coma, was taken to the nearest hospital. He lay unconscious for four days. Brusso, meanwhile, was handcuffed and led away by police. He was charged with assault causing bodily harm and flatly warned the charge would be upgraded to manslaughter if O'Grady died. Bail was denied, possibly because the authorities feared he would leave the country. As a Canadian, Brusso could have crossed the border into nearby Windsor, Ontario, without any problem and it might have proven difficult to extradite him. He was let out of jail only when he asked permission to visit O'Grady in the hospital, and then only with a police escort.

To his credit, Noah appeared more worried about O'Grady's health than his own future. As he sat in his cell he held up his hands and muttered, "If I've killed a man with these I'll never fight again, so help me God."[3] Sam Biddle tried to assure him that O'Grady's injuries had been a fluke, that the boxer had been hurt more by his head's contact with the floor than by Brusso's punch, but Noah was inconsolable.

O'Grady pulled out of the coma on the fifth day, but he was in poor condition. Three years later the *Detroit Times* reported the unfortunate fighter had suffered permanent brain damage — Brusso's last punch had "made a lunatic out of O'Grady."

Brusso still faced assault charges, but they were dropped after one of Noah's lacrosse buddies, a man named Allan McDonald, smuggled O'Grady and his manager out of Detroit. The badly injured boxer was returned to Buffalo, where he spent another eight days in hospital. Without O'Grady's testimony, the police knew they had a weak case against Brusso. In the end, they agreed to drop all charges if the Canadian would promise not to fight in Michigan for at least a year.

That wasn't the end of the Brusso-O'Grady saga. Years later, when Noah was World Heavyweight Boxing Champion, the two had a bizarre encounter. Brusso was appearing as the main attraction in a Buffalo burlesque show; his role was to stage three-round exhibition bouts with anyone in the audience willing to take him on. O'Grady, who was running his own health club at the time, asked the champ to spar with him, explaining that it would help promote his business. But, not anxious to end up back in the hospital, he asked Brusso to go easy on him. Noah agreed, promising to let him make a good showing.

When the bout was scheduled to begin, however, O'Grady was nowhere to be seen. Brusso turned to leave, only to be punched in the mouth as he stepped through a door at the rear of the stage. The blow landed with such force that a tooth was driven through his lower lip. Lunging out instinctively, he grabbed his attacker in a bear hug. In the next instant he found himself face to face with Ben O'Grady. Someone called the police and reporters began clamouring for a street fight. But Noah insisted it was all a mistake, that O'Grady hadn't intended to hurt him. The American was released, and the Buffalo newspapers had a field day suggesting the heavyweight champ was afraid of the local boy.

The Canadian didn't want to fight O'Grady because he had no desire to end up back in jail. As for the Buffalo fighter, other than his cowardly ambush of the champ, his fighting career was over. He never boxed again professionally after the day Noah put him in a coma.

Ben O'Grady wasn't the only one who would never step into a ring again. The bloody Brusso-O'Grady battle had also put an end to the ring career of Noah Brusso. Noah's mother had been appalled by his vocation for some time, but she was now almost hysterical about it. The negative publicity from the O'Grady affair had humiliated her. Sofa wrote her youngest boy a letter all but begging him to abandon the sport. He was, she told him, doing dishonour to his late father's good name.

Sofa's feelings were shared by many. Indeed, it was against the Criminal Code of Canada to stage a prizefight. Boxing contests were allowed under federal law provided that the participants were both members of an athletic club. In such cases, however, the spectators were all supposed to be club members as well. In some cities, including Montreal, even those bouts were outlawed by municipal statute. In the United States, meanwhile, boxing was illegal in several cities and states. In 1881, the year Noah was born, it had been declared "a crime against the peace" in New York City.[4] Anyone caught staging a fight could be jailed for up to three years. Similar laws were passed and unpassed over the years in the United Kingdom and South Africa. In essence, large segments of the western world saw pugilism as a dangerous and barbarous pastime that should be banned.

Besides considering boxing a disreputable occupation, Sofa worried constantly about Noah's safety. A handful of fighters were killed in the ring every year, and the deaths all received prominent news coverage. She also feared that her son might kill someone else.

Sofa's words hurt Noah, but he had no intention of giving up now, just as he was reaching his prime. Instead, he decided to hide his occupation from her by changing his name. He'd never liked his given name anyway, and he wasn't especially fond of his surname either. Like Tom McCune and many others before him, he decided on an Irish alias. At first he opted for "Ed Burns," but after a few weeks decided he didn't like the sound of it and changed it to "Tommy Burns," which was the name of a popular Canadian jockey of the era. Although no one had ever heard of this new prizefighter, within two years he'd be the most famous athlete on the planet. And his cover would be blown even sooner than that. The moment he started winning important fights, newspapers in Ontario let everyone — including Sofa — know that the

Burns in a rather mean-looking pose.

rising young star named Tommy Burns was none other than Noah
Brusso of Hanover.

A confrontation with gangsters

Tommy Burns chose Chicago as his new home in February 1904 because it had an excellent reputation as a fight town. As the *Chicago Tribune* noted in an editorial that month, "Chicago is one of the best, if not the best, fight towns in the country." Fans were so crazy for the sport they'd pay up to $3 even for "poor attractions." By way of contrast, most boxing tickets in Michigan could be purchased for 75¢. The Chicago referees, it added, were "generally honest and not swayed by crowds." In such a place Burns hoped to make money and improve his game by competing against more skilful opponents than those found in Detroit.

At first Burns loved Chicago. It was a huge city, with a population of 1.7 million people. More than that, it had a futuristic feel to it. An elevated railway loop, built in 1890, wound its way through the tallest skyscrapers in the world. The buildings, which one writer has described as glass and steel "monuments of the new age,"[5] looked like nothing he had ever seen. One of them, the Board of Trade, soared a staggering 110 metres into the air. In a letter to his mother, Tommy said he got dizzy just looking up at it from the sidewalk. Renting a waterfront apartment for $14 a month, he found awe-inspiring sights at every turn. At night, the docks could be achingly beautiful. Describing Chicago's shoreline at the beginning of the twentieth century, historian Finis Farr wrote, "At evening, the lights on the masts and gleaming from the cabins of ships, at piers along the river, or riding in harbour, added the feeling of Oriental lanterns to the fascinating mystery of Chicago."[6] During the early mornings, when Burns went for his jogs, mist rose from Lake Michigan, enveloping the highest buildings and adding further to the mystical atmosphere.

Unfortunately, Chicago had a dark side to it that would soon threaten Burns's future. Dishonest judges, police officers and politicians were routinely bribed by organized criminals who ran brothels, seedy saloons, decrepit hotels, dance halls and boarding houses. They controlled at least five thousand prostitutes, many of them young girls, and were beginning to rig horse-races and prizefights.

The year Burns arrived a special investigator hired by a group of concerned Chicago businessmen released a report that concluded the police department was out of control. According to Farr, the report found some constables were "no better than uniformed hoodlums, and addicted to morphine and cocaine. The police force failed in such primary duties as controlling traffic and protecting citizens in the streets, and many officers shared in thieves' loot, sent in false duty reports, and loafed in saloons when supposedly on patrol. During the winter of 1905–6, residential streets became so dangerous that the people in north side neighbourhoods hired private watchmen to patrol after dark. In other parts of the city, one risked meeting holdup men of such inhuman brutality that they not only robbed the victims, but tied them to posts, tortured them with knives, and sometimes left them dead."[6]

This deplorable situation would not have an impact on Burns during his first two months in Chicago. He defeated a boxer named George Shrosbree on February 26, 1904, then fought old foe Mike Schreck to a draw in a fight staged, incredibly, the very next night in Milwaukee. Following that he took part in a pair of bouts with a tough little Italian-American fighter named Tony Caponi, obtaining a draw on March 18 and a win on April 9.

Burns had won only two of four fights in his new home, but that was the least of his problems. He'd been approached prior to the second Caponi fight and offered money to take part in a fix. Under the proposed plan, he'd let Caponi win in exchange for $1,000. It was a lot of money, but the Canadian turned it down without thinking twice about it. He wanted to go somewhere in boxing and he could hardly do that if he started taking dives. When a burly underworld character threatened to break his legs if he didn't participate in the con game, Burns lost his temper and told the man to "go to hell."[7] Despite the show of bravado, he took the threat seriously, going so far as to buy a revolver for protection. And just to be on the safe side, he left Chicago heading to Salt Lake City for a match with a big heavyweight named Joe "Kid" Wardinski. The heavily muscled Wardinski was the betting favourite, but Burns caught him in the first round with his destructive left hook, knocking him cold.

In a poker game after the fight, Burns won the deed to a gold mine in Alaska. Anxious to put as much distance between himself and the Chicago gangsters as possible, he decided to head north to take a look at his new possession. It was a move that would embroil him in some of the most hair-raising adventures of his life.

North to Alaska

In the summer of 1904 there were few more romantic places on the face of the earth than Alaska. Gold had been discovered there five years earlier, launching a stampede that sent tens of thousands of thrill-seekers converging on the place from every corner of the globe. Eight thousand miners left Dawson City in Canada's Yukon Territory in a single month in the summer of 1899 to make their way to Nome, Alaska. And no wonder. One shovelful of gold dust and nuggets could fetch a lucky prospector $800, or the equivalent of about 18 months pay for the average person.

Burns boarded a steamer in Seattle in May and sailed to Nome, located on the frigid shores of the Bering Sea. He never forgot the sight as the ship rounded a bend and the fabled city of gold rose out of the mist. Nome was shimmering in the afternoon sunlight, a magical place located on the edge of the Arctic Circle, in the middle of nowhere. Saloons, hotels, false-front dance halls, three newspapers, an opera house, motion-picture theatres, church steeples, warehouses, brothels, shops, markets, shacks and tents could be seen crowded along a narrow strip of land between the beach and nearby tundra. There were only two streets, each stretching for two kilometres. Both sported sidewalks and telephone poles. In all, 8,000 people lived in a town that hadn't existed just a few years before.

The sun stays up around the clock during a Nome summer, so there was still plenty of daylight as Burns walked up the main street looking for a hotel room. Colourful banners and signs read, "Gold bought and sold." On the wooden sidewalks prospectors could be seen wearing fur hats and snowglasses, even though it was a warm day. The items were, Burns guessed correctly, considered to be badges of honour. A drunken donkey that had been plied with whiskey by intoxicated miners was staggering down the street, chased by yapping dogs.

Burns soon found that the whole city was one gigantic bazaar. You could buy anything, whether it was a tusk from a prehistoric woolly mammoth, ostrich feathers or peanuts and ice cream. The prices, however, were astronomical. Nome was a long way from anywhere, which made the cost of bringing in goods from the outside world prohibitive. Besides, the merchants had a captive market and they knew it. It could cost five hundred dollars for a keg of beer and a dollar for an egg. Even considering the fortunes made by the miners, the prices were ridiculous.

Around dinner-time a carnival-like atmosphere took over. Saloon-keepers appeared in the doorways of their establishments with megaphones in hand, trying to lure customers inside. As Burns walked past the Northern Saloon, he was attracted at once by the sounds of piano and fiddle music. Intrigued, he stepped inside and immediately found himself in his element. Whiskey flowed at an oak bar; red, white and blue poker chips clattered on green table tops and a pair of scantily dressed young women could be seen dancing up a storm on a makeshift stage. Burns bought himself a bottle of whiskey, took his place at one of the 15 gambling tables and settled in for a long evening. He didn't realize that he was no longer dealing with the amateur gamblers of the American Midwest. These were real pros. More than that, they had plenty of money and played for high stakes. One of Nome's gamblers, "Silent Sam" Bonnifield, had once lost $72,000 and his hotel in a card game. Just as he ran out of money, however, a buddy showed up and lent him enough cash to stay in the game. Five hours later he'd won back the hotel and all his loot. And an hour after that he'd cleaned out his opponent. Another gambler, who went by the name of One-Eyed Riley, once won $28,000 in a single evening, then lost it all in a card game a few weeks later.

Although Burns didn't have that kind of money to lose, by 2 A.M. he'd lost almost $400 of the $500 he'd brought with him from Seattle. Fortunately, the card game was coming to an end. But on the stage the two thinly clad girls, known as the Oatley Sisters, were still going strong. Burns had never heard of them, but they were legendary figures throughout the north. The *Dryea Trail*, a weekly newspaper in Alaska, described them as the "queens of the gold fields." It added, "Their capacity for drink, if nothing else, should attract a good patronage out of mere curiosity to see two girls who are put to bed drunk every night and yet who retain the bloom of youth, bright eyes, good voice and lively heels. They are the wonders of their kind."[8]

As Burns looked on, the girls sang "Break the News to Mother," "A bird in the Gilded Cage" and "I Love Her, Yes I Love Her Just the Same." The prizefighter and the miners, all thousands of kilometres from home, fell silent, each man lost in his thoughts, as the sisters' lovely voices carried across the saloon and out into the street. A miner who had seen the sisters perform in Dawson City a few years earlier wrote, "I stood there with my mouth open, listening to the Oatley sisters sing those sad ballads. I never knew them personally and didn't have enough money in those days to really get a good look at them. But they sure helped me to put many a lonesome night behind me and gave me something to think about when I crawled into my bunk at night and packed my weary head on a pillow made of two high boots."[9]

Burns was so taken with the girls — and so drunk — that he got up on the stage and began singing with them. After the place closed, they both offered to take him to bed for $50. Unsure which one to choose, he took both, paying them his last $100. He was so intoxicated that he passed out before anything happened. When the three of them got up around noon the next day the girls took pity on Tommy, offering to buy him lunch. He was, after all, marooned in Alaska with nothing more than the deed to a gold mine in his pocket. In the course of the conversation they found out he was a boxer and suggested a way he could earn enough money to stay in Nome long enough to inspect his mine. He could, they said, stage a prizefight.

When Burns asked who he could fight, the girls both blurted out, "Why 'Klondike Mike' of course!"[10]

Burns vs. Klondike Mike

Of all the intriguing characters who descended on Nome during the gold rush, Klondike Mike Mahoney was among the most memorable.

Klondike Mike Mahoney,
champion of Alaska and
the Yukon.

He certainly cut an imposing figure. His biographer, Merrill Denison, described him as "six-foot two, with an athlete's build and a luxurious mop of copper-red hair that seemed literally aflame. He had a big head and a wide, square-boned face tanned the colour of a ripe tangerine."[11]

Born on a farm near Buckingham, Quebec, Mahoney had grown up chopping wood in the lumber camps of the Gatineau forests. A husky man, he could neither read nor write but was exceptionally strong, becoming a feared boxer and wrestler in the lumber camps. In 1892, after moving to Michigan, he won the state's amateur heavyweight boxing title. He headed west after that, settling in Seattle in 1897. That summer word of a great gold find in the Yukon reached the Pacific coast, sparking widespread excitement. Nowhere was it more keenly felt than in Seattle, the seaport into which the first gold-laden ship had sailed. More than two tons of gold were unloaded from the vessel, creating a sensation in the city. "Seattle has gone stark, raving mad on gold," the *New York Herald* reported. Indeed it had. Outfitting shops sprang up overnight, selling everything from shovels to fur coats to the tens of thousands of adventurers who poured into the city. Mahoney was so broke he couldn't afford the fare on a steamer headed to Skagway, Alaska, but he got a job as a deck-hand and sailed north. Once he reached the Yukon he put his amazing strength to work, making thousands of dollars a month carrying goods over the infamous Chilkoot Pass. The treacherous Chilkoot was long, narrow and so steep that at some points travellers could crawl on their hands and knees and still appear to be standing in an upright position. Those who moved a metre or two to the right or left could tumble into a ravine, never to be seen again. And just to complicate matters, banshee winds howled through the pass much of the year. For decades after the gold rush ended, items that had been tossed aside by weary miners anxious to lighten their loads were still in evidence along the trail. Everything from boots to trunks was discarded. But those who hired Mahoney didn't have to worry about leaving prized possessions behind. To this day, Yukon residents insist Klondike Mike once carried a piano through the pass. He eventually set up shop in Dawson City, operating a dog team from there to the gold fields. He moved to Nome after that, where he spent most of his time at the Northern Saloon, which was run by legendary boxing promoter Tex Rickard. On many nights Mahoney could be found in the Northern, taking on all comers in boxing matches staged in the hotel's back room. So when Burns approached him with the idea of holding an exhibition bout, he quickly agreed.

Burns was in for a shock when he entered the ring. Mahoney walked over to his corner and announced that, since he was on his home ground, he'd fight "lumberjack style." And that included both punching and kicking.

Tommy had expected little more than a friendly sparring match, a brisk workout in which neither man would attempt to seriously hurt the other. But Klondike Mike had other ideas. He wanted to enhance his reputation by scoring a knockout. And the assembled crowd was hoping to see the same thing.

As the men waiting in their corners, the announcer called for silence. Raising a megaphone to his lips, he cried out, "In the red corner, straight from Chicago, the former middleweight champion of Michigan, weighing 158 pounds, Tommy Burns." There was a smattering of polite applause before the announcer continued. "In the white corner, weighing 208 pounds, the champion of the Yukon and Alaska, 'Klondike Mike' Mahoney!"[12] The thunderous roar that greeted the announcement shook the Northern's glass chandeliers.

Burns told what happened next in an account he wrote at Klondike Mike's request 38 years later. "We wore six-ounce gloves and for two rounds I hit him with everything I had. He was bleeding from the mouth and nose at the start of the second round, but big Klondike Mike

African-American middleweight Billy Woods became a friend of Burns.

still kept boring in for more. I was always shifting to my right side and boxing him all the time, as he had too much weight and height on me. I kept forcing the fight and peppering him with everything I had, sure that it would be a cinch to win the hundred dollars."[13]

When he got back to his corner at the end of the second round, a panting Burns told his second, an African-American prizefighter named Billy Woods, "This guy's going to kill me if I don't knock him out."

"If you knock him out," Woods replied, "this crowd is going to kill us both."[14]

Late in the third round the bout came to a sudden halt. "I was tiring or maybe a little careless," Burns admitted later. "He kept shifting to my left and never letting me rest. All at once, like a shot out of a gun, it seemed to me, he sent his right foot into my solar plexus and I went down. I could hear everything, but I was paralyzed for a couple of minutes."[15]

Some accounts say the referee stopped proceedings and declared the bout a draw. But Burns admitted he'd lost. After becoming world heavyweight champ he sent Mahoney a card inscribed with the message, "To my friend Klondike Mike Mahoney, the only man who gave me a KO to the solar plexus."[16]

Burns genuinely liked Mahoney. After the fight, he recalled, "We shook hands and had some food and drinks."[17] Fortunately, the setback didn't go into the record books as an official loss because it was a kick-boxing match, not a regular prizefight. In any case, with the Mahoney fight out of the way, Burns borrowed money from an acquaintance and headed for the gold fields the next day. He offered Woods a few dollars to help him carry supplies. Burns seemed drawn to the black man, possibly because the two of them were the only professional boxers in Nome at that time.

Shoot-out in the gold fields

Tommy Burns and Billy Woods left Nome to take a look at Burns's gold mine on a warm morning in the late spring of 1904. They carried packs filled with bacon, beans, coffee and a shovel. After riding the Wild Goose Railway across 10 kilometres of tundra, they reached Anvil Creek. Here the smell of brier roses filled the air, and nearby meadows were teeming with flowers and wild fruits. It was a beautiful day and Burns was in a jubilant mood. Before long, however, Woods began to suspect they were being followed. It wasn't uncommon for robbers to hold up prospectors on the trail.

By the time the men reached the mine, Woods was certain he'd spotted a pair of shadowy figures lurking in the brush a few hundred metres behind them. Not sure what to do, the pair scurried down the mine shaft and hid in the dark. A few minutes later the men following them appeared in the entrance with rifles at the ready.

"This is a holdup! Come out with your hands up and nobody will get hurt!" one of them yelled.[18]

Burns was frightened but he had no intention of giving up without a fight. Digging into his backpack, he pulled out the revolver he'd purchased to protect himself from the Chicago gangsters. Crouching low, he took aim at the nearest man and squeezed off a shot. Later, he admitted he was trembling with such fear that he missed the man's head by more than a foot. In the next instant the two riflemen dropped to their knees and opened fire. Burns clearly saw muzzle flashes and heard at least one shot whiz past his ear. Then he detected the unmistakable sound of rifle bolts being flipped back, as the bandits prepared to shoot again. Not waiting for the second salvo to come his way, the young prizefighter fired off his five remaining bullets in quick succession. The fusillade of slugs slammed into wooden beams and hard granite rock, sending hot lead ricocheting all over the mine. No one was hit, but the two robbers were so alarmed by the sudden burst of fire that they fled as fast as their feet would carry them.

Burns and Woods spent the rest of the afternoon huddling fearfully in the mine. The young Canadian found he liked the black fighter, despite his own notions of white superiority. He even agreed to meet him in a match, should they both get back to civilization intact. When they finally ventured out, there was no sign of the thieves.

The next morning Burns found that getting gold out of a mine was almost as tough as boxing for a living. The mine shaft was narrow and claustrophobic, and dropping 15 metres below ground made him feel as if he were buried alive. Furthermore, the ground was permanently frozen, which meant wood fires had to be kept going all the time to make further digging possible. Fires thawed the ground beneath them, but the sides of the mine remained impenetrable. Complicating matters further was the lack of wood available to keep the fires burning. Before long Burns decided there was very little gold to be found, so he sold the mine and headed back home. But he had no intention of returning to crime-ridden Chicago. Woods, a Los Angeles native, had convinced him his future lay in that California community.

5

Becoming a "Blubberweight"

She was standing at the opposite end of a Portland, Oregon, dance-hall, a glass of punch clutched in her dainty hands. A tall young woman with dark eyes, a round face, full lips and long brown hair wound up in a bun behind her head. She was wearing a colourful, floor-length dress and a stylish hat.

Burns, who had stopped in Portland on his way to California from Alaska in the summer of 1904, spotted her the moment he entered the building. Stopping dead in his tracks, he stood staring at her for the longest time, unable to move. Not since Nellie Sweitzer had he felt such a strong rush of emotion. It was, he later admitted, the most intoxicating thing that he'd ever experienced.

Then, unexpectedly, as he continued to stare longingly in her direction, she turned and spotted him. For a moment their eyes met — and locked — then she quickly looked away. But the connection had been made. Burns moved across the dance floor and introduced himself. His friends looked on in bewilderment as Burns, the man who had been avoiding females because he feared they'd ruin his career, swept the beautiful young woman onto the dance floor.

Tommy was as startled as his pals. In recent months he'd been absorbed by one preoccupation — boxing better than any other living fighter. His life had become little more than a series of prizefights to be won or lost. But with Julia Keating, he found a kindred spirit who made him feel at ease. Within a few days they were inseparable. Not long after that, they were married.

Julia was nothing like Irene Peppers. While his first wife had been a spunky, playful woman, his new bride was refined, almost delicate. She'd been raised in Birmingham, Alabama, but had lived in recent

Jewel Burns

years in Minnesota. When Tommy met her she was visiting relatives in Portland. One newspaper reporter described her as a "tall, graceful girl who is fresh from a convent school. She is bright and engaging, a good talker and fond of sport and amusement." Another praised her as "very charming." She enjoyed nothing more than buying fashionable clothes — including her much-admired hats — and hosting tea parties. In that regard she was no different from other ladies of the era, who seldom went outside without a hat garnished with lace, ribbons and flowers. Indeed, American females spent a staggering $1 billion a year on clothing, including $14 million for corsets alone.

Julia called her husband "Tommy" but insisted that others address him as "Mr. Brusso." She went by the name of "Mrs. Noah Brusso." For his part, he called her "Jewel."

Jewel may have been fond of most sports, but she hated boxing. She fainted at the sight of violence and, in all the years they were married, she never attended one of his bouts, preferring instead to wait by the telephone for calls that he usually made from ringside. Tommy was utterly devoted to her and always made a point of calling to tell her he was unhurt, often before the referee handed down his decision. Nevertheless, the vigils were almost unbearable for her. "I do hate him fighting," she told one reporter. "You don't know how it affects my nerves. I am ill for days after each fight, and I was in bed for three weeks" after one tilt. "He is always going to stop fighting, but he never does — just one more, he says, and so it goes on."[1]

As it turned out, the rest of the Keating family had no qualms about Tommy's profession, possibly because he was now a name boxer who was making good money. They were especially impressed when he bought Jewel a Fiat automobile for Christmas. But her parents made it clear they didn't approve of his periodic bouts with blacks, and Jewel also found this conduct socially unacceptable and embarrassing. After Tommy became world heavyweight champion, the *London Free Press* reported, "Mrs. Brusso is a member of a prominent

Tommy and Jewel.

old southern family with an aversion to the Negro. For this reason Brusso avoids Jack Johnson, and it is doubtful whether the pair will ever meet." In fact, despite pressue from Jewel to avoid African-American fighters, he steadfastly refused to draw the colour line against Johnson or anyone else.

Despite the arrival of a new woman in his life, Burns still appeared to sports writers and fans as the same old fighter. But inwardly he'd changed. He seemed fearless in the ring, but for the first time he began to worry about getting injured or killed. He admitted to friends that he sometimes found his palms damp with sweat before fights. He'd pace around outside the arena for a couple of hours prior to the start of some bouts, worrying about what might happen. Only after he got into his dressing-room and started to tape his hands did his anxiety level begin to fall.

Rocky start to a marriage

Tommy and Jewel began their married life by moving into a modest home in Los Angeles. For Jewel, the experience would soon prove to be trying. Her husband was often away, fighting in other cities, leaving her in a hot, dry climate during an age without air conditioning. Few women of the period worked outside the home, and it would be several years before the Brussos' first child was born. In the meantime, Jewel had virtually nothing to do. She was a long way from her family and friends and didn't know anyone in town. This isolation may have sown the troubles that would later plague their marriage.

As for Los Angeles, Tommy liked the fact that oranges grew outside in midwinter, but he wasn't overly impressed with the city. Los Angeles at the beginning of the twentieth century was not the entertainment mecca we know today. "It's a big Hanover, without the snow," he complained.[2] Indeed, the city, with a population of only 100,000 at the time, had little to offer in the way of nightlife or diversions. In his book *California Rich*, author Stephen Birmingham described its shortcomings:

> As late as 1915 most of the streets were still unpaved. The streets of Los Angeles ran up to the edge of the foothills, where they ended, and from the foothills onward there was nothing but sagebrush and wild mountains filled with coyotes and rattlesnakes and little wild deer that came down into the town at night. There were a few automobiles, but not many, and a couple of street cars — with signs at the back saying "Don't shoot rabbits from the rear platform!" — and the "red trains" that ran from the centre of town out to the beaches. Otherwise, transportation was primitive, and the most sensible way to get around was on horseback.[3]

A contemporary journalist, Willard Huntington Wright, found the place downright stuffy. "You will look in vain for the flashing eye, the painted cheek, the silken ankle. The current belief in Los Angeles is that there is something inherently and inalienably indecent in that segment of the day between 12 midnight and 5 a.m.," he wrote. "Hence, the Quakerish regulation of the public dance halls. Hence, a stupid censorship so incredibly puerile that even Boston will have to take second place. Hence, the silly legal pottering about the proper length of bathing suits at the beaches, the special election to decide whether or not one should be permitted to eat in saloons, and the fiery discussions as to the morality of displaying moving pictures of boxing matches. Los Angeles is overrun with militant moralists."[4]

The only interesting thing to happen during this period was the arrival of a motion-picture company from the east. Folks were curious about the development, but few got excited because, as Birmingham noted, "No one thought that movies would last."[5]

With few good restaurants in the city, Tommy and Jewel usually ate at home. And Jewel's cooking seems to have agreed with Burns because he soon became fat. Not long after returning from his Alaskan odyssey, the 23 year old found he weighed an astonishing 185 pounds — a full 27 pounds above the middleweight limit. Sarcastic reporters began referring to him as a "blubberweight." It was no laughing matter, however, because he'd already signed to fight William "Cyclone" Kelly in Tacoma, Washington, on August 20, 1904. Kelly was a mediocre fighter with a record of 11 wins, 18 losses and 5 draws, but he had a good punch. In fact, five of his wins had come via the knockout route.

Desperate to get down to the legal limit, Burns half-starved himself for a fortnight. "I have a few melancholy recollections of the days before I entered the heavyweight class," he wrote later. "I used often to find any amount of difficulty in getting down to 158 pounds and on one occasion I had to get rid of 27 pounds, and had only 12 days in which to do it. That was no joke, I can assure you."[6]

The day-to-day life of an athlete in training could be incredibly tedious back then. Nineteenth-century British boxer Tom Cribb was largely to blame. He hiked 30 miles a day to get ready for his fights, and as if that wasn't enough, he *walked* the 300 miles from London to the scene of one of his most famous bouts. Cribb's winning streak persuaded prizefighters the world over to copy his methods. But not Burns. The Canadian agreed long walks improved a man's stamina and wind, but he found such monotonous activity sapped the spirit. Instead, he came up with his own revolutionary forms of training that would soon be copied by athletes in all the major sports.

The secret to good training was to make it as varied and interesting as possible, he believed. An Australian reporter who followed him around for a week wrote, "His training exercises — they range from tree-climbing to swimming in snow-fed rivers, and from sprinting up hills to horseback riding — scandalize the old-time pugilists."[7] Nor was he in favour of rising at the crack of dawn. Instead, he slept in until 8

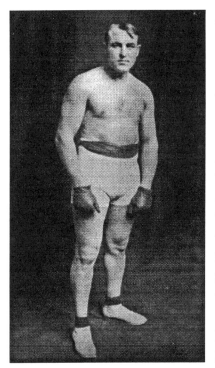

*Burns in a relaxed pose after
a workout.*

A.M. and had a breakfast consisting of oranges, a pair of eggs, toast and tea. Afterwards, he took a strong dose of salt, believing it would thin out his blood and cleanse his system of any impurities. Thus fortified, he headed out into hilly country for his roadwork. There he walked briskly for a mile, then sprinted for a hundred yards or so, continuing the routine until he had covered about five miles. Returning to the gym, he followed a rub down and shower with a light lunch.

After resting until about 3 P.M., Burns would hit the gym for what he called "the serious work of the day."[8] Once again the key was to avoid a boring routine. The athlete who performed the same exercises over and over again would soon become stale, he said. To strengthen his stomach muscles for the pounding they would surely take in any fight, he lay on his back, raising his legs to right angles with his body, and then relied purely on muscle power to sit up. To make things even more challenging, he'd hold dumb-bells in his hands in order to put extra weight on the abdominal muscles. After sit-ups he'd stand erect, then stoop down and touch his toes without bending the knees.

The most remarkable part of his routine came when he put the gloves on for sparring sessions. Instead of sparring for the traditional three-minute rounds, he'd go for six solid minutes. And to keep himself on his toes he used three sparring partners, each man fighting him for two minutes. That way, he was up against a fresh opponent the whole time. Such workouts were tough to take, but they prepared him well for his fights. Indeed, he found some of his official bouts almost restful in comparison to what he did in the gym.

Burns was down to 158 pounds by the time the fight with Cyclone Kelly rolled around. The boxer lived up to his nickname, charging around the ring at top speed, continuously forcing the action. He backed Burns into the ropes in the third round, but a left upper-cut from the Canadian took the wind out of the Cyclone. In the fourth, Burns knocked him out with an awesome display of combination punching.

Giving another black fighter a chance

Burns travelled to Seattle next, for a September 16, 1904, showdown with Billy Woods, his sidekick from Alaska. The 21-year-old Woods was in many ways a black version of Burns. He was the same height as the Canadian and weighed just four pounds less than Tommy. Like Burns, he also had massive shoulders and 13-inch forearms. And he had the same swarming style of attack. After leaving Nome he'd gone to Dawson City, where he'd scored three wins over little-known local fighters, bringing his record up to at least 10 wins against only 3 losses. He also had a number of draws, including a memorable 20-round stand-off with famous black middleweight Joe Walcott. Clearly, he was a major talent. The *Seattle Times* referred to him as "very strong and a hard hitter." But like all African-American fighters of the era, Woods had trouble getting bouts with whites. Burns, however, had promised Woods he'd fight him if they ever got out of the gold mine alive, and it was a pledge he kept. It marked the seventh time he'd gone into the ring with a black man, a record matched by few white fighters of the era.

The two men fought for 15 gruelling rounds, and when it was over Burns admitted it had been the toughest contest of his career. The Canadian started the fight using what sports writers today would call "trash talk." He insulted Woods, calling him a "nigger" and a "yellow cur" in a bid to psych him out.[9] Woods responded by almost knocking out his tormentor with a swing to the stomach in the opening minutes. But the Canadian held on and mounted a furious comeback. A ringside reporter described the breathtaking action:

Burns put up a great exhibition, but his blows lacked force. Woods' peculiar crouch was hard for Burns to reach, but Burns' blocking of Woods' rushes was little less than phenomenal.

Both were strong at the end, and made a whirlwind finish. Such cleverness as was exhibited by Burns has never been seen in Seattle before. He had the Negro worried because of his inability to hit. But Burns's cleverness was the only thing that saved him from being defeated, as his blows had no effect on the Negro.

The *Seattle Times* thought Burns had won, but referee Charles Reno, who had the best view of the action, called it a draw. His verdict was booed and hissed by a partisan white crowd. After the fight, Burns felt guilty about the way he'd verbally abused Woods. He apologized and even offered to buy him dinner.

According to Joe Louis, Woods graciously accepted the apology, telling Burns, "I'm just thankful you agreed to fight me, most whites won't come near me. I'm more interested in a man's actions than in what he says or thinks."[10]

As for dinner, Woods pointed out there was no eatery nearby that would serve him. But when Burns suggested they dine in a black part of town, he quickly accepted. The dinner gave the Canadian a glimpse of what it was like to be a member of a minority. When the two boxers walked into a black-owned restaurant an hour later, the jaws of everyone present dropped in astonishment at the sight of Tommy's white skin. More than a few people shot hostile glances towards him. Woods noticed the cool reception and called out, "It's OK fellas, he's with me." Before the night was over, Burns and Woods had restored their friendship.

Suffering another setback

Events took an unpleasant turn for Tommy Burns in the fall of 1904, when he showed up in Milwaukee after a tiresome four-day train ride from Seattle. He'd come to the beer capital of America to fight a tough middleweight named Hugo Kelly. Had Kelly actually been his opponent, Burns would have had his hands full because the American was a genuine contender for the world championship. But when he got to Milwaukee Burns was informed that Kelly had backed out of the fight, and that his adversary was to be none other than the fabled Philadelphia Jack O'Brien.

O'Brien is largely forgotten today, but for much of the twentieth century he was considered the greatest light-heavyweight boxer who ever lived. Born in Philadelphia in 1878, the 171-pounder was a tall, lanky individual who stood a shade under six feet. He was the darling of sports writers, almost all of whom were in awe of his fancy footwork. He was popular with fans, too, possibly because in May 1901 he'd become the first American boxer to defeat an English champion. And he did it in England, knocking out heavyweight George Chip in a bout staged at Newcastle upon Tyne. Moreover, "Foxy Jack" seemed to almost live in the ring. Although he'd only started his career in 1896, the 26-year-old had fought no less than 133 bouts by the time he met up with Burns. Of those, he'd won 85, including two dozen by way of knockout. He'd lost only 3 fights and tied 11. The rest of his contests were "no-decisions" in which both boxers had agreed ahead of time that no verdict would be rendered unless there was a knockout. More impressive still was the fact that O'Brien had beaten or drawn some of the best boxers on the planet, including Marvin Hart, Stan Ketchell and Bob Fitzsimmons. The 23-year-old Burns, by way of contrast, had a record of 28 wins, 1 loss and 5 draws.

But it wasn't just O'Brien's fantastic number of victories or the calibre of his opponents that impressed fight fans so much. It was the way in which he put his men down. One New York writer described him as "a shifty, two-handed fighter who can get away from a swing or hook with lightning-like rapidity. He is a great ring tactician, is courageous and is one of those men who never say 'die.' O'Brien is endowed with the faculty of being able to strike a really hard blow. He has been known to knock a rival out with one smash." A San Francisco reporter was even more gushing, describing him as "the most polished artist in his line." After he demolished feared heavyweight Al Kaufman, another newspaper reported O'Brien had given his opponent "a beating such as seldom has been suffered in the history of San Francisco fights. Kaufman, a strong 19-year-old with a punch, could not land on the shifty man from Philadelphia. O'Brien's sidestepping, ducking and general footwork was a marvellous exhibition of skill."

He was also a dapper, impeccably dressed individual who sounded more like a university professor than a prizefighter when he opened his mouth. Asked what he thought of boxer Stan Ketchell, for example, O'Brien told a reporter, "He's a bum distinguished only by the tumultuous but ill-directed ferocity of his assault." As for Sam Langford, he said the Nova Scotia fighter had "a mystic quality. When he appeared upon the scene of combat you knew you were cooked."[12]

Perhaps understandably, Burns complained bitterly to the promoter and even threatened to pull out of the fight. He suspected he'd need a few more years of experience under his belt before he could hold his own against the redoubtable Philadelphia Jack. But when the promoter assured him it would be just an exhibition bout, Burns agreed to participate. "O'Brien will go easy and give the crowd a nice, friendly show," he was told.[13]

Unfortunately, either the promoter lied or no one bothered to tell Philadephia Jack that the battle was going to be anything but a grudge match. The fight, the first of three epic clashes the two men would stage, occurred on October 4, 1904. O'Brien took Burns by surprise in the opening round, throwing punches that would fell an ox. Suprisingly, the Canadian weathered the storm and gave a good showing. Still, he was clearly in over his head, as one newspaper account of the action describes:

In the first four rounds O'Brien and Burns sparred for openings and Burns, by some clever work, at times managed to break down O'Brien's guard and do some good work infighting. O'Brien, at such times had to do some quick leg-work to get out of reach. As a general thing O'Brien's reach and height stood him in good stead in giving him the advantage, except in the fourth round, when Burns was able to make a fair showing against the Philadelphia boy. There was little clinching and the referee had an easy task. In the sixth round Burns braced up and for a time it seemed he would be able to get a draw, but O'Brien's reach again came in handy and Burns was worsted. Burns got in several stiff punches and short-arm jolts but O'Brien was continually swinging and landing on Burns's body.

O'Brien won the fight on points, but there was a price to be paid. For in Tommy Burns he'd just created an enemy. The Canadian developed an intense hatred of O'Brien, whom he called a "double-crosser." At the end of the bout, as he leaned on the ropes in his corner, an exhausted and battered Burns muttered, "O'Brien, I'll get you for this. I'll get you." Later that night, he scrawled a single line in his diary. It read: "Get Jack O'Brien."[14]

Middleweight contender Jack "Twin" Sullivan.

Despite the loss, 1904 had been a good year for Burns, at least on the financial front. He'd fought 9 times in 12 months, earning $2,000 (today's equivalent of about $50,000, tax-free).

Becoming Pacific Coast champion

Tommy Burns started off the New Year on the right foot, knocking out a native American heavyweight called "Indian Joe" Schildt at Ballard, Washington, on January 31, 1905. He followed that victory up by tackling one of the best middleweights in the world — the infamous Jack "Twin" Sullivan. The Cambridge, Massachusetts, native was the twin brother of fellow prizefighter Mike Sullivan. They were, in fact, identical twins, who delighted in fooling opponents by changing places in the ring. On occasion, the slightly smaller Mike would show up for the weigh-in, while Jack would do the actual fighting. Because both men had a receding hairline and a crossed, floating left eye, no one ever noticed the switch. Before his career ended, Jack Sullivan would take part in 137 fights, losing only 18. Included among his many bouts was a draw with Philadelphia Jack O'Brien.

Burns and Sullivan squared off on March 7, 1905, in Tacoma, Washington. The next day, under the headline, "Brusso's Good Showing," the *London Free Press* reported, "Noah Brusso, formerly of Galt, Ontario, fighting under the name Tommy Burns, fought 20 fast rounds to a draw last night with Jack 'Twin' Sullivan, of Boston. The bout was one of the fastest ever seen in the state. The Canadian fighter made an excellent showing in this his first important go, and placed himself in the first rank of his class."

Burns had done so well, in fact, that he caught the attention of another top-flight boxer — United States Pacific Coast champion Dave Barry. Barry was a Canadian from Montreal who had moved to the U.S. in 1901. He'd gained national recognition that year by knocking out a good middleweight named John Brien. Now he was hoping a victory against an up-and-comer like Burns would vault him into contention for a crack at the world championship.

The two Canadians trained for their fight in the same gym and, for a few days, were on rather friendly terms. All that changed, however, when Tommy noticed Barry was making eyes at Jewel. The Montreal fighter became bolder as the bout approached, going so far as to invite her back to his apartment for an afternoon romp in bed. Jewel reported this to her husband, who vowed to dismember his foe once they got into the ring. When they met in San Francisco on May 5, 1905, reporters quickly picked up on the palpable hostility that was present even before the opening bell. Burns scowled at Barry during the introductions and refused to engage in the traditional glove-tapping show of sportsmanship at the start of the fight.

"The bout was a hot one, some trouble during their training having caused bad blood between the men," one reporter told readers. He added, "Both men took a great amount of punishment, Burns landing the harder blows. The former Detroiter showed himself faster on his feet and more clever in ducking." The match went the full 20 rounds but "Burns was much the fresher man at the end."

When referee James Carroll awarded the decision to Burns, there was widepread applause. Barry remained unconvinced that he'd lost, however, loudly shouting that he should have been given the verdict. Nevertheless, Tommy Burns had won his first title belt since he'd relinquished the Michigan middleweight crown more than a year earlier. As U.S. Pacific Coast champion, he soon found he was receiving more offers from frontline boxers. That meant more opportunity for money and advancement, but it also greatly increased the risk of injury and defeat.

The wars with Hugo Kelly

Burns returned to his old stomping ground of Detroit for the first time in a year and a half on June 7, 1905, for a contest with Chicago fighter Hugo Kelly. Kelly was a dangerous boxer who, one reporter noted, could "hurl a bomb that ought to shake up every scrapper in the country." He was, indeed, one of the few men who had ever beaten Philadelphia Jack O'Brien, which he accomplished just a few months before lacing on the gloves with Burns. It had been an emotion-charged bout in which the two fought like tigers. A reporter wrote afterwards, "The air was so full of gloves that you could hardly see the boys in the ring for the haze of flying swings and jabs and jolts. Jack was darting around like a toad on a skillet, and Hugo was there every time with his long, straight left, chopping Jack's features with the regularity and effect of a prize butcher mincing hamburger steak."

Burns and Kelly battled to a 10-round draw. Although he failed to get the win, the Canadian managed to impress the *Detroit Free Press*, even if the newspaper was still refusing to call him by his new name. "Noah Brusso's showing in the bout at the Light Infantry Armoury this past week was gratifying to his friends here," the paper's sports editor wrote. "The former local boxer has improved his work a great deal since he went west. He isn't so much faster, but he utilizes his speed to great effect. It is only fair to say that Wednesday's show gave no correct line on Brusso's present form, because of the boxer's physical condition. He didn't pay any serious attention to the matter of weight until within a few hours of the contest, and as a result went into the ring weak and exhausted. When Kelly began to land Brusso had nothing to come back with. The good right hand punch that he landed at the beginning of the ninth round was the only thing that saved him from worse than a draw."

What the newspaper didn't say was that Burns was having serious difficulty keeping the weight off. He had run himself ragged for days on end just to get down to the 158-pound limit. He was so tired going into fights at this point that he was having trouble making it to the final bell. Against Kelly he'd built up a big early lead, then wilted. Only by an excruciating effort in the final two rounds was he able to salvage a tie.

The deadlock wasn't satifactory to either boxer, so they boarded a train and headed for Los Angeles to settle the issue of superiority once and for all. This time, according to newspaper accounts, Burns easily outperformed Kelly, although the referee once again declared it a draw.

The Dave Barry rematch

Dave Barry began stalking Burns. The Montreal fighter taunted him in the newspapers, pointing out his two draws with Kelly, combined with the deadlocks with Billy Woods and Jack "Twin" Sullivan and the loss to Philadelphia Jack O'Brien, had left Burns with only two wins in his last seven fights. And that, he said, was hardly the record of a champion.

Burns, who was still smarting from Barry's pass at Jewel, quickly agreed to a rematch to be fought August 31, 1905, in San Francisco. The following excerpt from a story in the *San Francisco Examiner* shows just how much the normally clean-fighting boxer hated Dave Barry:

> In the 15th round Burns got the upper hand and he improved it by holding Barry around the neck with his left glove and pummeling him dizzy. The Irishman went to the floor and some people wondered why referee Shaughnessy countenanced this holding and hitting at the same time on Burns's part.
>
> Barry recovered and pulled through until the 20th round was nearly over. Burns then landed one hard right-hander on the jaw and followed it up with a shower of rights until Barry went down and out.

This was one of the few times in his 63 professional bouts that there was even a suggestion of dirty fighting by Burns. No doubt his intense dislike of Barry led him to behave in a manner that was out of character for him. He somehow got away with hitting and holding without being disqualified by the referee. And in the process he'd recorded his thirtieth victory.

While Burns was trading fists with Barry, the middleweight division was being hit with a bombshell. Champion Tom Ryan suddenly retired and the two top contenders, Jack "Twin" Sullivan and Stan Ketchell, both declared themselves the new champ. The two boxers wouldn't settle the issue until they met in the ring three years later. Until then, there would be two disputed world champions.

Twin Sullivan put his piece of the title on the line for the first time on Oct. 17, 1905, against Pacific Coast champion Tommy Burns. Although it was a crack at only a share of the world title, this was an important match for Burns. If he could beat Sullivan, a man he had battled to a draw only seven months earlier, he'd get a shot at Stan Ketchell and the undisputed middleweight championship. Unfortunately, a frankly tubby Burns was finding it almost impossible to get down to the middleweight limit. He worked like a dog and went whole days without eating. Finally, just hours before the weigh-in, he got down to the magical 158 pounds. As a result of his starvation diet, however, he went into the ring feeling so weak that he couldn't put forward his best effort. Sullivan still had his hands full, but he managed to outpoint the Canadian over 20 rounds.

So ended 1905. Financially, Burns had done very well. Fights with such good boxers as Sullivan, Barry and Kelly had helped him make a total of $6,240, or the modern equivalent of $156,000, tax-free. But from an athletic viewpoint it had hardly been a banner year. Over 12 months he'd compiled a rather pedestrian record of three wins, one loss and three draws. Worse than that was the undeniable fact that he was losing his battle to keep the weight off. He could no longer get down to the middleweight limit with any degree of comfort, so he decided to quit the division. The logical step would have been to enter the light-heavyweight ranks, where the weight limit was set at a more manageable 170 pounds. Burns, however, wasn't interested in this category. He figured if he was going to move up he might as well go straight to the top and become a heavyweight. That, after all, was where the big money was to be found. He'd fought heavyweights before, of course, but from now on that would be the only kind of opponent he'd face. Tommy Burns was about to enter the land of the giants.

6

The Upset of the Century

Tommy Burns entered the heavyweight ranks at the beginning of 1906, just as chaos was breaking out in boxing's glamour division. In a move that shook the sport to its very foundations, enormously popular champion Jim Jeffries announced his retirement. The boxing world had always counted on the heavyweight champ to create publicity and, until that moment, he had furnished the sport with a larger-than-life character at the top.

The first champion of the modern, gloved era, John L. Sullivan, was an almost mythical figure during his time. Known as the "Boston Strong Boy," he was a hulking bear of a man who liked to boast he could "lick any son-of-a-bitch in the house."[1] Born in Boston in the fall of 1858, Sullivan developed his huge muscles as a labourer. He had little future in the construction business, however, because he was constantly getting into fights with his employers. Like Tommy Burns, he got into prizefighting almost by accident. He'd gone to see a touring strongman and was goaded into a fight with him. The battle ended with Sullivan knocking his man into the orchestra pit. In that instant a legend was born. From there he toured the United States, offering $100 to any white man who could last three rounds with him. In an age in which brute strength was almost worshipped, the burly brawler with the handlebar moustache was widely believed to be the strongest man on the planet.

Sullivan became World Heavyweight Boxing Champion on February 17, 1882, when he defeated Paddy Ryan in a bare-knuckle contest. He held the crown for a decade before being dethroned by Gentleman Jim Corbett in the first gloved championship fight in history.

The stylish Corbett was king of the heavyweights until he met up with Bob Fitzsimmons in a surreal bout that looked more like a high-noon showdown than a prizefight. Legendary sheriff Bat Masterton was at the arena entrance, collecting six-shooters from fans. Inside, equally famous gunfigher Wyatt Earp sat at ringside with both of his pistols drawn.

The fight, the first ever to be recorded by the new kinetoscopic motion-picture camera invented by Thomas Edison, was a bloodbath. "It was as if a bucket of red paint had been poured over the two men," one reporter said.[2] It ended in the fourteenth round when Fitzsimmons, a former blacksmith, laid Corbett low with what he called his "solar plexus punch." In reality, it was nothing more than a hard shot to the body, but the public was tricked into believing the colourful Fitzsimmons had invented a new punch.

When the two fighters shook hands afterwards, Corbett demanded a rematch. Fitzsimmons refused, saying, "I will not fight again."

"You'll have to," Corbett told him. "If you don't, I'll go at you in the street."

"If you tackle me in the street," Fitzsimmons said menacingly, "I will kill you."[3]

Tensions eased and the pair never met again, in the ring or on the street. But the public never forgot the bout or Fitzsimmons. The freckle-faced redhead became tremendously popular, not only because he was seen as an inventive fellow, but also because he was such an unlikely-looking champion. Although he was 6'1, he weighed only about 175 pounds, giving him an unusually lanky appearance. He was also popular because, although born in England, he'd assumed American citizenship and made his home in the U.S. Despite his popularity, he didn't last long as champ, losing his title to James J. Jeffries.

Jeffries, known as the "Boilermaker," was arguably the most popular heavyweight champion of them all. Standing 6'3" and weighing 225 pounds, he was an absolutely massive man for his era. He was also a handsome, charismatic figure who *looked* like an ideal hero. Despite his size, he wasn't just another straight-ahead brawler. In fact, Jeffries was surprisingly fast on his feet. He used his great footwork and powerful punch to make seven successful title defenses before announcing he was through with the fight game.

Scores of boxing promoters, sports writers and ordinary fans tried to talk him out of his decision. But Jeffries, who had made enough money to buy his own pub, said, "Fighting is not what it's cracked up to be. And I've promised my mother not to fight anymore; she's opposed to it and she is pretty old now."[4] He also hated the singing and dancing acts that the public had come to expect heavyweight champions to perform on stage between bouts. Corbett had been a master at it, touring the U.S. in *Gentleman Jim*, a play penned just for him. When reporters continued to press him to reconsider his retirement, Jeffries growled, "All I got out of the title was embarrassment. They wanted to put me on exhibition like a prize pig, but I wouldn't give them a show like Sullivan or Corbett."[5]

What Jeffries hadn't said was that he was tired of the rigours of training. Few people have any idea how hard a professional boxer trains. Then, as now, the prizefighter is usually the best conditioned of all athletes. In addition to his weariness, Jeffries was no longer in good health. He'd recently broken both his hands in a fight and had come close to death during a bout with pneumonia. He was also developing a drinking problem. In fact, he claimed to have cured his pneumonia by drinking half a case of whiskey in one day. His doctor declared, "If an ordinary man took even one-third the dose of this drug you are taking regularly, James, he would die." When Jeffries miraculously recovered, the doctor said, "I still don't believe it. You are simply not human, Jeffries."[6]

Whatever his reasons, Jeffries was leaving the ring with an undefeated record of 18 wins (15 by way of knockout) and 2 draws in 20 fights.

Jeffries was so popular that there was little grumbling when he announced he would promote a tournament to find his successor. Right off the bat he declared the two best black fighters — Jack Johnson and Sam Langford — would not be participating. At first, he proposed a tourney involving the top four white boxers in the United States. The newspapers had a field day suggesting who should be chosen. Heavyweight contenders Marvin Hart and "Fireman" Jim Flynn were usually

Jack Johnson, who held the "Negro Heavyweight Championship" in 1906.

mentioned, along with light heavyweights Philadephia Jack O'Brien and Jack Root. A few papers in Ontario and Michigan argued that Tommy Burns should be included, but no one, least of all Jeffries, took the idea very seriously. In the end, Jeffries decided it would be more dramatic to pit Hart, the top heavyweight contender, against Root, the reigning light-heavyweight champion.

The two men met on July 5, 1905, in Reno, Nevada, with Hart knocking out Root in the fourteenth round. After the fight, the gracious loser described the newest World Heavyweight Boxing Champion as a "truly formidable scrapper."

As soon as news flashed around the world that Hart had won, people wanted to know who he was. For one thing, Marvin Hart was a fanatical white supremacist who had been taught since boyhood that blacks were inferior beings. Born in Louisville, Kentucky, on September 16, 1876, he had left home at 18 to become a plumber's assistant and part-time chicken farmer. Not satisfied with either occupation, he turned to boxing at age 23. Standing 6'2" and weighing 203 pounds, he was an imposing figure in the ring. In his first professional fight he scored a knockout against veteran boxer William Schiller. Before long, it was obvious he was a decidedly good fighter. In addition to his win over Root, he'd defeated Jack "Twin" Sullivan and had fought draws with such respected figures as Philadelphia Jack O'Brien, Gus "the Akron Giant" Ruhlin and George Gardner.

But Hart's most impressive win of all had come against a young Jack Johnson, who held the so-called Negro Heavyweight Championship of the World. Hart had always drawn the colour line but, as Johnson started to gain national attention, he decided a win over the big black fighter would dramatically improve his stature.

Before the fight, which turned out to be one of the most controversial bouts in history, Hart was oozing confidence. "Before the 20th round is reached — probably several rounds before — there'll be a nigger prostrate on the canvas," he said.[7]

Hart tried hard to live up to his bold prediction by pressing the action for the first five rounds. The white man was well ahead on points at that stage, but Johnson recovered and dominated the middle rounds. He punished Hart severely, cutting him over both eyes before drawing blood from his nose and mouth. Confident that he had the fight in the bag, Johnson took it easy the rest of the way. In the final round he looked tired, spending most of the last three minutes clinching or covering up.

It had been a fairly close fight, but most observers believed Johnson had won. A few, including at least one ringside reporter, thought it should have been declared a draw. Instead, referee Alex Greggains awarded the decision to Hart.

Johnson was outraged, claiming he'd been "robbed" by a bigoted referee. But Greggains stood by his decision, saying the black man had "dogged it." He added, "I always give the gamest and most aggressive man the decision."[8] Greggains' verdict was not as outrageous as some have suggested in the years since. Johnson had a laid-back style that sometimes made him appear lazy. He was, for all his great talent, basically a defensive fighter who often failed to press the issue. This was a case where his relaxed attitude cost him the decision.

Whether he deserved to win or not, Hart had shown pluck and considerable ability by lasting 20 rounds with Johnson, a man who was to go down in history as one of the greatest heavyweights of all time. And, just as he'd suspected, his win over the vaunted black boxer had vaulted him into first place among heavyweight contenders.

Now that he had the heavyweight title, Hart wanted to enjoy it for awhile. Like Sullivan, Corbett, Fitzsimmons and Jeffries before him, he immediately drew the colour line, publicly declaring he would not give any black man a shot at the crown. His decision smacked of hypocrisy. Hart had already fought Jack Johnson, demonstrating he wasn't opposed to tackling a coloured fighter when it suited his purpose. So he could hardly claim he was boycotting African-Americans now for moral reasons. The only possible explanation is that he was anxious to avoid dangerous black contenders. This wasn't the first time a champion had done the same thing. Joe Woodman, who managed Sam Langford's career, said white champs had repeatedly ducked his fighter simply because they were afraid they'd lose. "They used his dark skin to hide their own yellow streaks," he said in a 1960 interview.[9]

Philadelphia Jack O'Brien was clamouring for a match, but Hart put him off, too. He wanted to pick up some easy money by fighting a few "lemons" before risking his belt against a legitimate contender.

His first outing, which came on January 16, 1906, in Butte, Montana, pitted the new champion against a completely unknown fighter named Pat Callahan. Callahan, a husky coal miner by trade, caught the champ by surprise in the first round, knocking him on his backside. Enraged, Hart sprang to his feet and knocked out the challenger with a series of blows to the jaw. A few days later Hart got together with boxing promoter Tom McCarey to discuss his next title defense. McCarey wanted to line up a fight with "Fireman" Jim Flynn because he knew it would attract a good gate. But Hart would have none of it, insisting he deserved another easy fight first. Going down the list of possible opponents, he came across the name Tommy Burns. "This guy's a lemon," he declared. "I'll fight him next."[10]

But getting Burns into the ring was easier said than done. When McCarey offered the Canadian a shot at the title he hesitated. He feared a second straight loss would seriously hurt his future. Besides that, pointing to Hart's vital statistics, Burns said, "He's a big, tough fellow."

"I'll give you $15,000 to fight him," McCarey said.

"I'll take it. Send for him."[11]

The negotiations that followed were acrimonious in the extreme. McCarey, it turned out, couldn't raise $15,000 for both boxers, never mind for one of them. In fact, he could only promise them a share of the gate receipts, and Hart wanted most of it. Burns suggested they split it 50–50, but Hart refused. He demanded the winner get 70 per cent, with the loser settling for 30. When Burns objected, Hart interrupted him with the wave of his hand. It was going to be his way or the fight was off. "After all," he said haughtily, "I'm the champion."[12]

When the fight was announced the press reaction was hostile. Reporters had been willing to grant the champion one easy fight without raising a fuss. Now they thought it was time for him to face a serious contender.

By any measuring stick Burns's defeat was a foregone conclusion. He was five inches shorter and nearly 40 pounds lighter than the champion. Besides that, the 24-year-old Burns had won only 3 of his last 9 bouts. The 29-year-old Hart, on the other hand, had lost only 3 of his 36 fights.

The *Chicago Journal* openly mocked the challenger, declaring he could no more beat Hart than he could "drop kick a steam engine." The newspaper even poked fun at his small-town roots, telling readers Burns was from "Muskratt Falls, Canada." The champion, it predicted, would dispose of Burns in two to four rounds. Famed boxing reporter George Siler wrote,

> The coming battle is not causing the interest that a battle of its importance should, presumably because Burns is not considered classy enough to take part in a championship battle. The champion will have a decided advantage over Burns in height, weight and reach, and as he has been under Tom Ryan's tutorship for months, there is no doubt he will have it on Burns in science.
>
> With all these advantages, to which should be added hitting powers, there is no reason why he should not knock out his smaller opponent within 10 rounds. In fact, that is expected of him, and if he fails to accomplish the trick within that limit his championship stock will fall below par. This will be Tommy Burns's first heavyweight battle and although he might have improved his skill and weight, he still seems far outclassed.[13]

Jim Jeffries thought it was a mismatch, too. "Hart will tear him to pieces," he predicted. "That Canadian shrimp won't last to hear the bell for round two."[14]

Hart, for his part, was trying to drum up interest in the fight by playing up the international angle. Wrapping himself in the Stars and Stripes, he told reporters, "I am thoroughly American. My father was born in Pennsyl-

World Heavyweight Champion Marvin Hart.

vania and my mother was a Kentuckian. My ancestors were in the American Revolution; still others of them helped preserve the Union [in the American Civil War]; and one of my near relatives was in the battle of San Juan Hill."[15] Burns answered this tiresome bit of self-promotion by declaring, "The only really tough athletes in the world are Canadians, who played lacrosse as roughly and toughly as the Mohawks ever did."[16]

Hart also seemed anxious to establish his credentials as a brawler, telling the assembled scribes, "As a boy I could whip any of the youngsters my age and in wrestling could handle larger lads than myself. As I grew older I became interested in fighting and I studied the champions as they developed. There was Sullivan, the son of Irish parents, Corbett's parents were Irish and Fitzsimmons was born in England. I am going to do my best to retain the honour of being a Kentuckian, and the son of distinguished American parents. I feel as if I am justified styling myself as a new American type of pugilist."

When someone suggested the undefeated Jeffries was still the real champ, Hart bristled. "Youth counts and my claim must not be overlooked. Corbett, Fitzsimmons and Jeffries are great pugilists but they are going back while I am coming along. I feel myself improving. I am hitting faster and harder. I am not as awkward as in my early days in the ring and I can take care of myself!"[17]

Just to be on the safe side, Hart was counting on more than his youth to see him through. Visitors to his camp reported he was working hard to get into top condition. One reporter said he looked "as strong as a bull." The champion was, he added, "running 10 miles a day, doing some heavy bag work and sparring eight rounds."[18]

Silk O'Loughlin, a famous baseball umpire, and several major-league ball players watched the champ work out, then pooled their money, betting $500 that he would win. It was a lot of cash, but with the odds standing at 17-to-1 in Hart's favour, it seemed like a sure bet.

Burns, for his part, was training every bit as hard. This was the chance of a lifetime and he had no intention of blowing it. The day before the fight, looking relaxed and fit, he told reporters, "I am trained to the minute and never felt better in all my life. I am handicapped in weight in the battle, but my speed and cleverness will balance his weight. He will never get near enough to me to land a clean blow. I will tire him out in the first eight rounds by forcing him to step lively; then I will cross over my right. He is big, and the harder I hit him the harder he will fall. The fight will not last 10 rounds."[19]

The journalists humoured Burns and dutifully reported his remarks. But few thought he had any hope of winning. About the only paper that suggested he might have a chance was the *Detroit Times*, which stated "Brusso (we will always think of Tommy Burns as Noah Brusso), if he becomes champion of the world, would bring a distinct shock to the sporting world in general. It would be another sad commentary on the dearth of real heavyweights since Jeffries retired and all that. But most of all, it would be a solar plexus punch to those who have refused to take Noah Brusso seriously."

The newspapers didn't know that Burns was getting ready to spring a trap. Ever since he'd signed for the fight he'd been trying to figure out a way to win and now he thought he'd found it. To be more precise, Jack "Twin" Sullivan, whom he'd hired as a spy, had found it for him. Sullivan had gone to Hart's camp, watching intently as the champion worked out. When he returned he had two important pieces of information. The first was that Hart was a hothead who easily lost his temper. Sullivan reported the champ would become agitated for no apparent reason and then start yelling and screaming at his sparring partners. Secondly, he was a relatively slow fighter who relied on brute strength.

"Use your jab all night long," Sullivan advised Burns. "Whatever you do, don't let him get his right working. Dance away, or hold on whenever it looks like he might land one. Do those things and you've got a chance."[20]

The trap is laid

When Tommy Burns and Marvin Hart climbed through the ropes at the Pacific Athletic Club in Los Angeles on the evening of February 23, 1906, a collective gasp went up from the crowd of four thousand fans. The size difference between the two fighters was absolutely startling, and Burns purposely made himself look even smaller by crouching low.

As referee Charles Eyton summoned the boxers to the centre of the ring, Burns was ready to put his plan into action. Hart immediately noticed the Canadian was wearing several layers of tape around his hands, and he demanded they be removed.

"Why Mr. Hart, I didn't think a big champion like you would mind that a little man like me used a little bit of tape," Burns said mockingly.[21] He followed up the remark by giving Hart a poke in the chest and shouting, "Get out of my corner, you cheese champion!"[22]

Just as Burns thought he would, Hart went berserk, calling him "a little rat" and throwing a punch that the Canadian easily ducked. The referee stepped between the two men and guided Hart back to his own corner as the crowd booed and hissed. Few fans had seen Burns's initial shove, and those who did took it for a playful gesture. As far as the crowd was concerned, Hart was a bully.

With boos still ringing in his ears, the champion bolted from his corner when the bell rang, determined to teach Burns a lesson. Writer Stanley Weston best described what happened next: "At the opening bell, Hart rushed across the ring to make short work of Burns. Burns, much faster, easily avoided the rushes and peppered long lefts into Hart's face. Burns kept Hart broiling throughout the fight by taunting him. In the fifth, he closed Hart's right eye. From then on, Burns danced in the direction of Hart's blind eye and belted the so-called champion at will."[23]

Another reporter thought Burns looked "very nervous and lacked confidence in the opening round." But he agreed the challenger soon gained the upper hand. In the second round, he wrote,

Burns quickly sized Hart up and began a systematic attack on his face and body with straight lefts. In the third round he started the blood flowing from Hart's nose and kept it running in almost every round thereafter. In the fifth Burns caught Hart over the right eye and in the following rounds battered the optic until it was closed. The left eye was badly marked and Hart's face presented a bloody sight practically throughout the fight.

Hart failed to show any championship form of any sort. His persistent attempts to 'rough it' in the clinches earned the disapproval of the crowd, which appeared to be with Burns almost to a man. Burns' style of attack was to shoot his left to the face or body and step inside of Hart's swings, allowing them to go around his neck or ducking them entirely. Hart simply could not land on Burns, and towards the latter part of the fight tried to wear Burns out by using his weight in the clinches.

Hart rallied somewhat in the second half, winning the tenth and twelfth rounds. But Burns almost knocked him out in the fourteenth, staggering the bigger man with a right and left to the jaw. "Quickly seizing the advantage, the challenger hammered Hart about the face and head, forcing him to cover up," one newspaper reported.

As he walked back to his corner at the end of the fourteenth, Burns could sense a knockout was coming. But Jack "Twin" Sullivan urged him to be cautious. He'd won 12 of the first 14 rounds and couldn't possibly lose the fight now. Not unless he got knocked out himself. The key, Sullivan said, was to stay out of range of Hart's dangerous punch. Hart, who also knew he needed a knockout, attacked frantically. But Burns was easily able to sidestep every rush. He even managed to score a few more points with telling counter-punches. Both men were still standing at the end of the twentieth and final round, but there was no doubt about who was going to get the decision. As one newspaper said the next day, "Burns outfought the bigger man, outgeneralled him and beat him at every point of the game. At times Burns, although handicapped in weight and height, made Hart look like a novice." Most reporters concluded Burns had won no less than 18 of the 20 rounds.

The referee agreed. Moments after the final bell, he called the two men to the centre of the ring. Hart was bleeding and bruised, while Burns, one reporter wrote, "didn't have a mark on him." A moment later the referee rendered his decision, raising Tommy Burns's right arm into the air. The heavyweight championship of the world had passed into the hands of a Canadian for the first time in history.

It didn't take long for the stunning news to be flashed around the world. In Pittsburgh, four Canadian professional hockey players were boarding a stagecoach at the train station when a middle-aged man wearing a green visor emerged from a nearby telegraph office and shouted, "Burns! The Canadian, Tommy Burns. Decision! In 20 rounds!"

Another man standing nearby shook his head and muttered, "Well, I'll be damned!"[24]

The hockey players were slapping one another on the back in giddy celebration when superstar Joe Hall suddenly jumped into the driver's seat. Pushing the driver out of the way, he took the reigns and went galloping off into the night. "With a roar from Joe," one writer recounted, "the vehicle took off over the cobblestones, careening through the dark Pittsburgh streets like a stagecoach pursued by a band of Apaches. Miraculously, the wild ride eventually led to the hotel, with all passengers safe and sound but plainly shaken. Having revived, the cabbie began shouting for the constabulary but was mollified when Joe grandly slipped him a dollar tip, bowed and ambled happily off to the desk to check in."[25]

The aftermath

The next day Marvin Hart was a sorehead in more ways than one. Nursing a severe headache and a badly swollen face, he complained bitterly about the work of both Burns and the referee.

"I am not through," he told reporters. "My record entitles me to a match. I want Burns. If I fail to stop him in 20 rounds, I do not want a cent. But I do insist on a referee who will give me a square deal and make Burns fight fair. In our 60 minutes in the ring, he hugged me 40 minutes of the time, butted me with his head, gouged me in the eye with his gloved thumb, and refused to stand up and fight. Though I boxed straight Marquis of Queensbury Rules, referee Eyton threatened to disqualify me if I hit in the clinches.

Burns tries on his World Heavyweight Championship belt.

"I shall continue to fight, meeting all comers, and convince the public that I can fight. I was not defeated. I do not charge anybody with being dishonest, but referee Eyton is not competent or consistent."[26]

Reporters were generally unsympathetic. Almost to a man they had picked Hart to win and he had embarrassed them by going down to such a shocking, one-sided defeat. "Hart started the trouble himself when he first came to Los Angeles," one journalist wrote. "His managers had talked him into thinking Burns was a nice, easy piece of peach pie. He is so completely dejected and dispirited that it is doubtful if he will ever fight again. His heart is broken."

His wallet wasn't in much better shape. The crowd was so small that only $4,800 had been raised. Of that, just $2,400 went to the fighters. And because Hart had insisted the winner get 70 per cent, Burns walked off with $1,650 while he got only $750.

Hart was all but finished as a prizefighter, too. He never got another serious match and, a few years later, quit the game to become a police officer in Louisville. His reputation lay in tatters, despite the fact that he retired with a record of only 7 losses in 47 fights. He died at the relatively young age of 53, still bitter about his loss to Burns.

Burns was in a jubilant mood when he met with reporters for post-fight interviews. "My fight may not have been spectacular," he said, "but I wanted to win and fought the way I knew I could turn the trick. Hart didn't hurt me once."[27]

When a reporter asked if he would follow tradition and draw the colour line, Burns startled them with his reply. "No," he said emphatically. "I will defend my title as heavyweight champion of the world against all comers, none barred. By this I mean white, black, Mexican, Indian, or any other nationality, without regard to colour, size or nationality. I propose to be the champion of the world, not the white, or the Canadian, or the American, or any other limited degree of champion. If I am not the best man in the heavyweight division, I don't want to hold the title."[28]

The answer did not sit well with the press. "They knew he'd already fought a number of blacks," sports writer Red Wilson said later. "More than one muttered, 'If he's not careful he's gonna lose the title to a nigger.'"[29]

Another reporter asked if he would give Hart a rematch. Burns said he wasn't interested in a second fight with the big Kentuckian because there was nothing left to prove. He also doubted whether there'd be much fan interest in such a contest. What he didn't say was that he had other challenges in mind. Now that he was champion of the world, Tommy Burns planned to tour the globe, fighting all the best boxers in every country where prizefighting was legal. And he would start with the United States.

The Conquest of the U.S.A.

Tommy Burns couldn't get any respect.

The newly crowned World Heavyweight Boxing Champion returned to his Los Angeles home in late February 1906 to discover few people were taking him very seriously as the king of the big men.

Sports writers in particular were skeptical that this little fellow was really the toughest man on the planet. They kept insisting James J. Jeffries was the real champ because he'd never been defeated in the ring. Jeffries continued to point out he was retired, but few people believed he'd stay away from the sport for very long. Even if the much-loved former champ hadn't been lurking in the background, Burns would have had trouble convincing many people he was truly the best professional boxer in the world. That's because just weeks before Burns beat Hart, Philadelphia Jack O'Brien had won the world light-heavyweight championship. Fight fans were asking how Burns could become heavyweight champion of the world in 1906 *after having lost a bout with the new light-heavyweight champion as recently as October 1904.* Still others pointed out the Canadian had been defeated by middleweight champ Jack "Twin" Sullivan just five months prior to the Hart fight. In other words, the reigning heavyweight champion of the world had lost recent contests with both the light-heavyweight and middleweight champions.

There was a perfectly good explanation. Tommy's losses to those two gentlemen had come at a time when he was struggling to stay within the middleweight limit. During his last months in that weight category he was often so weak he could hardly fight. Once he moved up to boxing's glamour division he'd become a much stronger, more relaxed and considerably more dangerous fighter. But it didn't matter what Burns said, people still didn't think he was a reputable heavyweight champion.

Burns in fighting pose, wearing his heavyweight championship belt.

His old lacrosse buddy, "Dad" Stewart, hurt his reputation even further, telling reporters Burns wasn't the rough and tough lacrosse player that he'd led people to believe. "I roomed with the kid in Woodstock and used to warm him properly in friendly tussles on the field and in our rooms. Champion of the world, eh? I believe I could trim him yet."[1]

Burns, who had a fragile ego at the best of times, was anxious to do something about the situation as quickly as possible. Remembering that his 1902 stunt of challenging two men in one night had created a sensation in Detroit, he latched onto the idea of trying the same thing again. This time, his opponents would include burly Pittsburgh fighter James O'Brien, who outweighed him by 20 pounds, and Soldier Walker, a brawler from Battle Creek, Michigan, who had once fought Tommy Ryan for the world middleweight title.

Some ring historians have dismissed these fights, which took place in San Diego, California, as mere exhibition bouts. But this was not the case. As boxing historian Larry Roberts pointed out, there were no governing bodies in the sport in those days, which meant a champion's title was on the line if he said it was. Both encounters were, in fact, advertised in newspapers as being for Burns's belt. Furthermore, both Burns and the promoter of the fight card went on record saying these were championship tilts. Had he lost either contest, there is no doubt that Burns would have been stripped of his title on the spot.

So it was on March 28, 1906, just over a month after he had defeated Hart, that Tommy Burns became the first and only World Heavyweight Boxing Champion of the modern era to take on two adversaries in one night. James O'Brien, who had gone the distance with Burns before losing a 10-round decision on points back in 1903, was the first up. Burns realized he couldn't afford to go 10 rounds with him again — not if he wanted to have a realistic chance against Walker. Fortunately, he didn't have to. He toyed with the bigger man, flooring him four times before O'Brien was counted out two minutes and 18 seconds into the first round. Walker was able to last a few seconds longer, but he too was knocked out before the end of the first round. Afterwards, newspapers damned the champ with faint praise. "Burns' footwork was good and he seemed capable of taking on 20 such men in as many rounds," one reporter wrote. The key phrase here was "such men." Clearly, the writer didn't think much of the fighting skills of either O'Brien or Walker. Another reporter was even less kind, calling the two boxers "dubs."

Perhaps they were. But Burns planned to silence his critics with his next bout, which would be against legitimate heavyweight contender Fireman Jim Flynn. It's important to take a good look at Flynn's record because over the years countless writers have claimed Burns didn't face any name fighters after winning the title. Flynn, a former Colorado miner with matinée-idol good looks, was the kind of athlete who fought up or down to the level of his opponents. If he found himself facing a mediocre boxer he'd come into the contest poorly trained and basically uninterested. But if matched against a champion, he'd show up in top condition and highly

Heavyweight contender Fireman Jim Flynn.

motivated. Born on Christmas Eve 1879 in Hoboken, New Jersey, Flynn's real name was Andrew Chairiglionne. But like so many pugilists of the era, he had adopted an Irish moniker. Turning professional in 1901, the 22-year-old scored a fourth round knockout in his first fight, then reeled off 11 wins in a row. At 5'10" and 188 pounds, he was a decent size for a heavyweight of that era. He also had a clubbing punch, as he proved by knocking out future world heavyweight champion Jack Dempsey in one round. Flynn has been described as an "unpredictable trial horse for champion and challenger" and indeed he was. In all, he took part in 113 fights, winning 54 and losing 23. The rest were draws or no-decision bouts. In addition to his big win over Dempsey, he once beat Jack "Twin" Sullivan and fought draws with Philadelphia Jack O'Brien and French champion George Gardner. Flynn could also be a dirty fighter, as he demonstrated in a bout with Jack Johnson. Realizing he was behind on points, Flynn literally jumped off his feet in a bid to head-butt the black fighter. Johnson avoided the charge and knocked out Flynn after 11 tough rounds. Nevertheless, Flynn was clearly a man to be reckoned with. He was also the betting favourite, not only because he had more than 30 knockouts to his credit, but also because he was three inches taller than Burns and outweighed him by 17 pounds.

There was so much interest in the fight, which was staged October 3, 1906, in Los Angeles, that eight hundred people had to be turned away at the gate. The next day, they found out via the newspapers that they'd missed the battle of the year. Flynn was on the offensive from the opening bell and dominated the early going. Amazingly, he kept up the torrid pace for round after round. It was a fight, one reporter said later, in which "there was not a moment of rest for either man. At times Flynn fairly outfought the champion and his blows seemed to carry more steam."

Burns had his hands full, but this was a contest in which brains would prove to be more important than brawn. And Tommy Burns was a little smarter than Jimmy Flynn. As the fight wore on, one reporter said, "Burns displayed a great deal of cleverness. In clinches he used his head as much as Nelson [Battling Nelson, a famous light-heavyweight of the era] did, and while resting it on Flynn's shoulder sent in blows on the body. Not until the last three rounds did Flynn respond with any effective infighting and then it was too late."

In the last rounds Burns began to dominate. Flynn was knocked down three times in the fifteenth round, twice for the count of nine. "It was apparent he was all in, but he finished the plucky fight by coming back for more," one reporter wrote. "A succession of well aimed right uppercuts to the jaw sent Flynn to the floor for the fatal count. It was fully 10 minutes before he was able to rise."

At the end of the fight there was a tremendous ovation for Burns. He had fought like a champion, coming back from an early deficit to take the bout. Burns also won some grudging respect from sports writers, although more than a few were now saying he couldn't be considered the best in the world until he beat Philadelphia Jack O'Brien. O'Brien, who attended the fight, agreed, saying he was the real heavyweight champion because he'd once beaten former champ Bob Fitzsimmons.

The private Tommy Burns

The status of World Heavyweight Boxing Champion had changed Tommy Burns. For one thing, he was making — and spending — a lot more money. He moved into a posh home in a fashionable section of Los Angeles, bought property in Long Beach and purchased his own pub in the same community. With some of the proceeds from the Flynn fight he also secured a half interest in an oriental art goods business. To Burns, money was obviously not something to be saved for a rainy day. He'd had enough of poverty in his childhood. Now that he was wealthly, he intended to enjoy it to the fullest.

One writer described him as "a cigar-smoking dandy who was a regular at the California race tracks, sporting a chesterfield coat and squiring a beautiful woman."[2] That beautiful woman was, of course, his wife, Jewel. There is no evidence whatever that Tommy was a womanizer. Indeed, newspaper accounts of the era reported that Jewel went everywhere with him, except to his fights. He was, more than one reporter wrote, "devoted" to her.

Nevertheless, the first signs of serious trouble in his marriage were beginning to surface. Jewel undoubtedly enjoyed the bigger home, which was shaded by palm and eucalyptus trees, but she still didn't have much to do as the couple remained childless. She was often deeply depressed and difficult to live with. It would later be said she suffered from mental illness.

Burns, who loved her deeply, would stand by her for years to come. He even considered changing careers to keep her happy. At one point he tried his hand at egg farming. He bought incubators and announced he'd leave the ring for good if all went well. But he gave the enterprise up when he discovered it was costing him five dollars per egg. Later, he talked about building a string of playhouses. "I am building a $100,000 theatre in Vancouver now, and hope that later on we will be able to get into Spokane and Seattle," he said in a 1910 interview. "It's the theatrical business for me, not as an actor, but as a manager."[3] But that venture, like the egg-farming scheme, ended in failure. Generally speaking, however, he was a good businessman. He dabbled in everything from real estate to arena construction, making money on most of his schemes.

He also made a considerable amount of cash around this time taking part in vaudeville acts. John L. Sullivan had started the tradition of the heavyweight champion appearing on stage, participating in a number of shows in the 1880s. Ever since, fans had come to expect the reigning champ to do the same. Few were any good on the stage, but it hardly seemed to matter. The champion was a celebrity people would pay to watch, no matter what he was doing. Gentleman Jim Corbett had proven that by making a small fortune as an actor.

Burns, who had always been a bit of a ham, was a natural on stage. His act consisted of jokes, films of his fights, a bag-punching demonstration and an exhibition of sparring. During the spring of 1907 he travelled throughout Canada and the United States to put on these shows. His sparring partner at each stop was black heavyweight Klondike Haynes, who shared the same hotel room with Burns.

This was a time when vaudeville theatres were located in virtually every town in North America, and they were often packed to the rafters. Movies were still in their infancy, and the vaudeville shows were often great fun. At the beginning of the century, one historian has noted, "Vaudeville had a speed, charm, glitter and glare that it had not known before. Plain folks could get six acts of variety for a nickle; fancier fare cost up to a dollar. New York shipped both plain and fancy to the country's 2,000 theatres."[4]

Performers such as Harry Houdini, Buster Keaton and Charlie Chaplin vied for attention with talking dogs, acrobats, comedy teams, dramatic actors and even a fellow with a 17-foot-long beard. And by 1907 the entertainment was becoming almost racy. People accustomed to lofty Shakespearean prose were suddenly exposed to gritty plays and monologues in which profanity was sometimes used. At one show, an entire audience stormed out and a *New York World* critic fainted when the word "goddamn" was spoken.

Burns and his fellow performers found the audiences could be tough in other ways as well. As one historian has pointed out, "Reaction was decidedly mixed to the usual vaudeville collection of ventriloquists, jugglers, singers and animal acts. The standard gags from rapid-fire comics — 'I sent my wife to the Thousand Islands for a vacation: one week on each island' or 'You can drive a horse to drink, but a pencil must be lead' — might receive any response from belly laughs to strong silence."[5]

One travelling troupe was pelted with rotten fruit and vegetables so often that it took to performing behind a net. But Burns was exceptionally popular. When he came to Calgary to fulfil a one-week engagement in a local auditorium, he was met at the train station by a brass band and taken on a motorcade ride through the city. He loved the life, but found it a major threat to his boxing career. After only a few weeks of touring he had gained 20 pounds of fat. One critic went so far as to write, "You have no idea of the size Burns grew to while he was taking life easy. He looked more like an alderman than a pugilist, and if he can remove that load of flesh and take up boxing where he quit he is one man in a million." In a letter to a friend, Burns admitted, "They can say what they like, but theatrical work is the worst thing in the world for a fighter."[6]

Burns' mother, Sofa Brusso, right, with his aunt, Sarah Dankert.

Despite all he spent on himself, Burns had not forgotten his mother. When *Detroit Free Press* sports writer Joe Jackson journeyed to Preston, Ontario, around this time to visit Sofa, he found her living in a cosy brick home she'd purchased with $2,000 sent to her by her famous son. She was still opposed to his boxing career but, Jackson thought, her opposition was a little less pronounced than it had been in years gone by. After Jackson read her an account of Tommy's latest fight, she exclaimed, "Oh! If only I could have been there!"[7] The champ also found time to raise funds for the poor. Once, at Christmas, he put on a stage act to help collect money for the needy. A huge crowd turned out and many were moved to tears as Burns spoke about the poverty of his youth.

Other than his mother, however, Burns did not keep in touch with family members, including his brothers and sisters. In a letter to the editor of the *Globe and Mail* written in 1971, Reseda Brusso of Preston, a neice of Tommy's, complained that he "never was very active in writing to his family, not even his sister, who lives in Hamilton."

Burns seemed to enjoy flaunting his wealth, holding a series of parties attended by some of the most important people in California, including the governor of the state and the mayor of Los Angeles. Jewel was thrilled to have such people in her home, but she was not amused when Tommy invited Billy Woods to dinner one night shortly after the Flynn bout.

"It's OK to have *them* in the gym, but there'll be no coloureds in this house!" she snapped.[8]

Burns insisted his friend was going to stay, but Woods put an end to the argument by turning on his heel and walking out. After that, the two men met socially only in Burns's pub or at Woods's home. Before long, Tommy hired Billy as a sparring partner and made him one of his cornermen.

Burns did not show the same loyalty to all his friends, however. Sadly, he allowed money to destroy a friendship he had formed with a young white fighter named George Memsic. Memsic was just a teenager when he showed up on the champ's doorstep announcing he wanted to study Tommy's methods. Burns took him under his wing, treating him like a kid brother. For a time, the two worked out together, with Burns passing along tips to the younger man and lining up fights for him. He constantly promoted him, telling sports writers that his young protégé had the talent to become a world champ. Memsic was so enthralled with the heavyweight champion that he went so far as to change his name to Jimmy Burns. But when the younger man borrowed money from Tommy and failed to pay him back, the older boxer became so enraged that he cut him out of his life.

Besides his hot temper, Burns had other unattractive traits. His inferiority complex drove him to grasp for attention in a shameless manner. He was, indeed, becoming a braggart. Wounded by the fact that he wasn't getting the credit he thought was his due, he began to boast at every opportunity. While the Detroit newspapers had always described Noah Brusso as modest and humble, media accounts of Tommy Burns were not so flattering. Acording to one story written by an English reporter in 1907, "Burns was prepared to tell anyone who would listen that he was in a class by himself. As champion he was arrogance itself during the preliminaries leading up to his fight with Gunner Moir, the best English heavyweight. In view of his offensive conduct it is not strange that for once the National Sporting Club members permitted partisanship to sway them. It was not so much a case of plumping for Moir, as it was a devout hope that the braggart and mannerless visitor should be taught a salutary lesson."[9] Tommy protested, claiming some English reporters had been misquoting him to make him look arrogant. But a year later, an Australian writer described him as being "puffed up to the bursting point with his own self-importance."[10]

Referee Eugene Corri found Burns could also be an autocratic, mistrusting man with "dictatorial ways." Once, he recalled in his memoirs, the champ selected the gloves to be used in a match, then insisted they be "sealed up in a box to be opened in the ring on the night of the fight."[11]

Showdown with Philadelphia Jack O'Brien

One man who thought he could teach Burns a lesson was Philadelphia Jack O'Brien. And why not? Since they'd last met two years earlier, O'Brien had scored 11 more victories, bringing his overall won-lost record to a mind-boggling 96–4. What's more, five of his last six fights had ended with his opponent stretched out on the canvas. Newspapers and fans were also clamouring for a showdown between the two men. Burns, who knew he'd have to beat O'Brien if he ever hoped to gain recognition as the best boxer in the world, agreed to a November 28, 1906, match in Los Angeles.

The bout created widespread interest, with O'Brien the clear fan favourite. "The tall boxer is one of the best entertainers who follows boxing for a livelihood, and he grows popular after he has been training in one place for two days," the *San Francisco Examiner* declared. The paper added that O'Brien was running eight miles daily, rain or shine — in fact he enjoyed jogging in the rain because he didn't get sweaty or dehydrated. After his romps, which usually lasted about two hours, O'Brien would work out in the gym before large, admiring crowds. Even the *Detroit Free Press*, normally kind to Burns, thought the cham-

*Legendary heavyweight
Philadelphia Jack O'Brien.*

pion was in over his head. It speculated he might have been coaxed into the fight "in undue haste." It added "O'Brien is more dangerous to him than Hart, for O'Brien is a man that no boxer in the ring can show up when it comes to a question of speed and cleverness." Perhaps not surprisingly, O'Brien was a 10–6 favourite in the betting.

Burns was angry about stories that suggested he wasn't as good a boxer as O'Brien, but what really upset him was a playful article that poked fun at his attire. Until now, he'd always been better dressed than his opponents. But with O'Brien things were different. They were both stylish dressers, a fact that was not lost on the press. Under the headline, "Battle of Clothes," one reporter suggested O'Brien was a better dresser than Burns. Although it was all in good fun, Burns was so upset he threatened to sue. Perhaps it was his insecurity that made him so angry, or maybe it was his hatred of O'Brien. Whatever the reason, the reporter had struck a nerve.

When the long-awaited Burns-O'Brien showdown came in Los Angeles, the five thousand wildly enthusiastic fans in attendance couldn't have cared less which one of them was the better dresser. The only exception may have been former champion Jim Jeffries, who refereed the fight wearing a white shirt, silk tie and top hat. He was allowed to handle the bout despite the fact that he had told reporters ahead of time he thought O'Brien would win.

It was, in many ways, one of the most amazing prizefights ever seen, pitting as it did two of the fastest boxers in history against each other. And because both weighed in under the 175-182 pound light-heavyweight limit, there were no less than two title belts on the line. The winner would be declared both heavyweight and light-heavyweight champion of the world. It was also one of the first fights ever filmed, which meant large, red-hot lights were directed at the ring. Under the glare of the lights, the fans looked like white-faced zombies, and the blood from the boxers would look pitch black.

With so much at stake, the men were at each other's throats before the gong sounded for round one. O'Brien started the quarrel, complaining to Jeffries that the Canadian's belt was inflated.

"Under the rules he can't wear anything except bare trunks," he pointed out.[12]

Burns countered by noting O'Brien's right elbow was bandaged. Finally, after haggling for 15 minutes, Burns agreed to remove the belt. A smug O'Brien, who was allowed to keep his bandages, bowed to the crowd, only to be greeted with a chorus of boos. He'd won the argument but had lost the support of the fans, most of whom thought his protests petty.

The verbal fight was nothing compared to the confrontation that followed. This is how one reporter described the heart-stopping action:

From the first to the last Burns plunged in viciously with undiminished anxiety to end the fight with a knockout. O'Brien, on his part, showed remarkable footwork and a greater degree of gameness than he is usually credited with. All of Burns' rushes ended in clinches, and in every clinch O'Brien caught Burns' gloves under his armpits or grasped Burns around the forearms until Jeffries ordered the men to part.

In each clinch Burns struggled, twisted, and tugged trying to get his arms free. Now and then he would get a free hand and whale away with it until O'Brien was forced to free Tom's other arm and then beat a fast retreat. In the fifth round, Burns caught O'Brien with a fearful right hand that broke O'Brien's nose and covered him with blood. Thereafter, except for momentary bursts of action, O'Brien had to be content to hold the retreat.

So it went, round after round, with Burns boring in like a bulldog and O'Brien prancing away like a greyhound. The Canadian almost knocked his man out with a blow to the jaw in the eighth round, then opened a nasty cut over O'Brien's left eye in the tenth. At the end of the fight, one reporter noted, the light-heavyweight champion's face was "a ghastly sight. Jeffries' white shirt was bloody, owing to his interferences in the clinches." Most observers thought Burns won 15 of the 20 rounds, but referee Jeffries stunned journalists and fans alike by calling the bout a draw. The bloody fight had resolved nothing. Both men would be allowed to retain their respective titles.

After the contest O'Brien blamed a sore elbow he'd picked up in training for his inability to get the win. But he was essentially gracious, describing Burns as "a wonderfully improved fighter. He has improved ever since he fought Flynn, I think. His strength, too, is prodigious. He surprised me and showed that he is a dangerous opponent for any man."

As for the referee's verdict, he said, "I am very well pleased with the decision. Jeffries did the right thing. I outpointed Burns, I think, but I was a little light for him."[13]

Burns was not so gentlemanly. Asked what he thought of Jeffries' ruling, he said,

> I won fairly and I think the decision was bad. I chased O'Brien miles all over the ring. Just compare our faces and draw your own conclusions. Those who saw the bout give O'Brien the best of the first three rounds, and some of them think that he had a shade in the last two. That leaves quite a stretch in which I had the better of it. When you see the pictures you will see O'Brien running away in round after round, his back turned to me, when I was doing all that I could to make a fight of it and to end the thing. I couldn't do any more. It's hard to finish a man who is sprinting away. O'Brien is clever and has a good head but I think I am just as fast and I know I can hit harder and take more punishment. My footwork is just as good as O'Brien's, though he may be more showy. He wastes a lot in his fancy work with his feet. I cover more ground by making every move count.[14]

Jeffries defended himself, saying, "There was nothing warranting a different decision in favour of either. Both were strong at the finish. There was not enough leading done to justify a selection of the better man."[15]

So who *really* got the better of the historic fight? All the ringside reporters thought Burns was the winner. One account had him landing twice as many blows as O'Brien. Another reporter went so far as to say,

"Burns beat O'Brien in every minute of their 20 round fight. Jack was nearly out on his feet as he sped away from the savage onslaught of the Canadian. As Tommy rushed in O'Brien actually turned his back and ran. It's beyond me how the fight ended in a draw. Burns won hands down." There seems little doubt that Jeffries was biased in favour of his buddy, O'Brien. *New York World* boxing critic Bob Edgren declared that Jeffries had proven himself to be "a lobster referee for not handing the decision to Burns."

So ended 1906. During the year Burns had fought five times, winning four and drawing one. Along the way he'd won the World Heavyweight Boxing Championship and had successfully defended it four times. On the financial front, he'd made $12,300 in the ring alone, or more than $315,000 tax free in modern terms. It had, in other words, been a year of unprecedented success for him. But Tommy Burns was far from a happy man. He was the king of the boxing world, but he knew he had a long way to go before his subjects would show him any respect.

Burns meets the Iron Man

Despite his strong performance against Philadelphia Jack O'Brien, few people thought Burns was a true champion. Most figured Jim Jeffries would have been able to knock O'Brien out without any trouble at all. Desperate to rectify this perception, Burns decided on another gimmick. This time, instead of fighting two men in one night, he proposed to travel to Philadelphia to meet Iron Joe Grim. What followed was one of the most bizarre and pathetic bouts in the history of the heavyweight division.

Grim has been called the "toughest fighter who ever lived," and in many ways he was just that. He also appeared to be completely oblivious to pain. Born Saverio Gianonne in Italy in 1881, he'd moved to the United States with his family as a nine-year-old. Poorly educated and not very bright, he went to work as a shoeshine boy outside a local boxing club. One day, when a fighter failed to show up for a bout, 17-year-old Gianonne filled in for him, receiving $1.50 for his troubles. After that he changed his name to Joe Grim and started fighting for a living.

Iron Joe Grim.

It's doubtful if the prize ring has ever seen a worse boxer. Grim weighed only 145 pounds, but he fought in virtually every weight category, from welterweight right up to heavyweight. In all he fought for about a dozen years, taking part in an estimated 400 bouts. Of those, he won exactly 10.

Despite his terrible record, however, by 1907 he'd become one of the best-known and most popular pugilists in the world. While virtually everyone was able to knock him down, absolutely no one had been able to knock Joe Grim out. In one fight he'd landed only three punches, while his adversary, according to a newspaper account, got in more than a thousand. But when it was all over the Iron Man was still on his feet.

Before each fight Grim would enter the ring by somersaulting over the ropes. Once inside, he'd take his robe off, revealing garish pink-and-blue trunks that one reporter said, "were so loud that announcer Bright had to use a megaphone to be heard."[16] After each contest, bleeding and battered, he'd stagger over to the ropes and shout to the crowd, "I am Joe Grim! I fear no man on earth!"[17] After one match, in which he was floored a dozen times, a Milwaukee newspaper called him "a nerveless and brainless freak of human idiocy." Following a contest in Boston, a Massachusetts paper editorialized, "To a disinterested observer, it seems strange that no one has yet been found with enough intelligence or public spirit to keep this foolish fellow out of the ring. Although these performances are billed as boxing exhibitions they are neither more nor less than torturing matches, just as brutal and revolting as the worst slaughtering exhibitions in the arena during the decadence of Rome."[18]

Before long all the best boxers from every weight division were in an unofficial contest to see who could become the first to knock out Grim. Bob Fitzsimmons tried on October 14, 1903, knocking the Iron Man down nine times in six rounds. But he got up each time, gamely waving

Fitzsimmons on. When Fitzsimmons hit him with his famous solar plexus punch Grim burst into hysterical laughter. At the end of the fight Iron Joe was still on his feet.

Jack Johnson was the next big name to take him on, knocking Grim down no less than 18 times in six rounds. Each time he lifted himself up, one newspaper said, as if he were going to get his hair cut. At the conclusion of the fight Grim was standing at centre ring with a goofy smile on his face. He even had the panache to taunt Johnson, declaring, "Joe Grim is still here and you can't knock him out!"

"He ain't human," Johnson told one reporter.[19]

Legendary fighter Joe Walcott said he once hit Grim with such force that he expected his glove to pass right through his body. Once again, however, the Iron Man was still upright at the end. Before long he was inviting non-fighters to knock him out. Once, he let a friend hit him in the stomach with an axe handle. On another occasion, a slaughterhouse employee hit him in the midsection with a sledgehammer. In both cases the blows had no visible impact on him.

Soon doctors were coming to Philadelphia to take a look at him. One, Dr. J. M. Craemer, published a paper in which he suggested Grim was too stupid to be knocked out. "Grim is not the physical giant I would imagine from the accounts of the battles," he wrote. "On the contrary, he weighs not more than 150 pounds when in condition, and lacks the development seen among most fighters. His body and stomach muscles are not developed in the least, and to see the Italian stripped ready for action, one would wonder how he could stand the punching." He then went on to suggest the Iron Man could take the punishment because "his brain matter is no more developed than his muscles. To cause a kayo, the blow must affect the brain. It is like an electric current that travels from the jaw to the brain through the nerves. Grim has no nerves, and he does not possess enough intelligence to realize any danger."[20]

Grim proved that diagnosis wasn't totally accurate when he got into the ring with Tommy Burns for a scheduled three-round bout on the night of January 10, 1907. When the Canadian took off his robe, Grim appeared genuinely startled. Perhaps it was Tommy's stocky frame, or the killer look in his eyes. Whatever it was, he suddenly demanded the rounds be reduced from three minutes each to just one. Burns protested vigorously. He'd travelled all the way from Los Angeles hoping to become the first man to knock out Iron Joe. But when Grim flatly refused to fight unless he got his way, there was nothing Burns could do but go along with him.

The Canadian went straight for Grim, knowing he didn't have to worry the slightest bit about defense. Totally unafraid of his opponent, he planted himself solidly in the centre of the ring and lashed into Iron Joe with everything he had. His first blow exploded onto Grim's jaw with stunning and immediate effect, knocking him on his backside. But the fiesty Italian bounced off the canvas like an India rubber ball and was back on his feet in the wink of an eye. Over the three minutes of fighting, the champion knocked Grim down four more times. It was a better knockdown percentage than Fitzsimmons or Johnson had managed, and the referee had no trouble declaring Burns the winner. But at the final bell the indestructable Joe Grim was still alert, standing over by the ropes, yelling to the fans, "I am Joe Grim! I fear no man on earth!"[21]

All of this would be funny if it wasn't for the fact that poor Grim's brains were getting rattled night after night. A few years after his fight with Burns, he was placed in a mental institution. For a time he had to wear a straitjacket so he couldn't harm himself.

The Jack O'Brien rematch

The story of how Tommy Burns got Philadelphia Jack O'Brien into the ring for their third and final clash is almost as pitiful as the tale of how he beat up the hapless Joe Grim. Since their draw the previous October, O'Brien had won another fight — his ninety-seventh — by beating a fellow who went by the name of Abdul the Turk. Given his fabulous won-lost record, a rematch with Burns seemed inevitable. But O'Brien didn't appear to be in a big hurry to get back into the ring with him. Their last fight may have officially been a draw, but O'Brien had taken a severe beating. In addition to his broken nose and cut eye, he'd been subjected to a terrible body battering. As one newspaper reported the day after the fight, "With doctors, his mother and sister attending him,

Philadelphia Jack O'Brien is a very sick man at his hotel. To anyone but the physically perfect man O'Brien is, Burns's punishment inflicted in the ring Thanksgiving evening would have meant death. For O'Brien a long spell of sickness seems ahead, due principally to deranged kidneys resulting from the terrific pounding he received at the hands of his hard-hitting Canadian adversary."

Frustrated with O'Brien's apparent aversion to a rematch, Burns began stalking him, much like Muhammad Ali did to Sonny Liston half a century later. Ali once went so far as to show up on Liston's front lawn in the middle of the night screaming and yelling that he was going to whip the champion. Burns didn't go quite that far, but he did follow O'Brien into a cigar store, where he made a scene, calling the light-heavyweight champion a "coward"[22] in front of dozens of witnesses. The flustered O'Brien agreed to a third fight, but he had an ace up his sleeve. When the two men got together to discuss contract arrangements, the challenger dropped a bombshell.

"If you lie down you can have the whole purse — $10,000," O'Brien told him.[23]

Burns poured himself a glass of whiskey and took a stiff drink. The men were deathly quiet, the silence masking the churning of minds. Tommy Burns may have been a lot of things but he wasn't a cheat. He feared, however, that if he turned down the proposal, O'Brien would never agree to another fight. And until he beat Philadelphia Jack, he knew he'd never be accepted as the true World Heavyweight Boxing Champion. Finally, after a long moment, he said, "You've got yourself a deal."[24] To guarantee his participation in the fakery, he posted a bond for one thousand dollars. What O'Brien didn't realize was that the notes were forgeries.

When the day of the fight arrived, on May 8, 1907, it was Tommy's turn to drop a bombshell of his own. He had no intention of taking part in a fix, and he planned to tell O'Brien that just before fight time. About 10 minutes prior to the bout, Burns called fight promoter Tom McCreary to his locker-room and told him of the proposed fix. Then he asked McCreary to instruct referee Charlie Eyton to inform the fans that all bets were off. As the fighters entered the ring, Eyton called out for silence. Cupping his hands around his mouth, he yelled, "Gentlemen, all bets made on O'Brien to win up to this moment are off. The fight will now commence. Gentlemen, you are free to make your bets as you will."[25]

A buzz of excitement swept through the crowd. The announcement could only mean one thing — there had been a cross, and now a doublecross.

O'Brien appeared shocked. Seconds before the bell rang to start the first round, Burns dashed over to his corner, grabbed him by the arms and snarled, "Fight your best, Jack. I'm out to beat you now. I've got you here at last. This is a real fight."[26]

The *New York Police Gazette* told best what happened next:

From the beginning to the end of the contest O'Brien resorted frequently to the marathon to keep out of the way of the vicious attacks of Tommy's right and left blows. In the seventh round, as Jack was retreating, Tommy crossed a right that staggered Jack, who fell into a clinch. In the ninth, Tommy slashed his right and left to Jack's face and opened a cut on Jack's left eye. The blood streamed freely from this wound. From this moment to the end of the fight, which was a great moment for Burns' rooters, O'Brien seemed eligible for the loser's end of the purse.

The Toronto *Globe* reported Burns repeatedly called for O'Brien to "come on and fight." But, the newspaper added, the American boxer "ran as though in terror of his antagonist. Now and then Burns would overtake him and beat him on the back, O'Brien attempting wildly to duck and dodge away, until Burns, weary of the foot race, would stand in the centre of the ring, with his hands to his sides, and wait for O'Brien to come to him. Each round was largely a repetition of the preceding one. Burns had the better of most of them." At the end of the 20 rounds both men were still standing, but no one was surprised when Burns was declared the winner on points.

Jim Jeffries, who was in the crowd, told reporters,

It was more of a running match than a fight, for the simple reason that O'Brien refused to fight. Burns was willing enough and never let an opportunity escape to mix it and mix it hard, but O'Brien was evidently afraid to let himself loose and for round after round he did little but run around the ring with Burns after him. It was one of the most remarkable contests in the history of championship fights. Instead of two perfectly trained fighters battling their best for the decision, the crowd saw one man rushing and rushing and rushing, while the other turned his back and ran. In but one round did O'Brien really do any fighting. This was in the fourth. In this round the Philadelphian sent in numerous straight lefts to the face, which brought blood from Burns' nose. This was the only round in which I could give O'Brien anything. In half a dozen rounds there was not enough doing to give the shade to either fighter, but in all the others it was all Burns.[27]

After the fight, a reporter pointed out that because both fighters had weighed under the 175-pound limit, Tommy was now both heavyweight and light-heavyweight champion of the world. But he appeared unimpressed with the light-heavyweight crown. "Forget it," he said. "I don't want that thing. Let O'Brien keep it."[28]

Burns would never acknowledge he was light-heavyweight champ, and he flatly refused to defend the title when others in that weight category challenged him. Burns knew the heavyweight crown was far more prestigious, and he didn't want to take any attention away from the fact that he was world heavyweight champion. As a result, few boxing histories list him as having ever been the light-heavyweight king. Despite his reluctance to accept the title, however, the fact remains that he *was* world light-heavyweight champ. Indeed, there were no further championship bouts in the division for the next several years. The championship was only declared vacant in 1912, five years after Burns had won the title. Finally, on May 28, 1912, Jack Dillon beat Hugo Kelly to replace Burns as the new light-heavyweight king.

After the Burns-O'Brien fight there were immediate demands to know why all bets had been called off. Burns shocked sports fans by issuing a statement that said, "Jack O'Brien was caught in one of his own traps. I could not get him to agree to enter the arena until I had promised to lay down and let him win the fight. I pretended to be willing to do this because I wanted to show the country that I was O'Brien's master. As for the bets being called off, I was instrumental in having that done for the protection of the public. I did not want to see the public tricked into losing any of its money. The calling off of the bets cost me $3,800, for I stood to win that amount by betting on myself."[29]

At first there was widespread suspicion that the outcome had still been rigged, that the fighters had agreed ahead of time to let Burns win. Some thought Burns was merely trying to cover up the fix with an elaborate story. The *Chicago Inter-Ocean* newspaper went so far as to say Canadians should be grateful that Burns had left their country to live in the U. S.

But such criticism vanished over the next few days, thanks to the testimony of other fighters. The first was none other than Jim Jeffries. He told reporters,

Jack O'Brien is the first and only man who ever came to me and asked me to do a crooked thing. Of all the fighters and managers I have known, this man is the only one who ever had the gall to ask me to fake a fight. Worse than that, he wanted me to lay down to him. Here is what happened. Shortly after the first fight with Burns, O'Brien called on me at my own residence.

'Jim,' said O'Brien, 'I have some business to talk over with you; it may interest you, and it may not. I do not know whether you have anything to do with a proposition of this kind. It is just this. I have found a certain party or parties in Nevada who say that they will give a $30,000 purse for a fight between you and me. They will place an additional $50,000 in the bank for you, making $80,000 in all — every cent of which will go to you.'

Then he stopped for a second and wound up with these identical words: "But you will have to take the count to get it."

It nearly paralyzed me — that he should come out with a bald-faced plan like that. I began to laugh at him, and he saw right away that it was all off. I told him that I did not need money that bad.[30]

After Jeffries made his comments, Hugo Kelly followed suit, saying O'Brien had once asked him to take a dive as well. O'Brien was, he said, "a big yellow-backed edition of a fighter."[31]

Burns's name had been cleared, but the anti-O'Brien backlash was so harsh that many fans thought a win over him was no big deal. This was nonsense, of course. Although he was a rogue who had doubtlessly participated in some fixed fights, the vast majority of O'Brien's bouts had been on the level. Newspaper accounts of his many bloody battles make that clear. But the damage had been done. O'Brien would only participate in four more fights before fading from the scene. And Tommy Burns found that, once again, people weren't all that impressed with what he had achieved.

8

Burns Rules Australia

They called him "Cyclone," "the Aussie Mystery" and "Killer Bill." But regardless of his nicknames, Australian heavyweight champion Bill Squires was thought by many in 1907 to be the finest prizefighter in the world.

So when the hulking brute from New South Wales stepped off the steamship *Venture* in San Francisco harbour on April 17 of that year, he created an instant sensation. Squires, who was born and raised in the Australian outback, was an imposing figure indeed. Standing just under six feet and weighing 185 pounds, he had powerful, sloping shoulders. From the waist up, Squires looked like a weightlifter. From the belt down, he resembled a sprinter. But what most people noticed about him straight away was the size of his hands. They were massive, twice the size, some said, of Jim Jeffries's formidable fists.

Fight fans had been talking about Squires for two years before he arrived in North America. Since turning professional five years earlier, the 27-year-old had won all 26 of his fights, 23 by knockout. Eight of his opponents had been put down in the first round, and most of the others hadn't lasted much longer. One of his adversaries, South African champion Mike Williams, had been blasted into oblivion only 45 seconds into the fight. Squires had pulverized celebrated East Indian fighter Peter Felix three times, knocking him out twice in the second round and once in the seventh. Another of his victims had been Irish champion Jem Roche, who was KO'd in the fourth. One Australian newspaper had declared, "In the ring Squires is more like a seismic disturbance than a man. He is the personification of the strenuous life adopted to pugilistic principles." After one of his fights, a reporter wrote, "His blows carried twice the weight of those of his opponent."

Promoters had been trying to lure Squires to the U. S. ever since Jeffries announced his retirement. But the crafty Australian had deliberately stayed away, waiting for public curiosity about the dynamic heavyweight with the awesome knockout punch to reach a fever pitch.

As he came down the gangplank at San Francisco a throng of reporters and photographers gathered around Squires, shouting questions and snapping pictures. One photographer asked him to smile. He scowled instead, asking, "Do you think I'm a comic actor?"

"What about Tommy Burns?" one of them shouted. "Can you trim him?"

Australian heavyweight champion Bill Squires.

"I will not fight a faker," he replied.

Squires, who apparently believed Burns was as dishonest as O'Brien, said he was gunning for Jeffries instead. He insisted Jeffries, not Burns, was the real champion of the world. "I have come half way around the world to fight this man Jeffries and will not be put off on anyone else."

Asked if he had any special training methods that he'd brought with him, he replied, "I brought no trainers, believing the American method of training is a good one, and I will adopt that system while here." With that he marched off, "quickly and gracefully," one reporter said.[1]

After he'd been in California a few weeks, Squires began to have second thoughts about boycotting Burns. Jeffries had flatly refused to fight him, making it plain once again that his retirement was permanent. So Squires could either return to Australia empty-handed or he could fight the reigning champion. Eventually, he agreed to take on the Canadian.

No sooner had the contract for the fight been signed than a flood of pro-Squires stories began to appear in the newspapers, all of them describing the big Aussie in the most glowing of terms. Each one put heavy emphasis on his hitting powers and conditioning. The *San Francisco Examiner* asserted,

Squires is not wasting any time loitering around sporting cafes, posing on public streets or giving exhibitions in a theatre. In the afternoon Squires begins work on a heavy bag. At this he is not as neat as some of the American heavies, but at the same time he displays great punching power. Like Jeffries, he uses swinging blows when assaulting the bag. He stands flat-footed, as though desirous of putting in solid licks rather than fancy touches, and he makes use of all the force at his command. The skipping rope seems to be the favourite form of exercise with Squires. He goes in for a series of extension motions with heavy dumb-bells, following this with a brisk spell of shadow boxing and then engages in stunts advocated by physical culture experts. He does very little sparring. He admits being bad at that game. He likes work that brings out all the strength. He has no use for anything that confines him to light tapping.

It was small wonder, reading these accounts, that Squires was the 10–7 betting favourite. The fight was scheduled for 45 rounds, but few people thought Burns would last anywhere near that long. The *Examiner*, recalling how much trouble the Canadian had had defeating middleweight Dave Barry at San Francisco in 1905, predicted Squires would cut him to pieces. A *Detroit Free Press* writer sent to cover the fight reported, "the town is flooded with Squires money and Squires talk. The general impression is that he will whip Burns inside of 10 rounds."[2]

Publicly, Burns appeared unconcerned. "I am ready and anxious to meet the Australian," he said.[3] But privately he was trying to find out as much about Squires as he could, hoping to find any kind of edge. He discovered that Squires was a coalminer by profession, who, like both himself and John L. Sullivan, had been prodded into his first prizefight.

He'd gone to watch a boxing exhibition given by a travelling fighter when the visiting pugilist challenged him to a bout. When Squires remained in his seat, the boxer chided him unmercifully, calling him a "big stiff."

Embarrassed, Squires shouted, "Stop right there!"[4] Jumping to his feet, he entered the ring, put on boxing gloves for the first time in his life and knocked his tormentor out in the second round. After that, it was Squires who was constantly on the road. Indeed, the life of a prizefighter in Australia was no picnic. Squires once told a reporter, "In America as soon as a fighter amounts to anything he quits his job, but in Australia the day after a fight I went back to my work in the mines. At one time, when I was new at the game, in order to beat the champion of one of the provinces, I walked 200 miles, trained for two weeks and fought for a $50 purse. That is the way a fighter in Australia has to fight in order to gain a reputation. A $250 purse is considered big in Australia."[5]

Squires had a bitter edge to him, probably because miners of the era were badly mistreated by their bosses. "Like most Australian working-men, Bill is a socialist," one newspaper reported. "A prominent member of the miners' union, he has for years been one of the foremost workers in the cause of the Labour Party in Newcastle." He was also deeply religious. He taught Sunday school and sometimes delivered unsolicited sermons to fellow miners during lunch-hours.

After reading everything he could get his hands on about Squires, Burns watched films of him in action. After that, he sought out former Australian boxer Joe Sleight, who was living in San Francisco, and asked him his opinion. "Squires has not merely one punch, but two," Sleight told him. "One hand is as good as the other and Squires mixes them up with deadly versatility. When in battle formation he crouches low, boxing close in."[6]

Armed with that information, Burns asked Jeffries how he'd fight the Aussie. "Squires keeps his chin up too high," the former champ said. "Feint low and aim high and you'll take him out."[7]

Based on all he'd seen, heard and read, Burns figured Squires was basically an unskilled boxer who relied solely on his raw hitting power. If he could avoid the bigger man's punch, he figured he could win. Leaving nothing to chance, he also trained hard. Ever the entrepreneur,

Burns, right, squares off against Bill Squires.

he charged admission to his sparring sessions. For one, in which he went four rounds with Billy Woods, three hundred spectators paid 25¢ each. Burns split the proceeds equally with his pal.

As the fight approached, Burns appeared relaxed and optimistic. In a letter to the Toronto *Globe* he wrote, "Of course Squires is an unknown quantity, to be sure, but I never felt more confident before, and you can tell my Canadian friends that the maple leaf will score a decisive victory on Americans' national holiday."

The Burns-Squires fight, which attracted a crowd of nine thousand, was held July 4, 1907, in the San Francisco suburb of Colma. Many of the fans had travelled hundreds of miles, anticipating a classic battle. Weather conditions for the outdoor bout were perfect and, one reporter noted, "A few women braved the gaze of thousands of men and occupied seats close to the ringside."

Squires, who was led into the stadium by a man carrying an Australian flag, was overheard to say he would go after the champion right away. "I won't waste a second of time," he said.[8] Burns, looking for an edge anywhere he could find it, marched in behind the Stars and Stripes. The American crowd gave the Canadian a loud ovation, but few believed he had much of a chance.

Burns was lucky from the start. He won the coin toss and chose the northwest corner, with his back to the sun.

"The gong sounded at 3:10 p.m.," one newspaper reported the next day. "Both men seemed to be in the pink of condition when they began what was thought would be a vicious and hardily-contested battle for the world's championship. Squires went after Burns with confidence, feinting and leading, while the crowd marvelled at his clever footwork. Burns appeared to be cautious at first, but the Canadian soon showed his mettle. After a clinch he landed a smashing right to Squires's jaw, and the Australian went down for the count of four. It looked like the fight was already over, but Squires staggered to his feet and clinched with his antagonist."

Burns had followed Jeffries's advice to the letter and it had worked. He'd feinted with his left, then sent a speedy right over Squires's slow-moving jab, catching the challenger by surprise.

Squires should have covered up and waited until he had recovered his senses before going back on the offensive. Instead, he charged forward, swinging wildly. Burns easily ducked, then unloaded another right that sent the big Aussie crashing to the floor a second time. Showing remarkable pluck, Squires rose to his feet and came at the smaller man again. As he bore in, ringside spectators could see a welt twice the size of an egg had already formed on the side of his head. A third punch caught him flush on the jaw and he fell flat on his face. He was still there when referee Jim Jeffries reached the count of ten. The fight had lasted exactly two minutes and eight seconds.

Tommy Burns had scored yet another stunning upset, but it did little good for his reputation. The next day, the newspapers savaged Squires unmercifully, dismissing the Australian champ as a "greatly over-rated lemon." One sneered, "he is a rough-and-tumble fighter who would have no chance with a second or third rate boxer." Another reported that fans who had paid up to $20 for their tickets left the arena "disappointed and disgusted." Many of them, the paper noted, had "come hundreds of miles to see what they believed would be a finish fight. The public was 'sold' again. The fight was a fiasco."

Even Squires's manager, Barney Reynolds, trashed his own man. "I have done with fighting and fighters," he said. "I guess we must have a pretty poor lot of fighters in Australia, because Squires was the best we have."[9]

Squires himself was sheepish, saying he'd been led to believe Burns did not have a knockout punch. Obviously, he hadn't done even the most elementary research before getting into the ring. If he had, he would have known Burns had scored 28 knockouts in his first 48 fights. With the exception of Squires himself, there was not an active heavyweight in the world with a better knockout percentage.

Burns, for his part, told reporters, "I saw the moving pictures of Squires in training. When I saw how he carried himself and how he acted, I knew I would not have any difficulty in defeating him. I went into the ring with the fullest confidence that I would be the winner." Then, not able to resist taking another shot at the hated Philadelphia Jack O'Brien, he added, "There was more fighting in one round with Squires than in 20 with O'Brien."

Tommy's secret

Instead of knocking fighters like Hart, O'Brien and Squires, reporters and fans should have been asking themselves, "What's Tommy Burns's secret? How is such a little guy able to knock out some of the biggest and best boxers in the world with such apparent ease?"

Burns could have told them, had they bothered to ask. He was already putting his thoughts together for a book to be published later that year. The days were gone, he would write, when fighters could expect to get by on brute strength and hitting power alone. Instead, a pugilist had to think and move quickly. "In modern boxing speed is nearly everything, and I have always considered my success to be primarily due to the fact that lacrosse and hockey had taught me to be spry and smart on my feet before I ever thought of donning a pair of boxing gloves." A good boxer, he continued, should balance his weight equally on both feet so he could be ready to dart quickly from side to side.

Besides being agile, he said a fighter who hoped to win consistently needed to play head games with his adversaries, keeping them constantly guessing about what was coming next. "Worry your opponent as much as you can," he wrote. "Cultivate quick, slight movements or tricks with the eyes, hands and feet, which will convey the impression of a sudden, rapid movement, which you will not really carry out. In many cases these tactics will cause your opponent to make a big lunge or a rapid jerk or spring backwards or sideways, such as will take a lot of steam out of him, without having distressed you in any way."[11]

A scientific boxer, he added, could beat a bull-headed fighter by waiting patiently for his opponent to get careless. He didn't even think it was necessary to hit such a fellow more than once or twice per round. Just to make sure his opponents lost their cool, Burns said he always taunted them. During clinches, he wrote, a good boxer should suddenly pull away and laugh at his adversary. The fans usually joined in, causing the other boxer to make crucial mistakes.

It was important, too, to make sure you kept your own cool, no matter what was going on. If you lost your head, he said, you'd almost certainly end up losing the fight as well. As for punching, he advised novice fighters to forget about big swings. Instead, they should get in close and deliver short, sharp jabs. With a much bigger opponent, it made sense to get between his arms and whale away at the body from point-blank range. Finally, Burns contended, a good boxer should crouch low and keep his chin down as much as possible. A blow to the jaw was, he said, the worst thing that could happen to you.

Jack Johnson issues a challenge

Racism was about to rear its ugly head in the heavyweight division once again. The catalyst was a telegram sent by black fighter Jack Johnson to Burns, challenging him to a bout. Burns told reporters about the challenge and added he would accept it, provided he could negotiate a contract to his satisfaction.

The Canadian's decision caused consternation in many circles. Jim Jeffries warned him not to fight either Johnson or Sam Langford. He'd always ducked both boxers, he admitted frankly, because he didn't want a black man to become World Heavyweight Boxing Champion. Jewel, too, opposed the match, warning she might leave Tommy if he disgraced her by getting into the ring with a coloured man again. Her objections were beginning to influence him. In fact, he mentioned them to a reporter, adding they could cause him to change his mind about fighting Johnson. The *Detroit Times* ridiculed him for his apparent flip-flop:

> A few days ago we got Tommy Burns, who crawled out of a match with Jack Johnson, the coloured champion, by putting forward the moth-eaten wifey-doesn't-want-me-to excuse. She's a southern woman, so we hear.
>
> Isn't it the limit? Why, things are getting to such a stage that no pugilist will be able to be considered unless he has a wife ready to take all the responsibilities of matchmaking, all the credit of victory and all the onus of defeat. And it's a humiliating spectacle, too, for the sporting world to see its professional eaters of gore, wound round the fingers of these weak women and reporting for orders after the fashion of mere men.
>
> Oh, pahaw! Oh, fudge! Oh, fury!

In the end, Tommy decided not to draw the colour line, probably because he didn't believe Jewel's threat was serious.

Over the years some historians have suggested there was such heavy pressure in the media for a Burns-Johnson fight that the champ had little choice but to eventually give in. But that's nonsense. Other than the *Detroit Times*, few newspapers had criticized his suggestion that he might not meet the big Texan in the ring. Burns could have ducked Johnson simply by issuing a public statement drawing the colour line. It had been drawn by all five champs before him and would be drawn again by several fighters who succeeded him. As late as 1919, champion Jack Dempsey announced he wouldn't fight blacks. The *New York Times* reported on July 5th of that year, "In the first statement he has made since becoming the heavyweight champion of the world, Jack Dempsey announced today that he would draw the color line. He will pay no attention to Negro challengers, but will defend his title against any white heavyweights as the occasion demands."

Dempsey did, in fact, hide behind the colour line for his entire reign, and there was hardly a whisper of criticism against him. In the United Kingdom, it would be against the law for blacks to challenge for any

British boxing title until 1947. In major-league baseball, meanwhile, the first African-American player wouldn't appear on the scene until 1942. Even the Detroit Tigers, who played in a city with a substantial black population, would not welcome their first player of colour until 1958.

Clearly then, in 1907 any white champion could have ignored black fighters without losing much public support. But Burns believed Johnson deserved a shot at the title. He'd read and heard stories about the fighter's early life that had impressed him. Born John Arthur Johnson in Galveston, Texas, on March 13, 1878, the big boxer was the son of former slaves Henry and Tina Johnson. Henry had been a bare-knuckle pugilist of note in his youth, but it was Tina who had steered young Jack towards a career in the ring. After he became a famous fighter she told reporters he had been "all coward" as a lad.[12] In fact, he often had to be protected by his sisters after getting into schoolyard tussles. But all that changed after Tina warned him she'd whip him herself when he got home if he didn't start defending himself.

Like Burns, Johnson was never much of a student, and quit school after the sixth grade to take odd jobs wherever he could find them. By the age of 15 he was already a giant, standing 6'1" and weighing 170 pounds. Before long he was entering the so-called Battle Royals being staged by Galveston's wealthy white businessmen. In these disgusting brawls, black youths would fight for pennies tossed to them by white spectators. Sometimes as many as a dozen boys would duke it out, with the last one standing to collect all the money. Occasionally, the combatants were blindfolded or even tied together by their hands and feet. Sometimes the organizers even insisted that the lads fight each other naked.

Johnson excelled at these contests, but it was hardly a way to make a living. So he left home at age 17, roaming the West. Everywhere he went he encountered hostility. He was once ordered out of Idaho City by the town marshall, who told him, "Nigger, if I ever see you again, I'm going to shoot you in the head, and then put the pistol in your hand."[13] From there he stowed away on a steamer heading up the Mississippi River. Discovered by the crew, he was virtually taken hostage and forced to work 18 hours a day for table scraps. The ship's cook, a burly white man, beat him constantly. Johnson eventually jumped ship and made his way to Boston, where he hoped to land a job as a sparring partner. He approached white boxer Billy Quinn, only to be told to take a hike. "Get out of this camp, nigger!" Quinn ordered. "If I ever catch your black ass back around here, I'll kick you out on your face."[14] These experiences, perhaps not surprisingly, turned Johnson into a bitter man who hated whites.

After stints as a painter, stablehand and longshoreman, Johnson finally became a professional boxer in 1897. His ring debut, against black fighter Klondike Haynes, ended in a seven-round draw. It was nothing to write home about, but in fairness to Johnson, he was often half-starved in those days. Never knowing where his next meal would come from, he bounced from town to town, taking on fights wherever he could find them. His big break came in 1901 when he tangled with a skilled Jewish boxer named Joe Choynski. Choynski, one of the very few whites of the era who would fight blacks, knocked Johnson out. But he had no time to savour the victory because both he and Johnson were arrested and jailed for violating Texas anti-boxing laws. The pair spent the next three weeks in the same cell, where a bored Choynski taught Johnson how to block punches and take advantage of his dazzling footwork.

After that there was no stopping the young fighter. Johnson beat all the best black heavyweights, including Sam Langford, Denver Ed Martin, Harry Wills, Joe Jeanette and Sam McVey, to become the so-called Negro Heavyweight Champion of the World. Along the way he'd challenged Fitzsimmons and Jeffries, but both world champs had drawn the colour line against him. After losing to Marvin Hart, it looked as if Johnson's chances of becoming world champion were dwindling. He kept plugging away, however, slowly building a reputation as one of the best fighters alive.

He was also becoming one of the most hated men in the United States. A free spirit, Johnson detested subservient blacks, refusing to play the role of the dim-witted Negro. Instead, he took a white wife, knowing that would enrage Caucasians, played the bass violin, flaunted his ability to read English, Spanish and French, sipped expensive wines out of a straw, wore the finest suits money could buy and drove the flashiest cars. Eager to shock the white establishment at every turn, he invited reporters to training sessions in which he coated his penis in several layers of gauze, giving it an absolutely massive appearance under his tight-fitting shorts. English boxing writer Lynch Bohum was so disgusted with Johnson that he wrote, "With money in his pocket and physical triumph over white men in his heart, he displayed all the gross and overbearing insolence which makes what we call the 'buck nigger' insufferable."[15]

After Tommy Burns became champion, Johnson was surprised to read a story which quoted the Canadian as saying he wouldn't draw the colour line. Johnson was skeptical, however, and didn't bother to issue Burns a challenge until four months after the 1907 Squires fight. He didn't expect an answer, but to his surprise a telegram came back informing him Burns was willing to discuss terms.

In years to come the story would spread that Johnson had to chase a cowardly Burns across the globe to secure a title fight. Johnson himself told the yarn with great relish. It has been repeated so many times since that it has become widely accepted as the truth. In fact, it's a bold-faced lie. Johnson could have had his shot at the title before 1907 was out if not for the fact that his manager, Sam Fitzpatrick, took Burns for a fool. Tommy had always been his own manager, figuring he was smart enough to make deals without anyone's help. He'd also reasoned that without a manager he could keep the entire purse for himself. The blustering Fitzpatrick underestimated Burns, who he assumed was just another unsophisticated fighter. He wired the Canadian, announcing Johnson would fight him only if they split the gate right down the middle. Burns, who had learned a thing or two about negotiations over the years, knew Johnson needed him a lot more than he needed Johnson. Accordingly, he fired back a telegram saying he'd be glad to meet the big Texan, provided he got 75 per cent of the proceeds, win, lose or draw.

Taken aback, Fitzpatrick decided to negotiate through the media. He issued a press release declaring, "First, Johnson will box him, winner take all. If that doesn't suit, Johnson will agree to stop him in 20 rounds. If he fails Burns may get 75 per cent of the purse. If Johnson does stop him, Burns may take 50 per cent of the prize. Nothing better. It is the best I will do. Many writers have assured me they will give us an equal break. All I want is to have the public know what we are willing to do, so if a match is not ultimately arranged, the followers of boxing may know wherein the fault lies. Burns will not be able to inveigle me into a match unless the terms are equitable. I've been in the match-making school too often and flatter myself that I know my little book, or part of it, at least."[16]

When Burns continued to insist he wanted an unconditional 75 per cent, Fitzpatrick announced to the media that Johnson might unilaterally declare himself the champion. The threat was laughable. No one in the mainstream press would take any black man seriously as the World Heavyweight Boxing Champion simply on his own say-so. Burns refused to be intimidated, deciding to bide his time. He knew Johnson would have to agree to his terms sooner or later.

Interestingly, Burns did all his negotiating privately. This tactic served to increase his popularity — when boxing fans cracked open their newspapers the last thing they wanted to do was read about contract squabbles. They turned to the sports page to escape from the drudgery of day-to-day life. Men like Fitzpatrick were seen by most fans as bloodsuckers out to line their own pockets. Indeed, the *Chicago Tribune* wrote around this time, "Champion Burns has the greatest manager of any pugilist that ever peeled a shirt. We don't know who he is and we have never heard of him. That is why we think so."

While he waited for Johnson to cry "uncle," Burns signed to fight former champion Bob Fitzsimmons in Essington, Pennsylvania. His new trainer, Sig Hart, wrote the *Detroit Free Press* a letter that boasted how well-conditioned a fighter the champ had become. His old trainer, Sam Biddle, had retired. "Tommy is in grand shape for his fight with Fitzsimmons," he declared. "He is working hard and to tell you the truth I never saw such an improved man in my life as he is. He is a revelation to me and to anyone else who knows anything about the glove game. Besides being fast and clever, he hits harder than any one of the big fellows that I have seen in many a day. I have big Klondike [Haynes] here to box and Tommy also boxes with Hock Keys, the Australian, and a few other lesser lights of the glove artists. Tommy weighs 174 pounds and he will enter the ring weighing about 170, and not a pound over, for that is his best weight."

Most experts were certain Burns would beat the ageing Fitzsimmons, but no one will ever know what would have happened because the governor of the state suddenly outlawed prizefighting. In fact, he sent police to stop the bout and order the two boxers out of his jurisdiction.

A fight with Gus "the Akron Giant" Ruhlin also fell through when Ruhlin, like Johnson, insisted on getting half the purse. The next challenge came from old foe Mike Schreck. Burns wired back saying he'd meet the southpaw, provided a promoter could be found to guarantee him $20,000. Burns placed this condition on the fight because he knew it would kill the bout. He'd achieved only a draw in two previous meetings with Schreck and didn't want to risk his title by facing him again. Furthermore, as the *London Free Press* noted, a Burns-Schreck fight "wouldn't draw flies and Burns knows it. He has taken this means of getting rid of the burly German."

So whom *was* he going to fight? Now that he had beaten Hart, O'Brien, Grim, Flynn and Squires, the only boxer left in North America or Australia the public wanted to see him fight was Jim Jeffries. Burns made offers, but the former champion turned them all down, insisting he would not come out of retirement. With the proposed Jack Johnson fight in limbo until the challenger agreed to meet the champion's conditions, there was very little left for Burns to achieve in the U.S.

Unsure what to do next, he returned to Canada to visit his mother. The world champ created a sensation as he drove through southern Ontario in a big red late-model car. As he approached Sofa's home in Preston, he came across a bridge with barricades erected on either side indicating it was closed.

The car stopped and Burns emerged to talk to a local farmer.

"I'm Tommy Burns, heavyweight boxing champion of the world," he said. "Why is the bridge closed?"

The farmer told him the cement had only been poured a day or two earlier and no one was sure it was hard.

"Hard or otherwise, I'm going to be the first one across that bridge," he said.[17] Burns tore down the barriers, walked back to his car and drove across.

One of those who saw him drive into town was a schoolboy named Jack Courtney. In a 1980 interview, he still vividly recalled the excitement Burns created. "I was going home from Hespeler Public School and saw a very well dressed man standing and shaking hands with a few of his friends in front of Flynn's Coal Office. He was dressed like somebody from a big city, and I was curious to meet him."

Jack was thrilled when Burns took a moment to greet him. "Hello there, young fellow," Tommy said as he extended his hand to the boy.[18]

While in Preston that fall of 1907, Burns told a Toronto reporter he planned to travel to Europe next to take on the best boxers on that continent. After he returned, he said, he'd meet Jack Johnson. "It will be Johnson next, and when I do meet him there will be no love lost. I haven't the slightest doubt that I'll trim him and trim him good."[19] Johnson, who was in Toronto at the time, replied by saying he didn't blame Burns for heading to Europe for some "easy money. He's going to need that money after I get through with him. He's small, but when we meet there will not be a difference of 10 pounds in our weights. I'll never have a better chance than this to be the champ. Burns can't come home too soon to suit me."[20]

Upon returning to the U.S. from Ontario, Burns was soon involved in an incident that very nearly ended his career — and his life. In early October, Burns took a train trip to New York. As the locomotive rounded a curve in the tracks, it derailed without warning, sending passengers and luggage flying through the air. Several people were seriously injured. Burns helped an elderly woman out of the wreck despite the fact that he had strained his back in the crash. The injury was serious enough for him to wire England's National Sporting Club, asking that his fight with British champion Gunner Moir be rescheduled from November 25 to December 2. He then boarded the steamer *Deutschland* and sailed for Europe.

9

The Invasion of Europe

The arrival of Tommy Burns was a major let-down for British sports fans.

They had expected to see a powerful symbol of firey manhood step off the boat at Folkstone in mid-November 1907. Instead, a fat little fellow in a bowler hat was in their midst. In the four months since the Squires fight, Burns had ballooned to 192 pounds, giving him a decidedly unathletic appearance. The champ was so out of shape that representatives from the National Sporting Club sent to greet him at dockside hadn't recognized him. A humiliated Burns was forced to introduce himself to Lord Lonsdale, the club's president.

On the positive side, the very fact that Burns was so small created enormous interest in his upcoming fight with British champion James "Gunner" Moir. English fans took one look at Burns and were immediately convinced that Moir could whip him and become the next World Heavyweight Boxing Champion. And the British were aching to have a world champ they could call their own. It had been 37 years since Englishman Jem Mace had ruled the heavyweight division. That was back in the days of bare-knuckle fighting, before the so-called modern era of the sport had begun. As far as the average British fight fan was concerned, Mace's rule was so far in the past it might as well have happened in another age.

Burns noticed right away that he wasn't being taken seriously. In a letter home he wrote,

London is a great place, and the sports fans treat me royally, but they look upon me as a farmer does on a turkey he is fattening up for Thanksgiving Day. I went to the National Sporting Club to see one of their fights and met Moir there. We were introduced and I was given a fine reception, but nothing to what they gave Gunner. They almost tore the house down when he stepped up to the ropes. While I was waiting to be introduced I heard remarks from all sides of the ring.

Some of them were saying that I was too small, others laughed at the size of me compared with Moir, and others said, "poor fellow, wait till the Gunner gets him."

Moir is a big fellow, weighing, I should say, 200 pounds, and is about three inches taller than I am. He is a big favourite over here, and I think they will bet the Bank of England on him in this fight.[1]

These observations weren't merely the result of Tommy's inferiority complex. Joe Jackson of the *Detroit Free Press* had been sent to London, to cover the fight and he noticed the same smug confidence oozing from British fans. "Among the Britons, a bit of pity is felt for the North American, because measured with the 200-pound Moir, he is such a little fellow," he wrote in his first dispatch. In Ontario, the *London Free Press* told its readers the British expected Moir to knock out Burns easily. "The English newspapers concede the stocky Canadian has no chance to win," it reported.

Indeed, after watching one of Moir's workouts, the British magazine *Sporting Life* painted a picture of a superbly conditioned athlete totally at ease with his craft. "Moir climbed a rope to the ceiling and came down as gracefully as the stage professional, and with the easy nonchalance of a sailor," it reported. "On the floor, over which was sprinkled rosin, Moir went through the varying phases of actual conflict, giving in all its details a graphic idea of his methods in dealing with an adversary. He moved here and there with easy activity, twisted and turned like a tee-totum, covered himself up cleverly in anticipation of danger, and with a blow on the mark, placed his man *hors de combat*."

The Associated Press also held out little hope for a Burns victory. It said the Englishman's vaunted hitting power and ability to "take a lot of punishment, meant the champion could only prevail by getting in close and working the body."

Moir was not only big for a man of the era, he *looked* like the archetypical prizefighter. A muscular, dark-haired fellow with heavily tattooed arms, he had what one reporter called a "terrible visage." He also had an impressive history. Born in Lambeth in 1879, he'd started his career as a wrestler. Unable to make a decent living at that profession, he joined the army, where he took part in a number of amateur boxing bouts, gaining a reputation as a fearsome knock-

British champion James "Gunner" Moir.

out artist. After being discharged from the military he turned professional, beating Tiger Smith for the United Kingdom middleweight championship and Jack Palmer for the British heavyweight crown. After that he toured Australia, where he won two more fights, including one over the great Peter Felix.

Returning to England, Moir found himself a national hero. No doubt his looks helped. He was a handsome, dark-haired man with a straight nose and a firm, square jaw. The newspapers further bolstered his image by saying he'd done the country proud in Australia. "He is a wonderfully improved man in his boxing — quicker and cleverer than when he left the old country — and admitted by Australian sporting men to be superior to anything they have out there, Squires included," one newspaper declared.

Moir lived up to his press clippings by scoring sensational victories over legendary strong man Iron Man Hague and against a top-ranked English heavyweight called Nutty Curran. Curran got his nickname from the fact that he charged opponents like a madman. But Moir handled him easily, scoring a second-round knockout. From there, he went to Europe, where he thrashed a number of boxers to become European heavyweight champ.

Burns tried to win some support for himself by telling reporters, "I am a Canadian citizen and, therefore, as much a citizen of the British Empire as Moir."[2] But it did little good. In fact, the papers were filled with inflammatory stories that compared North American boxers most unfavourably with British fighters. Pugilists from the New World, one editorialized, were dirty fighters who looked like they'd "escaped from a gaol [jail] or a museum for freaks." Some of them, it continued, had risen, like prehistoric beasts, out of "polyglot slums." And, it added, they were not gentlemen. They'd employ "a disgusting taunt, a contemptuous smile, a refusal to shake hands, a preposterous bet, to get the goat" of an opponent. British boxers, by way of contrast, were "long-limbered, modest, good-looking youths" who had "an innate sense of fair play."[3]

To top it all of, English boxing expert E. B. Osborn was quoted as saying North American fighters were ugly. The typical boxer from the former colonies had a "round cast-iron head with no chin, ribs that almost meet the stomach, the ape's curved, convulsive clutch and a low nervous organization indifferent to pain." In what he surely considered was the worst slight of all, Osborn concluded by saying the average North American boxer "seldom had more than a drop or two, if so much, of English blood in their veins."[4] Burns, who was of German descent, must have cringed when he read that one.

Such irresponsible reporting stirred passions so much that some Englishmen let their patriotism get the best of them, shouting insults at Burns as he walked the streets. One London police officer went so far as to assault the champ during his morning run. Burns was jogging along a sidewalk when the bobby gave him a two-handed shove that knocked him into the gutter.

"The road's the place for you," he snarled.

Burns had suffered an ankle sprain but he held his ground, shouting back, "Couldn't you have asked me to go off the sidewalk in a gentlemanly manner? You behave like a bully because you wear a policeman's uniform. I am training for a match, and I use this road every morning. I don't want you to annoy me again."[5]

The confrontation escalated, with Burns demanding to know the officer's badge number. The bobby responded by threatening to charge him with disorderly conduct. Fortunately for the boxer, there were several witnesses to the scene, and they leaked the details to the newspapers. The next day, a contingent of sheepish-looking London police officers showed up at Burns's door to offer a formal apology on behalf of the force.

Despite that public relations victory, Burns had no chance to win over British fans. And his statement that he was representing Canada, and not the United States, cost him American support as well. In Michigan, the *Grand Rapids Press* bristled at his tactics:

> Tommy Burns, who is now in England priming for his match with Gunner Moir, the British champion, has one advantage no other mittman can claim. It is his mingled nationalities.
>
> In America Tommy is a Yankee Doodle Dandy, for fair and his favorite song is "The Grand Old Flag." When Tommy goes up to his home among the French-Canadians in the Province of Quebec, it's the "Marseillaise" for him.
>
> Now Tommy is making his first trip to England and the first he handed out when he reached Plymouth was, "you know I am a Canadian and just as much a British subject as Gunner Moir." Before Burns fought Bill Squires, the Australian, he issued "believe me I shall do my best to keep the title in America" messages every 15 minutes.
>
> Every big fight Burns has engaged in was waged on soil governed by Theodore Roosevelt. Tommy learned the game from the American fighters and he developed into a top-notcher studying the methods of American fighters. Burns has spent all his fighting career in the United States. He met Americans at their own style and worked his way up to the top. He is as much an American, as far as the boxing game is concerned, as Jeffries, Kaufmann or any of the others.

In one of the few supportive media reactions, the *London Free Press* defended Burns's claim to be a Canadian fighter. "The fact still stands that the man was born and raised in the province of Ontario, and it was here that the grit, nerve and fighting spirit was instilled into him," it declared. "He was rounded into shape [in the United States], but we furnished the good, strong, raw material, and he will always be known by the unprejudiced as the great Canadian pugilist heavyweight champion of the world."

Outside of Canada, however, it was obvious Burns was losing the public relations war with Moir. In fact, he managed to alienate his hosts even more than the average North American fighter did during visits to the U.K. During final negotiations with the National Sporting Club, which was hosting the fight, he accepted the club's offer of £2,400, then demanded to be paid before entering the ring. In modern parlance, Burns was saying "show me the money." But in 1907 Britain, his conduct could not have been more insulting. Lord Lonsdale had a good mind to toss him out of the club on the spot, deciding against it only because he felt Gunner Moir deserved a chance to win the title. In the end, he agreed to have the notes drawn up and shown to the champ.

The National Sporting Club was no ordinary athletic organization. It was an exclusive group made up entirely of men from the upper classes. In addition to the Earl of Lonsdale, its board of directors included Sir William Eden, Anthony Eden's father, and a number of leading businessmen, politicians and members of the royal family. It was so dignified a place that all boxing cards were held after dinner and spectators were expected to dress in formal attire. Once the fight got under way, no talking or cheering was allowed. Fans sat in eerie silence, as if they were at the opera. The only noise came from the fighters, who groaned and moaned as they battled away in a ring located below the club's 1,300 seats.

Rebuffed by the fans and the press, Burns fled London and set up his training camp in a country estate called Wembly House. Before leaving he betrayed how much the negative publicity had wounded him, testily telling one reporter, "I don't care how big Moir is. The bigger they are the harder they fall. Hart and Squires were big and they were soft for me. I will beat Moir."[6] Despite the bravado, there's no doubt he took the fierce-looking Englishman seriously. That's evidenced by the fact that he rose every morning at dawn and ran up and down the rolling green hills until he got himself down to 172 pounds. And he had no time for parties. In an interview he said, "After hours I generally turn in pretty early. Out in the country we keep regular hours. I have not been up to London scarcely any since coming over. I shall leave that until after the fight, when I have won the championship. I think it is better to work now. The play will come afterwards."[7]

Moir, meanwhile, was training at a more gingerly pace. He set up shop in an old inn at the heart of London, where there were plenty of distractions for a national hero. Although he could be seen jogging through the streets early every morning, he was occasionally spotted in London's pubs, holding court with his fans, late into the night.

As he had done before his other major fights, Burns also did more than just work out. He travelled to London on a spy mission, sitting unobserved in the balcony of a small arena where Moir took part in an exhibition bout designed to raise funds for a local charity.

Dressed in a frumpy suit and an old hat, he sat among a group of working-class fans, none of whom realized the World Heavyweight Boxing Champion was in their midst.

As Burns waited for Moir to appear, the cockneys began to discuss his own merits. Most picked Moir to win, but one rough-looking character insisted the champ was the man to watch out for.

"Why, Moir'll have his bloomin' block knocked hoff wheen he meets Burns," the Englishman snarled.

Tommy, still unrecognized, turned and grinned. "Moir'll murder him," he said, faking his best cockney accent.

"Wot?" yelled the Englishman incredulously. "What do you know about Burns, you 'arf-grown rotter?"

"Burns isn't 'arf as big as the Gunner," explained Tommy. "'Ees a little fellow, like me."

The fight fan grinned derisively. "Little your grandmother. I've seen pictures of him. Blimey! 'Ees as big across the back as a bloomin' elephant. 'E'll knock Moir's block off, mark my words."

Burns continued to argue until the man threatened to "punch [his] bloomin' 'ead off."[8]

Before any trouble could erupt, Moir appeared and everyone in the balcony focused on the stage.

Afterwards, Burns went to a theatre that was showing films of Moir's fights. "I went to a show where they had moving pictures of his fight with Tiger Smith," he wrote home. "He went right after Tiger, and knocked him out in one round. I hope he comes at me the same way. If he does, there will be something doing immediately."[9] Confident that he could find a way to beat the bigger man, Burns located a bookmaker and bet $2,000 on himself to win.

The fight, which took place on December 2, 1907, was like no other Burns had been in. Besides the fact that the fans were dressed in tuxedoes, referee Eugene Corri wasn't even in the ring! Under British rules, the official sat at ringside, only climbing through the ropes if it became necessary to break up a clinch or to begin the count over a fallen boxer.

As the Canadian came into the arena he was briefly hissed by the sell-out crowd, which included King Edward VII. All 1,300 seats had been sold out for weeks, and hundreds of other fans were loitering outside in Covent Garden. It was an overflow crowd but, within seconds, the place became as quiet as a mortuary at midnight.

Corri never forgot the scene. "A little matter of etiquette on Tommy's part proved rather irritating," he wrote in his memoirs.

> [Burns] came into the ring with a cap on, and wore his ordinary trousers over his shorts. Seating himself in his corner, he quietly took off his boots and meanwhile enquired of someone near, "how are they betting on this fight?"
>
> In the opposite corner, looking very determined, sat Gunner Moir, all ready for the fray. Burns kept him waiting at least five minutes, while the members marvelled at the coolness of the little man.
>
> No two men were ever in better condition, and everyone liked the look of the Gunner, with his tattoed chest and arms, a very fine specimen of physical strength. Burns, by contrast, seemed to be better trained for speed.[10]

As the two boxers came to the centre of the ring for their final instructions, Corri announced that in the event of a knockdown there would be a silent count.

Burns instantly seized the moment, gaining a powerful psychological edge. "When I knock Moir down I want the count to be out loud so everyone can hear it," he shouted.[11]

Moir responded by licking his lips in nervous anticipation.

At 8:30 P.M. the gong shattered the calm, announcing the start of the fight. Burns and Moir came at one another with the World Heavyweight Boxing Championship on the line.

In the early going the British crowd was in a confident mood. It was plain to everyone that Moir was a much bigger man. Burns, as one newspaper noted the next day, appeared ridiculously small as he came out of his corner with his hands raised in his patented peekaboo style. The champion's "crouching attitude appeared to place him at a still greater disadvantage in height with Moir, who assumed a fairly erect position, with his arms widely extended, somewhat like a wrestler, and showing no guard."

The two men circled each other cautiously during the opening minutes. "The work in the first round was mostly at long range, the fighters sparring warily," sports fans read later. Then, late in the round, Burns "landed two heavy blows on the Gunner's neck and ear, the second sending him staggering to the ropes. The Canadian himself escaped without punishment, avoiding Moir's rushes cleverly."

The pace picked up in the second round, with the boxers battling at close quarters. The champ, who excelled at such infighting, peppered the challenger's body with several savage blows, forcing his knees to buckle. Moir looked to be on the verge of collapse, but he backed his tormentor off with a nasty jolt that caught Burns under the chin. Still, when the bell halted the action it was obvious the champion was ahead on points.

In the third and fourth rounds the men fought from long range, with Burns winning the third and Moir the fourth. Upset at having dropped a round, the champion launched a relentless assault in the fifth that ripped open Moir's face and sapped the strength from his husky frame. "Burns came back again hard in the fifth, forcing the fighting from the sound of the bell," newspaper readers were told. "He landed a right on the jaw and a long left swing cut Moir severely over the eye."

"The sixth round was all in favour of the Canadian, whose footwork completely baffled his opponent. Moir became very wild in his attempts to get in his right.

"In the seventh Burns sent home a terrific swing, which made an ugly gash in the Gunner's cheek. They came to close quarters, the

Englishman clinching and thus avoiding the force of two well-meant rights. Some holding caused referee Eugene Corri to enter the ring and separate the fighters. Moir then looked like a beaten man."

Moir, however, surprised everyone by coming out strong at the start of the eighth. For a few moments, at least, it looked as if he'd absorbed the best Burns could throw at him and was ready to launch a comeback. Drawing on the last of his reserves, he burrowed in close, landing several telling body blows. "Moir came back gamely, and with the evident intention of trying to stand off the Canadian," one reporter wrote. The champion responded by hitting the Englishman with every punch in his arsenal. Moir "was fought all over the ring and badly punished. Burns set upon him unmercifully in the following round, administering terrific punishment. Moir was now in a sorry plight, and the bell just saved him from being put out."

Sensing victory was at hand, Burns rushed to the centre of the ring at the start of the tenth round and went straight to work. "He sent the Gunner to the floor with a short right-arm jolt," one reporter wrote. "Moir rose, only to be floored again from a hard left on the jaw. He struggled to his feet, but was an easy victim for another cross on the jaw, and, going down, was unable to respond to the call of time. Although Moir showed marvellous pluck, he was equal to the Canadian in no other respect."

At the end of the fight Burns received his money, plus his side bet. At the same time, he learned a thing or two about the honesty of the gentlemen who frequented the National Sporting Club. During the bout the side bet had been given to referee Corri, who put it in the pocket of his dinner jacket. When it became necessary for him to enter the ring to separate the fighters, Corri took his coat off and flung it over his seat. He promptly forgot about it and had to go back for it after the fight. As anyone but Burns would have guessed, the cash was found still in the jacket pocket and given to the victor.

Seconds after Moir was counted out, Burns unexpectedly received a warm ovation from the crowd. One elderly gentleman even gave him a diamond ring. "Wear this for the old country," he said. Deeply touched, Burns slipped it on a finger.

Afterwards, buoyed by the reception, he told reporters, "I feel immense, and was just warming to my work when Moir cried 'content.' I felt from the beginning that I had him, although he punched hard. It was not a grueling fight; I have come through worse." He was full of praise for the European champ, saying Moir was a "plucky" fellow who had fought with more determination than either O'Brien or Squires.[12]

Moir told reporters he had done his best and expressed the hope that Burns would give him a rematch. But in truth he was finished as a prizefighter. He fought only nine more times, losing eight. After that, he turned to an acting career, appearing in several films in the role of an executioner.

Among reporters and fellow boxers, the reaction to the Burns victory was decidedly mixed. London's *Sporting News* was impressed with the champ. "There is something in the American style of fighting that we have yet to learn," it editorialized. "It is entirely a new game, and when we are confronted with the two, the old and the new, we readily realize which is the more effective. Moir fought up to the hilt in true traditional English style. He never showed anything which we had not seen before, nothing but the same old stereotype style. On the other hand, Burns was brimful of brand new methods hastily devised and equally hastily brought into play. He had a far greater variety of blows, and when he did land, it was done in the most effective manner. The result was inevitable. Burns was here, there and everywhere — and always at the right moment."

British middleweight champion R. C. Warnes was equallly effusive in his praise. "Burns played a waiting game," he said, "and the further the contest progressed the better he fought. He is the most artful fighter I ever saw." English featherweight titleholder Ben Jordan agreed, saying Burns and Moir were "in different classes." Jack Bart, another noted English sportsman, couldn't stop talking about the Canadian's "marvellous footwork."

Others were not so kind. Former British boxing champion Jem Smith claimed the fight was the poorest exhibition he had ever witnessed. "Neither of the contestants could fight," he groused, adding that Burns was a "third-rater."[13]

The *London Sportsman* admitted Burns had won easily, noting that while Moir was a bloody mess at the end of the fight, the champ had left the ring without a mark on him. More than that, "the parting of his hair was not disarranged." It suggested, however, that Burns didn't deserve much credit because his opponent was a useless excuse for a boxer.

It was not the fault of Burns that the splendid crowd that filled the National Sporting Club in every part had to sit out such a disappointing show," it said. "Moir is the man to blame. It is not our policy to go back on a loser, but Moir was absolutely painful. He went into the ring a model, well-trained man, evidently as hard as a board, and with a weight advantage of over a stone and the advantage of over two and a half inches in height. Yet his blows lacked the power of a featherweight. He was uncertain and ill at ease from the outset. Indeed his nervousness was so apparent that even Burns could not help smiling. Though outclassed and out-generalled, Moir seemed incapable of altering his method. He was thrown off his guard by the wily man in front and so worried by his seconds that at times he appeared altogether at a loss as to what to do.

We did not see the best of Burns, for the simple reasons that Moir could not extend himself an inch. The winner has a nasty habit of boring in with his head on the neck or cheek of his opponent. Moir was hampered a bit in this way and looked to be holding more than he really was. Under the most favourable conditions, however, Moir could never hope to make a show with Burns. He will experience very little, if any, trouble, in beating any who may be put up against him on this side of the Atlantic.

In the United States most reporters picked up on the same theme, dismissing British and European boxers as bums. Retired champion Jim Jeffries joined the chorus, saying, "Oh, it doesn't add anything to Burns' reputation. This fellow Moir has never beaten a good man. He was untried, and we all knew it was a cinch for Burns. It doesn't help a first-class man like Burns to go around beating dubs. What people want

African-American boxer Joe Gans was a Burns booster.

is a fight between two evenly matched men. Then there is interest in it."[14] About the only Americans who had anything good to say about Burns were black boxers. His history of fighting black pugilists and his public renunciation of the colour line had made him extremely popular with African-Americans. Indeed, black fighter Joe Gans told a reporter, "How are you going to get around handing it to Burns? They say he can't fight and that he is a fourth rater, but I notice he is beating them all as fast as they come."[15] The affection black fighters felt for him was further demonstrated during a chance meeting between the champion and Sam Langford. According to the *Vancouver World*, Burns was waiting to meet a photogapher when he spotted Langford across a crowded room and invited the great Novia Scotia boxer to join him. As the two shook hands, Langford said, "I'm mighty glad to meet you, Mister Burns. You are some man, Mister Burns. Yes sir, some man is right." He also expressed the opinion that Burns could "make trouble for" either Jim Jeffries or Jack Johnson. Deeply affected, Burns replied, "You don't look like any slouch yourself."[16]

But only in Canada was the media totally supportive. The Toronto *Globe* got closest to the truth, declaring Burns had taken a major risk by fighting Moir. Prior to the bout, it pointed out, little was known about the Englishman in North America. Previous heavyweight champs had studiously avoided going to Europe to test the waters, it said. By beating the best boxers in North America, Australia and Europe, Burns had become "the first man who has ever held a legitimate claim to the title 'world heavyweight champion.'"

Regardless of what the press thought of him, Burns was making a fine fortune. He'd been paid $12,000 for the Moir fight, bringing his 1907 ring earnings to just under $46,000, or today's equivalent of about $1 million, tax-free. On top of that, he was cleaning up in the music halls of London, where he had begun performing nightly song-and-dance acts. He made £300 in the first week alone and more was to follow. As soon as the film of the Moir fight was available, he went on tour with it, showing the moving pictures in theatres. After each viewing, he delivered a lecture and answered fan questions. A reporter who took in one of these sessions found the Canadian was popular with the crowd. "Burns, attired in a dark frock coat and looking a good deal more like a bank clerk than a fighter, thanked the audience in a few well-chosen words. In return his hearers made the place echo with 'For he's a jolly good fellow.'"

Originally, Burns had planned to defeat Moir and head home for a showdown with Jack Johnson. As recently as late November he had written his mother, telling her he hoped to be in Preston for Christmas. Now, however, he had other plans. He decided to stay in Europe for a few months, not to duck the formidable Johnson, but to pick up some easy money fighting a few more European boxers. He gave away his intentions in an interview that angered many Englishmen, saying, "I shan't return to the United States yet. There are still some juicy grapes here that I haven't squeezed."[17]

Burns wins his fortieth fight

Tommy Burns decided to follow up the Moir victory with another one of his stunts. This time, he proposed to fight three U.K. boxers in one night! The challenge went over like a lead balloon with the English press, which saw it as one more slight against British manhood. The *Sportsman* de-

scribed the challenge as a "gra-
tuitous insult" and an "absurd"
gesture. "Nobody disputes his
right to the title of champion of
the world, but such tactics are
not sports and would only de-
grade and place in peril the sport
of boxing, which with great difficulty has been raised to the
position of a legal pastime."

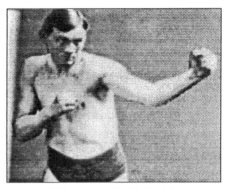

British contender Jack Palmer.

Burns quickly dropped the
idea of fighting English boxers in batches, but he ruffled British sports-
men still further by the condescending way in which he lectured them.
"The reason why England cannot find a heavyweight boxer capable of
winning the championship of the world is simple," he admonished.
"You find a pretty good man over here, but instead of going ahead with
him you stand still. What he wants is continual boxing, as in the States.
Here you give him one real contest in a year, the rest of the time being
spent in exhibition boxing against an inferior person. That sort of thing
will never develop a man as he should be developed. In the States we
are always at it until we reach the top. Your system is entirely wrong,
and until you treat your best man differently, the championship will
never return to England."[18]

Most British boxing fans now hoped Jack Palmer, a barrel-chested
fighter from Newcastle, would uphold the nation's honour by shutting
up the know-it-all from Canada once and for all. The two signed to
fight February 10, 1908, in Wonderland, London's big east-end music
hall. Palmer was a two-fisted brawler whom many thought would be
able to succeed where Moir had failed. "Palmer is considered a somewhat better fighter than Gunner Moir, whom Burns put away in 10
rounds, but has a reputation for hitting low," one reporter said.

A tall, good-looking, well-groomed man with the face of an angel and
the disposition of an axe murderer, Palmer had turned professional at
18. Equipped with powerful arms and large fists, he rose quickly through
the ranks, becoming British middleweight champion in 1902. Moving
up to the heavyweight division, he captured the national title in 1903 by

knocking out Ben Taylor. After that he hit the road, going on a successful tour of South Africa before heading to the United States. There he met his first setback, losing a 10-round decision to Jack "Twin" Sullivan. Palmer's next serious fight came in England, where he lost the British heavyweight title to Gunner Moir. Some observers thought he was well ahead on points before being disqualified for hitting Moir below the belt.

Now Palmer was gunning for a much bigger prize, and he worked out tirelessly in preparation for the clash. Burns, meanwhile, had to scale back his training during the week leading up to the fight because he was suffering from a severe cold and a strained tendon in his right foot. Nevertheless, he was a 6–4 betting favourite. Even Palmer was reluctant to gamble on himself, only accepting bets that he'd last six rounds.

The fight wasn't nearly that long. A ringside reporter described it this way:

> Burns climbed through the ropes smiling and showing his cus-
> tomary confidence, while Palmer displayed great nervousness.
> Without any preliminary sparring Burns went after him, and the
> first round had hardly begun before the Englishman was on his
> knees. He took the count twice and during the rest of the round
> was busily engaged in covering himself. This was repeated in each
> of the other rounds, Palmer being hopelessly outclassed and
> apparently without ability to either deliver a telling blow or to
> defend himself. In the final round he was sent to the floor several
> times and at the last was barely able to drag himself to his knees,
> where he remainded on his elbows on the floor, until after the
> count of 10 had been tolled off. The referee might have given a
> decision in the first minute of the contest, as Palmer was a beaten
> man from the moment he entered the ring.

Palmer, who had lasted less than four rounds, was quickly vilified in the press. "A more pitiful exhibition was never seen," the *London Express* declared. The Toronto *Globe* described the bout as "a farcical contest. The Canadian could have won at any stage."

Burns had had enough. He'd just demolished the second best boxer in England with consummate ease, only to be told, once again, that he didn't deserve any credit because his opponent was unimpressive. "Marvin Hart, Jack O'Brien, Bill Squires, Gunner Moir and Jack Palmer were all boomed to the skies before I beat them," he said in a public statement. "They had all established pretty decent reputations as boxers, and were acclaimed as such. If they were the 'lemons' which they have since been described as being, what must the men have been like at whose cost they gained their fame?"[19]

His protestations did no good, however. He couldn't even get any respect from world amateur boxing champion Johnny Douglas. Douglas, who had won an Olympic gold medal for England, fought Burns in a three-round exhibition bout staged in London. The Canadian's title was not at stake; the bout was supposed to be nothing more than a friendly match in which the two men would do a little sparring for the crowd. Everyone understood that no verdict would be rendered at the conclusion. Nevertheless, the vainglorious Douglas went after the professional champion, hoping to score a knockout. Taken by surprise, Burns had a difficult time holding his own over the nine minutes of fighting. When the bell rang to end the bout the Canadian was seething with rage. For one moment he considered making a scene. But with scores of people looking on, including several reporters, he thought better of it, deciding instead to congratulate the Englishman on his showing. "If this is what you call a sparring exhibition," he said in a jovial tone, "what is your honest-to-God fighting like down here?"[20] It was a wise move because Douglas was a much-loved figure in the U.K. In addition to his boxing gold medal, he was captain of the British cricket team. Any slight against him would have earned Burns still more censure in the English press. In a single stroke Burns had turned what could have been a public relations disaster into a triumph. Newspaper accounts of the fight were glowing, with one reporter saying Burns was "delighted" with Douglas's pluck.

Johnson turns up the heat

Jack Johnson was tired of waiting for Burns to return to the U.S. There was no doubt that the champion was going to fight him sooner or later — Burns had made too many public statements to back out of the bout

Jack Johnson as he appeared not long before his bout with Burns.

now. In fact, after the Moir fight, British reporters had asked him point
blank if he would fight the black boxer. "Of course I will," he shot back.
"I now claim the heavyweight championship of the world, and I will
certainly not refuse to fight any man who challenges me. More than
that, I announced publicly before I left New York that if I defeated Moir
I would fight Johnson as soon as I returned to America. I also gave
Johnson's manager that promise, and I was not joking."[21]

He continued to insist, however, that he should get 75 per cent of the purse, whatever the outcome of the fight. When the National Sporting Club offered a prize of £2,500 for a Burns-Johnson match, he turned it down flat, saying he wanted $30,000. Lord Lonsdale dismissed the counter-proposal on the spot, calling it "utterly absurd."[22] When another group offered £3,000 to Burns, he rejected that as well.

In an interview, the champ defended his position, declaring, "I propose to call every bluff Johnson makes. If he really wants to fight me he ought to be tickled to death to accept any terms I might offer. My terms are $30,000, win, tie or lose. Fitzsimmons demanded 75 per cent. Nelson took 80 per cent in his fight with Gans. So I'm only following precedent. Moreover, I'm the only heavyweight champion who has ever been ready to give a black man a chance."[23]

In a bid to turn the heat up, Johnson and his manager, Sam Fitzpatrick, travelled to London, telling anyone who would listen that Burns was afraid of the challenger. "We are going to get a fight with Burns or make him quit the ring," Fitzpatrick declared. "We will agree to almost any terms. Burns can have two-thirds of the purse if he so desires, but a real champion is always willing to agree to 75 per cent to the winner and 25 per cent to the loser, or winner take all. Whoever heard of John L. Sullivan, Jeffries, Corbett or Fitzsimmons demanding 11-10s of a purse, win, lose or draw? Burns will have to fight Johnson in England or admit he is afraid of him."[24]

Johnson, who proved to be surprisingly popular in English pubs, gained still more fans by declaring, "I am ready to engage Mr. Burns on any terms — and may the best man win. It is in the good name of my people that I stand ready to fight with Mr. Burns. And I will be the first to acknowledge him if I am defeated."[25] Johnson wasn't being completely truthful. At one point in the back-and-forth haggling a deal appeared to have been reached, but the American scuttled it, backing out at the last moment. The British syndicate that was trying to put the bout together became so annoyed it cabled Fitzpatrick a sharply worded message that read in part, "Syndicate disgusted with Johnson's action, calls everything off. Johnson knew terms."

But the public was led to believe Burns was to blame for the failure of the two men to meet in the ring. And Johnson's propaganda campaign took its toll on the champ's aleady weak popularity. One night, while attending a National Sporting Club fight card, Burns was spotted sitting in the crowd by the ring announcer. The man wanted to introduce the champion but hesitated, fearing a chorus of boos would follow.

"Go ahead," Burns told him, "introduce me."

"Ladies and gentlemen ... I would like to greet the World Heavy-weight Boxing Champion, Tommy Burns."

As if on cue the spectators responded with boos and catcalls. Burns waited a few moments, then raised his hand for silence. Standing up, he said, "Gentlemen, you abuse me because I have not yet signed to meet Jack Johnson. The fact is that I have refused to accept a purse of 3,000 pounds that has been offered for such a match. I am my own manager. Now, I put it to you that if you could get double that sum — 6,000 pounds — would you sign for the lower figure? Well, I know I can get 6,000 pounds to fight Johnson, and when I am offered that figure, I will fight him. That is a promise."[26]

There was polite applause from the crowd, but most believed Burns was running scared. That feeling was only intensified a few days later, when the King of England took a swipe at the champ. "Tommy Burns is a Yankee bluffer, and I shall take every means in my power to stop the battle between him and Johnson if it is arranged with the under-standing that Burns is to receive $30,000, win, lose or draw," Edward VII said in an extraordinary public statement. "The Burns proposition is not sportsmanlike, and England should be up in arms if a battle under any such conditions is permitted to occur."[27]

The king's comments could hardly have been more devastating to the champion. In Toronto, the *Globe* speculated, "Perhaps there is more truth than fiction that Burns fears Johnson. Burns figures that his title will be in danger if he takes on Johnson, and if beaten he would no longer be a money-making proposition. If he is to be beaten he wants to make a big cleanup and be comfortable for the rest of his days."

Johnson was quick to take advantage of the situation. "I want to thank His Majesty for his sentiments. But he has committed a typical British blunder. Tommy Burns is no Yankee, he is a Canadian. Never-theless, His Majesty is a sportsman, specializing in rats, so he oughta known about Tommy."[28]

Still, the defiant champion stood his ground. In an almost unprecedented move, he had leaflets telling his side of the story printed and distributed all over London. They read as follows:

BURNS VS. JOHNSON

FACTS, NOT FANCIES

Ladies and gentlemen:

Below I give you a few facts concerning Jack Johnson and myself. While in the music halls Jack Johnson has printed statements to the effect that he has defeated every man he ever met. His record as printed in the American Sporting Annuals, shows, on the contrary, that he has had 15 drawn contests, of which some are called 'no decisions.' Furthermore, he was knocked out by Joe Choynski in three rounds, he lost on a foul to Joe Jeanette in two rounds, and he was also defeated by Marvin Hart on March 28, 1905, at San Francisco, California, just 11 months before I defeated Marvin Hart for the championship at Los Angeles, California.

I am getting these bills out to prove to the British public that Jack Johnson is not telling the truth about his performances. It has been stated by the press that the offer of 2,500 pounds is a splendid offer, and should be accepted by me. Now, let me ask you a sensible question, for I judge that most of you are business people. If you were working for three pounds a week, and you knew that you could get six pounds a week for a similar job, would you take the job at six pounds? The same thing applies to the offer for Johnson and myself. Why should I accept this amount when I can get twice that amount elsewhere?

The figures given below will prove to you that the statement that 2,500 pounds is as large a purse as we could get, and no club would give the money I demand, is all wrong.

THE GROSS RECEIPTS AND LARGE PURSES
RECEIVED BY BOXERS.

Winner	Loser	Gross receipts	Boxers' share
Jeffries	Sharkey	13,200 pounds	7,293 pounds
Jeffries	Corbett	12,668	8,727
Nelson	McCoy	11,270	6,762
Corbett	Britt	9,662	6,289
Britt	Young	6,449	4,936
Jeffries	Fitzsimmons	6,350	4,452
Gans	Nelson	13,943	6,700
Gans	Britt	7,200	5,300
Burns	O'Brien	7,400	6,000

I admit that what I am asking is big money for this country, and there may be small possibilities of getting that amount here, but the reason that Johnson accepted the small offer of 2,500 pounds was because he knew that I would not accept such an offer because I know that I can, as I said above, get twice the amount for a match between Johnson and myself. Another reason why he accepted this small offer was because he thought he could excite ill feelings in the minds of the British public against me for my non-acceptance. Johnson has nothing to lose in this case, since he never received as much as 500 pounds for any contest he ever engaged in. But Johnson can say what he likes about me, and the British public will understand that it is not a question of fear on my part, for I stand on record as having, as I state above, defeated Marvin Hart for the championship. And this same Marvin Hart, by the way, stands six feet in height and weights 14 stone nine pounds.

I trust these few facts will convince you that I am absolutely within my rights in the stand I am taking, despite the ravings of those who are interested in getting this match for the money to be had out of it. I wish to state in conclusion that Johnson and I will meet in the ring just as sure as you are reading this bill, and the time is not very far off either.

Yours truly,

Tommy Burns[29]

Burns was losing the propaganda war, but he knew the more the press talked up a Burns-Johnson fight, the more interest there would be in such a bout. Sooner or later an ambitious promoter would come up with the money he was demanding. As it turned out, he was right.

A flamboyant Australian named H. D. McIntosh offered Burns $30,000 and Johnson $5,000 for a fight to be staged in Australia. Both tentatively accepted, agreeing to work out final details later. McIntosh, who liked to say his first two initials stood for

Australian promoter Hugh McIntosh put the Burns-Johnson bout together.

"Huge Deal," insisted the boxers keep the agreement a secret for the time being. He wanted the battle, which he planned to promote as the "Fight of the Century," to take place in December, when three American battleships were scheduled to dock in Sydney. He knew the warships would deliver four thousand sailors — almost all of them boxing fans — right into his lap.

McIntosh also wanted Burns to fight a couple of Australian boxers in the fall, just to drum up interest in the match. After that, Johnson would follow him to Australia and the fight would be officially announced.

From a financial point of view, Burns had done the right thing. But as far as his reputation was concerned, it would prove a mistake to keep the tentative deal a secret. The myth would spread that Johnson had been forced to chase the cowardly Burns around the globe, following him first to London, then to Sydney, before finally forcing a showdown. Nothing could be further from the truth. Burns had agreed to meet Johnson before he left for England and, the moment his conditions were met, he accepted the fight.

The St. Patrick's Day massacre

With the Johnson bout nearly 10 months away, Burns decided to stay in the U.K. and face Irish champion Jem Roche. Demonstrating he hadn't lost his flair for showmanship, he signed to fight him in Dublin on March 17, 1908 — St. Patrick's Day.

Despite what Burns had done to Moir and Palmer, most Irishmen had high hopes that the barrel-chested Roche could beat him. They took heart from the fact that Roche had bested Welsh champion Charley Wilson, a man who had once defeated Gunner Moir. On top of that, Roche, a blacksmith by trade, had thumped South American champ Joe Hagan, who was a cousin of Philadelphia Jack O'Brien. By virtue of that win, Roche was officially the champion of both Ireland and South America. In all, the 29-year-old former football hero had lost only 3 of 20 bouts. In addition to his big wins over Hagan and Wilson, he'd beaten a good American heavyweight boxer named Bob St. Clair and Irish middleweight titleholder Jack Fitzpatrick. Fitzpatrick had taken such a drubbing that he was convinced Roche was about to become the next world champion. "Burns will have to go to him to fight him, and with all his cleverness he won't get away without getting a couple of prods," he said. "When he's had a few he won't be looking so blooming clever."[30]

In a feature story about Roche, the *Irish Independent* depicted an invincible warrior with a powerful knockout punch. After watching him train before a packed gymnasium, the *Independent*'s writer reported, "His physique is magnificent. You must see Jem punch that ball. The thunder of it not only shivers the frame from which the ball is suspended, but sends a tremor through the whole building. A member of the audience was so carried away he shouted aloud 'Heaven, have mercy on poor Burns!'"

After that demonstration Roche went three brisk rounds with a sparring partner. When he was finished, he was "breathing as easily as ever." Following that, he dazzled onlookers with a lightning-quick skip-rope exhibition. "Jem skips steadily for 20 minutes," the Independent said. "Occasionally he varies the step, but there is not a pause for even a moment. He can do 40 minutes of this sort of thing. It is a great test of staying power and the audience applauded enthusiastically."

Following that he sparred with yet another boxer. "With head bowed, guarded by his left, he advances on his adversary with his right, and quickly puts him on the defensive," the reporter wrote.

Roche's manager, Nick Tennant, told an interviewer, "Jem is just the sort to make a world's champion — strong, fast, clever, cool and determined. He can give and take more than his share of punishment and this makes him a tall order for any living fighter. I fail to see how Jem can lose."[31] His man, he added, had every physical advantage. He was an inch taller than Burns and 28 pounds heavier.

Besides all that, Roche did not appear to be the least bit intimidated by the Canadian. After Burns knocked out Palmer, the Irishman was unimpressed, declaring, "Palmer fought like an old woman."[32]

A reporter sent to watch Roche train for the Burns fight found him cool and composed. "I have never met a quieter, more unassuming man, and except for the depth of chest and width of shoulder, one would think boxing was the very last thing he'd go in for," he wrote. "Of all the men in the room, Jem Roche himself appeared to be the least concerned regarding the upcoming event. At all events he will not suffer from stage fright; I don't believe he has a nerve in his whole composition."

When it came time for Roche to leave his Wexford training camp for the journey to Dublin, the reporter followed, gaining an appreciation of just how popular the Irish champion was with his countrymen. As they walked to the train station, he wrote, there were pictures of the boxer in every window. Roche was, the reporter noted, a handsome fellow with a square jaw, full mouth and straight nose. At the train station two teams of hurlers were just coming off a locomotive when they spotted the prizefighter. "Jem was at once recognized and the word went round 'that's Jem Roche!' In a few moments an open-mouthed, admiring circle was formed round our little group, staring, simply staring. I must say I felt a little embarrassed. I am not used to crowds. Some of the others shifted uneasily, but Jem didn't know he was the centre of attraction. How could he, seeing he was playing with two little girls of his acquaintance in the middle of the admiring circle?"

When the Irish champ got to Dublin there was a massive crowd on hand to greet him. Roche was leaning out a window as the train pulled in, shaking scores of outstretched hands. "I am confident, but not overcon-

Dublin's Dolphin Hotel, where Burns stayed in 1908.

fident," he told the throng.[33] Burns, he said, was a braggart who was about to get his come-uppance. With that, he headed off to the home of a friend, led by a fife and drum band.

Burns arrived the next day, creating almost as much of a sensation. A huge crowd gathered outside the posh Dolphin Hotel, where he had rented a suite of rooms. When he arrived, they let out an unexpectedly warm cheer. A few minutes later Burns appeared in a window, tossing coins to the fans.

In an interview with the *Irish Independent*, he was asked if he was afraid of losing.

"If I were there'd be no use in going into the ring, would there?"

"The opinion prevails that Roche may win," he was told.

"If Roche beats me I will be the first man to shake his hand."

His only complaint with Ireland, he said, was that he was being described in the country's newspapers as an American. "That's an error, for although I hold the heavyweight championship of the USA, I possess a birth qualification for Canada."

The reporter found Burns to be "very amiable and gentlemanly" and a man who "answered questions frankly."

What really drew attention was not what Burns said or did, but the patch over his right eye. Word quickly spread that he'd been injured in a sparring session. The wound was serious enough that the optic was closed for 12 hours before trainer Billy Neal was able to pry it open with hot lotions. Neal asked the promoters to postpone the contest, but they refused, saying all the tickets had already been sold. Burns was uncon-cerned, at least on the surface, declaring, "I have fought battles before with only one eye, and won."[34] The champion was so confident he bet £700 that he'd win the fight and be back at the Dolphin Hotel in time for supper, which was scheduled to be served only half an hour after the opening bell.

On fight night Dublin was in a state of frenzy. The *Irish Independent* captured the atmosphere best. "O'Connell Bridge and streets nearby were thick with people," the paper described. "Great crowds swirled to the crowded portals of the Theatre Royal. Hordes of people with excited features howled at the doors. There were strange sounds in many voices. One could catch only some words clearly. They were 'Tommy Burns' and 'Jimmy Boy.' 'Jimmy Boy' was repeated again and again with eager vehemence. Wexford versus America! Ireland versus the world! It was the night of nights."

Inside the theatre, the reporter was stunned by the size of the crowd. "What a spectacle! Not an inch of standing room. Electric lights sizzled through the house. All around those lights the cigar smoke of sportdom wreathed fantastic pictures in metallic blue. Every box was crowded to congestion; front seats presented great splashes of white shirt fronts. Up in the dress circle, near the curtain, were two ladies, closely veiled." In all, more than three thousand people were on hand.

Roche received a jubilant reception as he entered, wearing a bright red jersey and "smiling and with a confident air. The orchestra struck up 'The Boys of Wexford,' the spectators joining the chorus."

Burns, who had been watching the preliminary bouts, "strolled casually to the ring." Not knowing the words to "O Canada," and not inclined to play "God Save the King," the Irish band greeted the champion with "The Star Spangled Banner." The fight announcer introduced him as "an English citizen from Canada," a pronouncement that was greeted with thunderous boos.[35] One reporter noted his right eye still looked "red and discoloured."

As he climbed through the ropes Burns played one of his psychological cards. Earlier in the week he'd told Irish reporters he could hypnotize his opponents, and now he tried to get Roche off his game by glaring at him. As he stripped for action he kept looking at Roche, trying to make eye contact. He continued to stare at his adversary as the referee gave his final instructions and after Roche had gone to his corner. Roche, looking rather anxious, peered back from behind his trainers, making every effort to meet the champ's stare.

The bell sounded for the start of round one. What happened next has never been repeated in the history of the heavyweight division. "On the stroke of the gong Burns jumped to the centre of the ring and started his usual tactics of trying to draw his opponent," one newspaper reported the next day. "This seemed to annoy Roche, who angrily struck down Burns' arm and then covered his face with both gloves to protect it from a threatened blow. Burns, however, was looking for a better chance."

A moment later he found it. Feinting with his left, the champion shot a terrifying right that landed smack on the big Irishman's jaw. Roche spilled onto the canvas face first, almost as if he'd be shot. He lay face down for several seconds. Then, slowly and unsteadily, he tried to get up. "He was badly dazed," one reporter recounted, "and although he struggled to regain his feet, was unable to do so before the fatal count of ten."

The end had come just one minute and 28 seconds into the fight, making it the fastest knockout ever recorded in a world heavyweight championship bout. It is a record that still stands today, more than 90 years later.

The swiftness with which the battle ended shocked everyone. Even Roche seemed unsure it was over. As the champion helped him to his corner the groggy Irishman asked, "I'm not beat, am I Mr. Burns?"

"I'm afraid you are, Jem."[36]

For some fans the end had been just *too* quick to be believable. Cries of "fake" ecohed throughout the theatre. In some ways, one ringside reporter said, the shouts were understandable. The winning punch had been delivered with such blinding speed, he pointed out, that few fans had even seen it. He had, however, seen the fist land and was convinced the fight was not fixed. "There was no doubt Roche went in to do his best, but he was outclassed and altogether too slow for a man of Burns' quickness and ring craft."

After he had recovered his senses, Roche made no excuses for his loss. "He did it too quick, that's all," he told reporters.[37] Burns admitted the fight was the easiest he'd ever been in. "That Irishman stepped into one of the most perfectly timed blows of my career," he said.[38] He added he had wanted to end the fight as quickly as possible because "I had too much money at stake at long odds to take any chances." With that, he dashed out the door and took a cab back to the Dolphin Hotel, making it just in time to eat dinner and collect his £700 bet. Counting the $11,200 he'd made for the fight, it had been a most profitable night for him indeed.

There was one other winner that unforgetable evening. A quick-thinking Irish fan ran out of the Royal seconds after Roche hit the canvas, waving his ticket above his head. "I can't bear to look at it," he shouted to anxious fans waiting outside for news. "Roche is after murdering him. Is there anyone here who could bear to witness the horrid spectacle? He can buy my ticket for two pounds."[39] The crafty fellow got his money and disappeared into the night before the buyer realized he'd been conned.

Burns rules Africa

The Irish were stunned by the easy defeat of their hero, but they accepted it with good grace. The *Irish Times* was generous in its praise of the champ. "The affair, unhappily did not last long enough to judge the winner's full capabilities, but what we did see was sufficient to indicate that he is very fast and very clever and has plenty of dash and resource and beyond all doubt he is a worthy holder of the championship."

But despite his stunning achievement, Burns found the American press still wasn't warming up to him. Reporter George Considine, writing for the *New York Sun*, was dismissive of his latest win, declaring, "Burns picked up nearly $12,000 for licking Roche, but he did not increase the confidence of the American sporting public in his prowess. Nobody who knows anything about prizefighting will admit that such inferior boxers as Squires, Moir, Palmer and Roche were capable of putting Burns to a real test. Now that Burns has disposed of all the pugilistic lemons, sporting men say that he can offer no further excuses for not coming back here and meeting a real pugilist, either Jack Johnson or some other man of recognized ability."

South African contender
Joseph "Jewey" Smith.

Considine conceded that Burns had beaten two world champions in heavyweight Marvin Hart and light-heavyweight Philadelphia Jack O'Brien, but snidely noted he'd failed to knock out either man. He did not mention, however, that he'd written nothing negative about the abilities of Squires, Moir, Palmer or Roche until after Burns had beaten them. Like everyone else in North America, Considine didn't know beforehand whether they were great fighters or not.

Red Wilson, a sports writer during the first half of the twentieth century, recalled that "a lot of reporters didn't like Burns because he was a Canadian. They thought the heavyweight champion should be an American by divine right."[40]

Burns ignored the jibes and headed to Paris, searching for fresh opponents. Talented black boxer Sam McVey was in the French capital, and the two discussed a possible fight. The colour line at the heavyweight championship level would have been shattered then and there, except for the lack of a promoter who was willing to give Burns the $11,000 he wanted for the match. Every time he stepped into the ring now, Burns was risking his $30,000 purse for the Johnson bout. So he insisted on a good payday for each contest.

No one would give him that much money for a fight with McVey, but when a rising young star named Joseph "Jewey" Smith challenged him, he got the purse he was looking for. Smith's background is mysterious. Some sources claim he was a South African, while others list him as an Englishman, born January 5, 1884, in London. It's probable he was born in the U.K. and raised in South Africa. His record is also a bit of a mystery. Some newspapers hyped the Burns-Smith fight by claiming Smith was the champion of both South Africa and France. However, his list of official contests indicates he had only two victories

— a knockout win over Mike Crawley in London on March 21, 1908, and a win on points over Seaman Broadbent, also in London, on April 4, 1908 — prior to his crack at the world title. If he did have earlier wins over South African and French boxers, there's no record of them. Presumably he won amateur titles in those countries before turning professional. Such victories would not show up in his pro record. Whatever the truth, he was marketed as the "champion of South Africa." And since South Africa was the only country in Africa that practised boxing at the time, he was also portrayed as heavyweight king of the entire continent.

What is known for certain is that the 24-year-old Smith was a very good boxer. Indeed, he would eventually go on to win the British heavyweight championship on February 21, 1910, with a win over William "Iron" Hague. Along the way he'd also score an impressive triumph over respected British fighter Ben Taylor. Throughout his career, he would prove to be a man with a decent punch, winning 8 of his 26 recorded victories by way of knockout. He was also three inches taller than Burns and, at 196 pounds, outweighed the Canadian by 24 pounds. With all those credentials, there was widespread interest in their bout, which took place April 18, 1908. "The meeting of Burns and Smith was the biggest affair of the kind ever held in Paris, where something of a craze for boxing exists at present," the *Chicago Tribune* reported. "It was witnessed by a big crowd, who paid high prices for their seats."

Referee Eugene Corri thought Burns gained the upper hand days before the match, when the two boxers came together to sign the fight contract. Recalling the scene in his memoirs, he wrote,

Smith jibbled at something in the terms, when Burns walked over and said to him, "sign these articles like a good fellah. Don't be a quitter. I'll let you stay a round or two." Imagine the look on Smith's face as he surveyed the little man in the top hat, light overcoat with a brown velvet collar, and carrying a swagger cane, who dared to speak to him in that patronising manner. No doubt the rugged boxer, with great broad shoulders and enormous neck must have thought he would make certain of the dude who had tried to bluff him.[41]

Indeed, an angry Smith came out determined to provide the champ with a sterner test than the British boxers had been able to give him. Burns responded by knocking him out in the fifth round with what the *Chicago Tribune* called "a terrific right to the jaw." Still the excitement wasn't over. Near panic broke out seconds later, when a "photographic apparatus exploded, setting fire to the flags and decorations. Scores of spectators leaped to their feet, but they were prevailed upon to remain in their places, and the fire was speedily extinguished."

The fight also resulted in Burns making a friend with influence in high places. Baron Rothschild, one of the richest men in the world, visited Tommy's dressing-room just prior to the start of proceedings to invite the champ and Jewel to his home. Burns accepted, going so far as to shadow box a few rounds with the old gentleman, who was an exceptionally fat fellow with long whiskers. The pair had their picture taken together and Rothschild told everyone who would listen that he'd fought the world champion. To show his appreciation, the baron loaned Tommy his car and held a spectacular garden party in his honour. Fifty years later, Burns still recalled the beautiful women, the superb trees, the colourful flowers and the fact that his host showed up wearing black tights down to his knees!

For the next four weeks Tommy and Jewel toured France, Belgium, Holland and Germany. The trip helped them get reacquainted after a long separation. Jewel had not joined Burns the previous fall when he left for England. Instead, suffering from an unspecified illness, she went to Preston and spent several weeks with her mother-in-law. For much of that time she was bedridden. In fact, she claimed to be sick before most of her husband's fights, making quick recoveries as soon as they were over. Tommy, desperately lonely without her, sent one of his associates to Canada after the Moir bout to accompany her to England. She agreed to come, but was miserable until after the Palmer, Roche and Smith contests were over. Only when Tommy agreed to take a month off to tour the continent did her outlook improve.

Burns ended his astonishing European odyssey on June 13, 1908, with a fight in Paris against old rival Bill Squires. This time there would be no repeat of his first-round knockout of the burly Aussie. Squires, in fact, won the first five rounds and even managed to stun the champ momentarily near the end of the fifth. Burns rallied after that, scoring an eighth round knockout with a powerful stomach blow.

The champ had stayed in Europe much longer than he expected. But his tour had been a triumph. He'd won five fights, all by knockout. Now it was on to Australia for a showdown with Jack Johnson.

10

Race War Down Under

Tommy Burns sailed into Perth, Australia, in August 1908, to a hero's welcome.

While Americans had been unimpressed with his European triumphs, most Aussies were genuinely thrilled to have the World Heavyweight Boxing Champion in their country. This was the age of steamship travel, which meant a trip to the land of the kangaroo could take several weeks from North America or Europe. Consequently, few international celebrities ever made the effort to go there. So when the man who had defeated the best boxers in North America, Australia, Europe and Africa travelled halfway around the globe to be with them, the Australians were deeply appreciative.

Britons and Yanks had been disappointed by Tommy's physical stature, but the Aussies seemed to like him precisely *because* he was so short. Australia was still a small country — at least in terms of population — and its citizens saw themselves as underdogs on the world stage. As a result they took to the little man from Canada right away, treating him as a modern-day David who had slain a whole host of Goliaths. Australian newspapers began referring to him as "the Little Giant" or "the Napoleon of the prize ring." One reporter said he looked like "an American beauty actor," while another described him as a "keen, intelligent looking individual." There was also lavish praise for Jewel's beauty and elegance. Indeed, she took Australian high society by storm. In his 1998 book, *Boxing Day*, author Jeff Wells recounts that Jewel "arrived attired in a very smart coat and skirt of shepherd's plaid, with black-braid trimming, sable muff, and large black hat. She was pale, dark-eyed, attractive, ethereal. She epitomised the wife of the stylish new brand of professional, world-travelled athlete."[1]

*Tommy and Jewel are shown on the far right of this photo,
with a group of friends.*

For Jewel, the trip was undoubtedly a blessing, at least in the beginning. She still found herself largely unoccupied in Los Angeles. Now at least she was getting to see the world. And because it had been four months since Tommy had stepped into a boxing ring, her frame of mind was better as well.

The newcomers were immediately whisked away to a local arena, where Burns refereed a boxing match. Afterwards, he was presented with a walking cane with a gold mount. Within days the couple was the talk of Australia. Tommy was seen going to the races and even found time for fox hunting. Jewel, meanwhile, was the guest of honour at a major soirée hosted by some of the country's richest ladies. Here she was in her element. Jewel was, in many ways, the stereotypical nineteenth-century southern belle who enjoyed nothing more than socializing with other ladies. Before long, she was herself hosting tea parties for upper-class Australian women at every opportunity.

From Perth, located on Australia's western coast, the couple made their way to Sydney, situated on the eastern seaboard. It was a long haul — about four thousand kilometres by train — with frequent stops. And at every city and town along the way huge crowds turned out to greet the champ and his glamorous wife. When they reached Albury, a small community nestled between Sydney and Melbourne, five hundred fans appeared at the train station at 6 A.M. just to get a glimpse of them. August is a winter month in Australia, and people were nearly frozen by the time the celbrities appeared. Nevertheless, they cheered wildly every time Tommy opened his mouth. In many ways, Burns was greeted in the same way adoring fans welcome rock stars today. A few days later, when the train pulled into Sydney, eight thousand people were on hand to see him. A local politician named Colonel Ryrie praised boxers in general and Burns in particular. The sport, he said, produced real men, "not those milksops who cry out against it."[2]

When someone in the crowd asked the champ if he was willing to fight Jack Johnson, he said he was, never letting on that the bout had already been arranged. "There are a lot of newspaper stories that I don't want to fight Johnson. I do want to fight him, but I want to give the white boys a chance first," he said.[3]

One of the men listening on the sidelines was H. D. McIntosh. He'd already begun construction of a 25,000-seat outdoor stadium at Rush-chutter's Bay, on the outskirts of Sydney, where he planned to match Burns against Johnson. The stadium wasn't yet completed, but he decided to halt work for a few days to allow Tommy to meet Bill Squires for a third time. Some twenty thousand seats were ready for occupancy, and he figured he could sell most of them while, at the same time, drumming up interest in the Burns-Johnson battle.

Squires was exceedingly confident. He told reporters he'd almost won the world title in Paris when he hit Burns with a haymaker just before the bell ended the fifth round. Had he delivered the blow in mid-round, he said, Burns would not have come to Australia. Squires was right. If Tommy lost the title before December 26, the Johnson fight would be cancelled.

The day before the Squires bout, Burns showed up at a match between big Australian heavyweights Peter Felix and Sid Russell. When he entered the ring to shake hands with the hulking Felix, the crowd burst into laughter at the glaring size difference between the two men. More than a few just didn't believe this tiny fellow could beat Squires a third time.

As it turned out, all twenty thousand tickets for the Burns-Squires fight were scooped up almost the moment they went on sale. The scrap, which took place on August 24, 1908, turned out to be one of the greatest battles in the history of the heavyweight division. Not much was expected from it, because Burns had knocked out Squires twice before. But the champion was overweight after his long sea voyage and was suffering from a serious bout of influenza that had left him seeing double.

Sir Herbert Maitland, who was said to be Australia's finest physician, had checked Burns over before fight time, pleading with him not to enter the ring. But Tommy ignored him and got ready for battle. From the start it was obvious this would be no cakewalk. When Burns stripped for action, one reporter wrote the next day, he "looked to be heavy and not closely trained."

With the sun beating down fiercely on the ring, the two men came at one another cautiously in round one, both landing some good body blows in an evenly matched opening three minutes. In the second round, however, the big Australian took charge. "Squires drew first blood with a hard punch to Burns' nose, and had decidedly the better of the round," fight fans read the next day. The Aussie took the third round as well, drawing blood with a devastating shot to the Canadian's mouth. By now the crowd was going wild, sensing an upset might bring the title to Australia for the first time in history. Round four was a stand-off, but Squires took the fifth, sending in a jackhammer left that landed on Burns's jaw.

Tommy Burns was in deep trouble. He was having difficulty seeing Squires, not because of any damage done to his eyes by the Australian's punches, but because his illness had left him unable to focus clearly. The situation was so serious that in round seven he came within an eyelash of being knocked out. "Burns was distinctly groggy at the gong, and the round was strongly in Squires' favour," the reporter wrote.

The champ fought back gamely but he found himself in more trouble in the eleventh round. "Squires scored effectively with three right upper-cuts, following the blows with a staggering left to Burns' nose. Burns was decidedly groggy and staggered to his seat when the gong sounded."

By now the crowd was roaring non-stop. But the fans hadn't noticed that Squires was slowly running out of gas. He had won 9 of 11 rounds, but the Australian was not accustomed to such long fights. Burns, meanwhile, was planning a change in tactics. The champion had always been able to think fast on his feet, making strategic adjustments right in the middle of his fights. And if he ever needed a change in plan, it was now.

In round 12 Squires "again determinedly forced the fighting at the beginning." But Burns was no longer trying to slug it out with him. He was "becoming elusive, drawing his opponent on by swift sidestepping and dodging. And as the blows fell harmless, he steadied the Australian with two lightning punches. He then attacked vigorously and Squires, his fast work having plainly tired him, was on the defensive during the rest of the round."

As the men headed back to their corners, Squires was gasping for breath. He had all but punched himself out. In the thirteenth round an exhausted Squires tasted the canvas three times. The third time, he failed to get up by the count of 10.

Burns had shown rare compassion in this fight, imploring Squires to stay down when he hit the floor for the second time. But the proud Aussie insisted on staggering to his feet, leaving Tommy with no choice but to knock him out. It was several minutes before he came to.

Tommy Burns had just won the toughest fight of his life, retaining his title by a whisker. "To say that the Burns-Squires fight was a surprise is putting it mildly," the *London Free Press* said. "To begin with, it appears that Thomas was not properly trained. He has been beating so many of these aspirants that he doubtlessly has come to regard them lightly, and poor conditioning undoubtedly told. Kangaroo Bill put up a good fight and had Burns groggy in the tenth round."

Burns sets another record

Just nine days after his gritty, courageous victory over Bill Squires, Tommy Burns set a record that still stands today. This time, he was fighting an up-and-coming Australian star named Billy Lang. Lang was a big, tough rancher from the outback who had made a name for himself by defeating former world heavyweight champion Bob Fitzsimmons. Fitzsimmons was so badly battered that he retired for good after the fight. The victory ensured Lang, who was an arch-rival of Bill Squires, a place in boxing history. He would eventually eclipse Killer Bill in popularity among his countrymen by becoming British Empire champion.

That triumph still lay in the future when Lang squared off against Burns on September 7, 1908. Although he was not yet at the height of his fame, Lang was considered a legitimate heavyweight contender. Gentleman Jim Corbett described him as "a natural fighter" who had the potential to become world champion.[4] His won-lost record stood at an impressive 20–1. And he had a mean look about him. Photos show a man with a determined jaw, flat nose and angry, flashing eyes. One Australian newspaper noted, "Among the present talent in our own country, Lang has earned every right to be considerd a champion. He is a clever, cool, game fellow with a great, big, generous punch that will knock out any man who is foolish enough to let it land upon his chin." A former Australian Rules football star, Lang was also 35 pounds heavier and five inches taller than the champion.

The fight, staged in Melbourne in another hurriedly slapped-together outdoor stadium, drew a sell-out crowd of fifteen thousand. The following newspaper account of the bout shows just how good Burns had become at employing psychological warfare against his opponents:

> Burns is a ring general and a brainy fighter and he knows how to impress his antagonist. He studies his man, and, finding the least sign of nervousness in him, brings all his craft to work to heighten the effect he has produced. Yesterday, Lang was kept waiting for quite a long time in the ring while the motor car was sent away to bring a bandage for Burns' right arm, which was 'weak.' Finally, Burns got into the ring, in company with Pat O'Keefe, his sparring partner and trainer, and several bottle and towel men, one of whom carried a portmanteau [a trunk for clothes that opens into two equal parts]. Burns wore a big, fashionable box coat — light fawn and of the latest London cut — a motor cap, gloves and patent shoes. Pat O'Keefe carried a big bundle of snowy towels and another man carried a handsome morning gown. The champion's entry into the ring was like the arrival of a potentate. Burns

stood up in his magnificence and took a leisurely survey of his opponent, sitting patiently in his corner, huddled up in his over-coat, with plenty of time on his hands to cogitate concerning what might or might not happen. The irritating delay and other matters were not calcuated to make Lang any more cool and collected. Then Burns began calmly and deliberately to disrobe. When the process was about half completed he went to the middle of the ring to consult with the referee about the rules, and Lang had to be brought into the conference. Then he went back and took off some more clothes and again got up and spoke to the referee. All this time Lang had to hold himself down and there is no doubt whatever that the strain told on him. He was eager to attack and he was worried because he could not commence.

Lang's own manager delayed matters still further by insisting Burns remove the bandage from his elbow. The champion refused, and the referee sided with him, saying, "He's not going to do any fighting with his elbow."[5]

Despite the delays, Lang gave a good account of himself in the early going. "Honours were comparatively even in the first round, and in the second Lang knocked Burns off his feet with a heavy swing," one newspaper reported. Once again the champ appeared to be in trouble. He'd been floored for the first time since he'd won the title from Marvin Hart. But as he had done to so many big men before, the Canadian eventually got in close and cut Lang down to size with shattering body punches. In the third round, he sent the Australian to the canvas for the count of nine. After that he took charge, knocking the challenger down several more times before he was finally counted out in the sixth. When the end came, one reporter noted, "Lang was assisted to his corner while Burns just danced over to his. As soon as he could get his gloves off and shake hands with Lang, he was busy getting into his clothes. He had not a scratch on him."

Before Burns could leave the stadium trouble broke out. Unruly fans rushed the ring, smashing chairs. Police tried to stop them but they broke through, tearing the ring posts out of the ground. Amazingly, Burns single-handedly restored order. Standing on his stool, he called for calm. "Gentlemen, I've travelled the world, and must say you're the finest sports I have ever met," he shouted.[6] Suitably ashamed of themselves, the fans slinked away.

After the fight Burns took Jewel to visit Melbourne's colourful flower gardens. When a reporter caught up to them, the champ declared, "I am just as fresh as when I entered the ring this morning." As for Lang, he was gracious, saying, "To be successful in this infighting, a man must be trained for that particular kind of work and Lang has not been trained that way. He is a grand, game, clever fighter, but wants the proper kind of experience. He will be a much better man after this."[7]

With the victory, which went into the books as Burns' forty-fourth, Tommy had now scored a record eight consecutive knockouts in defense of his crown. No heavyweight champion has surpassed the mark since. Moreover, he had triumphed over three boxers who had — or soon would — defeat a fabled world champion. Marvin Hart had outpointed Jack Johnson, "Fireman" Jim Flynn would knock out Jack Dempsey and Billy Lang had flattened Bob Fitzsimmons.

Burns had baffled his critics yet again and, at least in the Australian press, he was finally getting some of the credit he deserved. "There is probably no boxer alive who has been more perfectly equipped by nature for the game he follows than Tommy Burns," one newspaper said. "He is a big man packed into the smallest possible space and overflowing with strength and endurance. He has been said to resemble the portrait of Napoleon. He does, but a better simile is George Hackenschmidt [a famous wrestler of the era]. His bodily and facial resemblance to that great athlete is wonderful, even to the sleepy, dreamy expression when placid and the hard, stony set of features and steel grey glint in the eyes when aroused."

A reporter with the Australian magazine *The Lone Hand* drew perhaps the finest word sketch of Burns ever written. This is how the champion struck his attentive interviewer:

I came into the dining room of a house five miles up Mt. Kosciusko, and a pair of immense shoulders heaved themselves slowly out of an armchair in front of a log fire. They belonged to Tommy Burns, champion heavyweight pugilist of the world. One notes other things in vague fashion — the pale, small-featured face, the impassive blue eyes, the short, straight legs, with their heavy thighs; but the shoulders outstand. They give to their owner, as he lolls back with his feet crossed (a favourite attitude), the appearance of a mighty wedge of flesh — a human triangle.

All Burns's movements — as an ordinary member of society — are slow, ponderous, almost ungainly. He walks heavily, sits down heavily, often uses his hands heavily. He suggests in his unprofessional moments, one who is tired and rather old. I never in my life saw a human being of his age — white, brown, or black — who was capable of sitting quite still for so long a time. He rises to show a hit he has "figured out." Straightway the lassitude is gone; every muscle is tense, under control, and in perfect relation, and the onlooker realizes in quick order that he is observing the fastest heavyweight fighter the world has ever known.

It is hard, even on a week's close association, to gauge Burns's mental equipment, and feel satisfied about the result. That his brains are above the ordinary there can be no doubt. He has conducted his various business negotiations with a skill and address that have won the rueful admiration of those who have engaged with him. But he cherishes a horror of "tall talk" and of "small talk" he has none — which traits handicap the character-student considerably.

Apart from his appearance, and apart from whatever mentality he has, Burns possesses another characteristic that impresses one — namely, his essential cleanliness. His health is literally perfect. He has not spent in the whole of his life a ten-pound note on doctors and dentists combined.

The long wait for Johnson

With the Johnson fight still nearly four months off, Burns found himself with far too much time on his hands. He and Jewel moved into a sprawling mansion above Sydney harbour and began to enjoy the good life. Sydney was a big city even then, with half a million people living in tightly crammed terrace houses. The red tile roofs, balconies and cast-iron railings, which can still be seen today, made it one of the prettiest cities in the world. From their front balcony the Burnses could see the shimmering blue waters of the harbour. Behind them lay rolling hills covered in grey-green brush. All around was the odour of tropical flowers, wet leaves and the pungent, dusty smell of dried apricots, peaches and pears. The couple loved the city, which was so well treed that it almost had a wilderness feel to it. But it was more than just the splendid vistas that pleased them. Tommy spent his days going to the races, while Jewel shopped for clothes and hats. During evenings, they could often be seen at the symphony.

From there they moved into a resort near Mt. Kosciusko, Australia's highest peak. Here, Tommy fished and swam, while Jewel spent her days looking out at the blue-green, snowcapped mountain. It was an idyllic setting. After visiting the place, writer Rodney Hall recalled seeing "icy streams knocking rocks together, and delicious crystalline water swirling invitingly around boulders. High on the ridges, great swathes and saddles of snow still held the coldness of last winter."[8] Reporters who visited found Burns hitting a punching-bag decorated with the flags of the United States, England, Ireland, Australia and South Africa. The banners represented his victories over the champions of those countries.

But all was not perfect in Burns's world. In the U.S., the *St. Louis Post-Dispatch* suggested he was a coward who was running from Jack Johnson. "It is up to Tommy Burns to heed the call of the fight fans," the paper chided. "They demand he get out of his hiding and set at rest for all time the matter of fistic supremacy between him and Johnson, between the white race and the coloured."

Days after the editorial appeared, H. D. McIntosh announced to the world that Burns and Johnson would fight for the championship at Rushchutter's Bay on Boxing Day, December 26, 1908. The declaration unleashed an outpouring of racial bigotry. Burns, who had been vilified in some quarters for not fighting Johnson, was now taken to task for giving a black man the chance to win the title. The *Sydney Illustrated Sporting and Dramatic News* declared, "Citizens who have never prayed before are supplicating Providence to give the white man a strong right arm with which to belt the coon into oblivion." The *Australian Star*

A poster promoting the Burns-Johnson bout.
Note the reference to Johnson as the "colored" champion.

offered the opinion that "this battle may in the future be looked upon as the first great battle of an inevitable race war. There's more in the fight to be considered than the mere title of pugilistic champion of the world." The *Australian Bulletin* went so far as to change the slogan on its banner from "Australia for Australians" to "Australia for the white men." But the prize for the most irresponsible journalism of all went to a weekly called *Fairplay*. It described Johnson as "a huge, primordial ape."

Johnson arrived in Australia in October and immediately began to hype the fight. In many respects he was an even better showman than Burns. Setting up camp at Botany Bay, he started staging flamboyant stunts designed to drum up publicity. In one, he raced a kangaroo, chasing the poor animal until, exhausted and terrified, it dropped over dead. In another, he ran down and tackled a squealing greased pig. In still another, he outran a jackrabbit! Despite these sideshows, however, it was obvious the challenger was taking the fight very seriously. For eight years he'd been trying to get a crack at the title, and now he finally had it. Just as Burns had done in preparation for his fight with Marvin Hart, Johnson worked tirelessly in preparation for the bout. As the battle approached, he wrote later, "My condition was superb. I do not recall another pre-fight period in my life when I felt better or more fit to enter the ring. My lungs were in especially fine condition, and no matter how strenuously I exerted myself it seemed that I never got winded."[9] His growing confidence was reflected in his pre-fight interviews. "How does Burns want it?" he asked defiantly. "Does he want it fast and willing? I'm his man in that case. Does he want it flat footed? Goodness, if he does, why I'm his man again. Anything to suit; but fast or slow, I'm going to win."[10]

A reporter who visited his training camp confirmed, "Johnson has been putting in the hardest kind of work with the gloves and on the road." He also noted Billy Lang was sparring with him and giving him tips about the champion's style.

Burns, meanwhile, was searching for a way to beat Johnson, who had every conceivable physical advantage. The challenger was seven inches taller, 30 pounds heavier and had a longer reach than the champ. Tommy had always been able to defeat bigger men by relying on his speed, but he'd watched films of Johnson in action, and the moving pictures hadn't provided him any solace. If anything, the American boxer was even quicker than Burns. He was also more experienced. While the 27-year-old Canadian had lost just 3 of 52 fights, the 28-year-old Johnson had lost only 3 of 62.

After much thought, the champion decided his only chance to beat Johnson was to intimidate and insult the contender at every opportunity. Such tactics might, he believed, throw the black boxer off his game. His first chance to do so came a few weeks before the fight, when they met face-to-face to iron out such details as who would referee the bout.

"You used to be a good fighter," Burns told Johnson, "but you are all shot now; you might as well take your medicine."

The challenger simply smiled.

Pretending to be enraged, Burns hurled racial slurs and profanities at the bigger man.

"Burns," Johnson replied coolly, "the newspapers are describing you as a gentleman, so be careful what you say. If you swear any more I shall give you a lacing right here."

At that, according to Johnson's autobiography, the champ became unglued. "This angered him beyond endurance," Johnson wrote years later. "Springing to his feet he made a gesture as though he would pull a gun, and I moved toward him. As I advanced, Burns grabbed a chair, which was snatched from him by McIntosh. He then seized an inkwell which was standing on McIntosh's desk, but before he could hurl it, McIntosh grabbed his arm and attempted to hold him."

Johnson had indeed mistaken this charade for genuine anger. But the outburst didn't have the desired effect. Johnson didn't slink away, fearing that he was up against an unpredictable madman. Instead, he told McIntosh, "Let him loose. He's tame and harmless." Turning to Burns, he said menacingly, "I'll remember this when I get you into the ring."[11]

Next, Burns tried to psych himself up by making brash statements to the press. By doing so, he was intentionally putting extra pressure on himself, hoping that would help motivate him to do his best. In an interview with the *New York World*, he accused Johnson of having a "yellow streak" and added, "I will bet a few plunks the coloured boy will not make good. I'll fight him and whip him as sure as my name is

Tommy Burns." One has to wonder whether he remembered at that particular moment that his real name was Noah Brusso.

For the next several days the two boxers traded insults through the newspapers. Burns was the worse of the two. He embarrassed himself on several occasions by calling Johnson a "nigger" in interviews. Later, he expressed regret for his shameful conduct. "We did not pull any punches, each scraping the bottom of the barrel for obscene reflections on the character of the other," he admitted. "I have always regretted the part which I played in the burlesque."[12]

Duel at Rushcutter's Bay

Tommy's popularity remained high, despite his unsportsmanlike comments. Ten thousand fans turned out to watch him fight Australian Olympic silver medalist Snowy Baker in an exhibition bout. Baker had lost the gold medal to Englishman Johnny Douglas, whom Burns had sparred with in London earlier in the year. The champ easily outboxed Baker, then thrilled the crowd by telling them their hero was just as good as Douglas. Following the bout, an audience of twelve thousand watched one of Burns's sparring partners fight one of Johnson's cornermen. The main attraction, of course, was the fact that Burns and Johnson were both in attendance. And when Burns opened one of his workouts to the public, five thousand people showed up, many of them women. Jewel tried to serve tea to the ladies until the numbers overwhelmed her.

To keep his wife happy, Tommy took her on a brief tour of Tasmania. The mountainous, heavily forested island, rich with flora and fauna, is one of the most scenic spots on earth and she was in a cheerful mood throughout the trip. She'd also enjoyed the train ride from their mountain retreat to the coast, squealing with delight when she saw kangaroos bounding across the countryside, covering 25 feet in a single leap. Her high spirits did not last, however, and she seemed depressed as soon as Tommy returned to his training.

As the fight approached, Burns became increasingly restless. Those who watched him train in the mountains near Dalton reported he looked nervous and uneasy, possibly even over-trained. One of his sparring partners admitted to the *Detroit Free Press*, "He's thinking about the bout all the time." In fact, Burns held out little hope he could emerge victorious. Even before sailing for Australia he'd told British referee Eugene Corri, "I will give him the fight of his life, although I don't think I can beat him."[13]

Reading between the lines of an interview Burns granted to the magazine *The Lone Hand*, one finds further hints that he knew his reign as heavyweight king was coming to an end. "A man is champion only once in his life," he said, "and not for long at that."[14]

Interest in the fight was now reaching a fever pitch. In the U.S., all the former heavyweight champions were polled for their predictions, with most favouring Burns.

Gentleman Jim Corbett said, "Burns, I think as a rule, is underestimated by the fighting fans. Tommy, for his inches, is one of the greatest fighting machines in the world. He knows both how to attack an opponent and how to defend himself when he has to. Burns has always shown that he knew how to take care of himself when up against a hard hitter or slugger."[15]

Jim Jeffries told reporters, "I think that it will be a great fight and I look to Burns being returned the winner. He is too clever, too strong and too courageous for the black fellow. Burns is better than he is given credit for being."[16]

John L. Sullivan favoured the Canadian, too. "I don't think the time is quite right for a Negro to pose at the head of the heavyweight boxers of the world," the old bare-knuckle champ said. "In the first place, I don't think they are advanced in the art as well as the white pugilists. Next, I don't think that Jack Johnson is game and for that reason I expect Tommy Burns to win out before the referee can render any decision."[17]

Jem Mace, the Englishman who had won the bare-knuckle world title in the nineteenth century, said much the same thing. Only Bob Fitzsimmons predicted a Johnson win. The black man, he said, "is bigger and a clever fighter in every way. I can't see Burns beating him."[18]

These endorsements, which were published in newspapers around the globe, had a major influence on the betting. As the date of the fight approached, Burns was a 6–4 favourite. But what the former champions didn't know was that Tommy Burns was now a very sick man. He had been stricken by a mysterious illness that kept him in bed for a week.

Doctors thought it was influenza, but others have suggested since that it may have been a form of jaundice. In any case, Burns was feeling so poorly that he wanted to postpone the battle. McIntosh insisted, however, that it proceed on schedule because twenty-five thousand tickets had already been sold. Eventually, Burns agreed to fight on Boxing Day, despite the fact that his weight was now down to just 163 pounds.

In the midst of the tension preceding the bout, one incident provided some comic relief. A bar-room brawl broke out as Burns and Jewel were passing by the door of a drinking establishment. Two drunks had been discussing the merits of the champion when one punched the other in the stomach. Hugh McIntosh and Pat O'Keefe rushed in to break it up, but Burns was held back by his wife. "Don't go in, Tommy, don't go in!" she shouted. "You might get hurt." The laughter that greeted this plea, one reporter wrote later, "went a long way toward restoring order."[19]

The night before the fight, realizing there was nothing more he could do, Burns was in a relaxed mood. He stayed up late, singing songs around a piano with his sparring partners and trainers.

Burns slept so soundly on Christmas night that he had to be shaken awake at 8 A.M., just three hours prior to the opening gong. It was cool and overcast, but the champ appeared to be in a cheerful mood. Meeting with reporters just before he left for the stadium, he said he'd get in close on Johnson and beat him with his superior infighting skills. Like many others, Burns subscribed to a preposterous theory of the time that blacks couldn't stand up to stomach punches as well as whites.

The scene outside the stadium, meanwhile, was bedlam. Forty thousand fans had shown up. Many had arrived the night before and had slept outside, hoping to buy a ticket from a scalper.

Inside the stadium, there was an almost festive mood. The eyes of the world were on Rushcutter's Bay and everyone knew it. Buoyed by this knowledge, the largely pro-Burns crowd even cheered Johnson when he entered the ring at 10:42 A.M. He greeted the unexpectedly warm reception by turning and bowing to all four sides of the ring. When he disrobed, there was a collective gasp from the crowd. As one reporter noted, "It would be hard to find among the world's fighting men a more magnificent physical specimen than the big Negro. He looks like an ancient bronze, finely proportioned, tall, clean cut and muscular."

An estimated 25,000 fans saw the Burns-Johnson fight.

When Burns appeared a few minutes later there was an even louder ovation than the one accorded the challenger. The Canadian was smiling as he climbed between the ropes, wearing a faded green hat and an old coat. But when he stripped for action there was no general intake of breath. He looked small alongside Johnson, and his skin, fans noticed right away, looked unnaturally yellow. Those in the front row thought he looked sick.

When Johnson came aross the ring and shook hands with Burns, the champ noticed both of the big Texan's fists were bandaged. He checked them out carefully to make sure they weren't rock hard. Once he was satisfied the bandages were of the soft variety, he announced he had no objections.

Johnson was not so magnanimous. Just as Lang had done four months before, he raised a ruckus over the bandage that Burns was wearing on his elbow. Turning to Hugh McIntosh, who had been chosen to referee the fight, he shouted, "Make him take it off, Mr. Mac. Make him take it off at once — or I quit the ring."[20]

"Either you come out fighting when the bell goes, or the fight's off — and you are disqualified," McIntosh replied.

"Mr. Mac, either he takes off that bandage, or I don't come out of my corner."

With that, Johnson pulled his robe over his shoulders and turned to leave. For one excrutiating moment it looked as if the whole thing was

Burns and Johnson engage in strenuous in-fighting.

off. Then Burns ripped the bandage from his arm and tossed it to one of his seconds. An enormous cheer went up from the crowd.

As the two men came to the centre of the ring for their final instructions, someone snapped a photo. In it, Tommy Burns is standing, his legs spread far apart, with a faraway look in his eyes.

McIntosh told the crowd that should police stop the fight he would render a verdict. There would not be a "no decision" handed out this day.

At 11:15 A.M. the gong sounded for round one. The fight of the century was under way.

Tommy Burns and Jack Johnson sprang out of their corners like two panthers released from their cages and immediately began trading punches. Both men blocked effectively, however, before falling into a clinch. McIntosh, who had never refereed a prizefight before, stepped in and yelled, "break." At the same time, he tried to pry the fighters apart, holding on to the champion's left glove as he did so. Burns was helpless, and the challenger took advantage, unleashing a dynamite upper-cut that landed on his jaw, lifting him off his feet.

"I dropped like a log," Burns admitted later. "The world spun crazily, a huge red blur obscured everything, but my fighting instinct brought me to my feet at the count of five."[21] The Canadian had hit the canvas with a thud, but he quickly signalled to his seconds that he was all right. Johnson, sensing victory, moved in for the kill. But Burns was ready for him. He was, he said later, like an enraged animal fighting for its life. "Momentarily equipped with the strength of a maniac," he chased the challenger all over the ring. One of his rights connected with Johnson's chin, snapping his head back so hard some thought his neck had broken.

Johnson had been stunned but, showing tremendous ring savvy, he pretended the blow hadn't fazed him a bit.

"Poor little Tommy," he taunted, "did someone kid you you were a fighter?"[22]

Burns, fooled by the outwardly calm behaviour of his wounded adversary, didn't press his advantage. Seconds later, his head now cleared, Johnson sent in a stinging left to the champion's face.

Midway through the round Burns herded his man into a corner and bore in with both fists. But Johnson reached out with his long arms, easily tying the champ up. "I continued my boring-in tactics throughout the first round; none of the modern 'feeling out' exhibitions, often witnessed in present day title bouts, were staged in this struggle," Burns wrote half a century later. "It was strictly a throwback — a couple of cavemen meeting on some long-forgotten path in an ancient forest, both disputing the right of the other to pass."[23]

As the bell rang Johnson almost danced back to his stool. Although briefly rattled by one punch, he'd landed a few telling blows of his own, one of which had resulted in a knockdown. Burns, the fans noticed, walked slowly back to his corner with a worried look on his face.

GONG! Round two. Johnson came out of his corner shouting at Burns. "Come right on." He followed up with a shot to the chin that sent the champion to the canvas again. Burns was up immediately and the two men fell into another clinch. This time, the Canadian complained loudly that Johnson was holding him.

Both men began hurling racial insults.

"Come and get it, little Tommy. Come and get it! Who told you I was yellow? You're white, dead scared white — white as the flag of surrender."[24]

Burns blocks a left rip from Johnson.

"Come on and fight nigger! Fight like a white man."[25]

Johnson backed up his taunts with superior boxing. By the time the round ended, Burns's left eye was swelling and he was bleeding from the mouth.

In the third round the champion finally changed his tactics. He realized he couldn't go toe-to-toe with Johnson. Not if he wanted to have any chance of winning. Crouching low, he went on the defensive, forcing Johnson to come to him. With his arms raised, he blocked virtually everything thrown at him, then launched a swift counter-attack that took the challenger off guard. Getting in close, he exhibited what one reporter described as "some wonderful execution at infighting, chopping his right to the ribs frequently." He also landed a solid shot to Johnson's head. It had taken him nine minutes, but Tommy Burns had finally won a round.

Round four went to Johnson, although not by much. Burns again planted a powerful right to the head, but the challenger answered with a right and a left to the skull and a smashing blow to Burns's ribs.

The fifth round was the Canadian's best. Literally running out of his corner, he dashed across the ring and caught Johnson by surprise with a smack in the mouth. The black fighter backed away, spitting blood from torn lips.

"See Tommy, the same colour as a white man's blood. The same colour as a yellow falla's blood,"[26] Johnson goaded.

Closing in, Burns landed six crunching blows on Johnson's ribcage. This was a consummate struggle. Johnson was ahead three rounds to two, but it was still anyone's fight. As the *Detroit Free Press* would report later, the action had the crowd in a constant uproar. "At times the slugging by both men was terrific," it said, "Blood was drawn by each fighter, and as the battle raged, 25,000 spectators went mad."

In the sixth round Burns again landed several punishing body blows. One reporter wrote that Johnson's body had been clearly "jolted." He was undoubtedly hurting on the inside but the challenger's face didn't betray that anything was wrong. Once again he masterfully pretended that Burns hadn't done a thing to upset him. Generations later, Muhammad Ali would employ similar tactics to trick his opponents into thinking they hadn't wobbled him.

"Hit me again, Tommy! Go on — harder this time!"[27]

Despite these clever taunts, however, the fight was now dead even, with each man having won three rounds.

GONG! Round seven. In this round the challenger gained the upper hand. Burns got in a left to Johnson's jaw but that was about it. During the rest of the three minutes of non-stop action it was the American who did all the connecting. One of his punches raised an ugly lump under Burns's right eye, and another dropped the Canadian to the canvas for the third time in the fight. Before the round ended Johnson was casually talking to the crowd whenever the two men clinched. Wrapping the shorter man in his powerful arms, he held on tight while shouting and smiling at fans.

Between rounds, Tommy's right eye had swelled shut. Pat O'Keefe managed to get it open only by sucking blood out of it.

Burns fought bravely in the late rounds against Johnson,
ignoring a badly swollen jaw.

Johnson won the eighth round easily, but the ninth was a draw, with
neither man doing much actual fighting. Both men, in fact, dished out
more verbal than physical abuse.

"Come on, Tommy, swing your right!" Johnson yelled.

Burns replied by calling the challenger a "yellow dog."[28]

One reporter wrote later, "There was not very much fighting —
probably more talking — during this round." In the tenth, he wrote,
both boxers appeared to be tiring. Each landed a number of punches,
but Burns's blows seemed to "lack steam."

Over the next two rounds Johnson had the clear edge, easily landing
twice as many blows as he received. The champ's jaw was badly swollen
and his right eye had been cut open again. Johnson was ahead seven

rounds to three, with two tied. But at the end of the twelfth, as he sat on his stool, the challenger was overheard complaining to his cornermen about possible broken ribs. Australian sports reporter W. F. Corbett, whose account of the fight has been largely ignored by historians, said Burns landed five body blows during the round. The champ, he told readers, still had the "vim of a tiger" at this stage of the fight.[29] Anxious to put an end to things, one of Johnson's seconds, a fellow named Rudy Unholtz, slipped under the ring apron. Scurrying under the canvas to the vicinity of the champion's corner, he began yelling, "Stop the fight, stop the fight," as soon as the action resumed in the thirteenth round.[30] Before long, the crowd picked up the chant as well.

Johnson, meanwhile, tried to end matters by battering away at Burns's injured jaw. But the Canadian held on grimly and was still fighting back when the round ended. Between rounds, convinced that Tommy's own corner had been crying for mercy, police entered the ring and warned McIntosh they were on the verge of stopping the fight. The referee went over to Burns and asked him if he was willing to continue. The Canadian, who felt he was getting stronger while Johnson was slowly running out of gas, snarled at the officers to mind their own business.

GONG! Round Fourteen. Johnson, realizing the police had been hoodwinked into thinking Burns was finished, went after the champion, hoping to further reinforce that false impression. He caught the Canadian with a heavy right to the head that sent him down again. Somehow, Burns managed to get back on his feet by the count of eight. But before either man could throw another punch a police officer climbed into the ring and ordered McIntosh to stop the fight.

Burns was incredulous. He made a huge scene, demanding that the battle be allowed to continue. But the officer ignored him and climbed back through the ropes. McIntosh immediately pointed to Johnson as the winner and a groan went through the crowd. The heavyweight championship of the world had passed into the hands of a black man for the first time in history. And the most spectacular chapter of Tommy Burns's life was over.

11

The Long Journey Home

Tommy Burns had not yet left the stadium at Rushcutter's Bay before the campaign to destroy his reputation got under way.

Jack Johnson started it. The new champion told reporters Burns was the worst fighter he had ever faced, that he could have knocked him out at any point during the fight. He had carried Burns for 14 rounds, he claimed, because he wanted to punish him for calling him names. None of the Canadian's punches had hurt him in the least, he said. "I never doubted the issue from the beginning. I knew I was too good for Burns. I have forgotten more about fighting than Burns ever knew."[1] Then he sneaked off to Manley Hospital in Sydney to have his broken ribs taped. While there, he later admitted to Joe Louis, he began urinating blood. Concerned physicians insisted he be kept overnight. The stay ended up lasting closer to a week, but the world didn't find out about it at the time because the new champion's manager swore the doctors to secrecy. When word did leak out, Johnson admitted he'd gone to hospital, but insisted it was only to undergo a routine check-up. He did the same thing as a precautionary move after every fight, he said. But the explanation was lame, and it contradicted his earlier claim that Burns had hardly laid a glove on him.

Johnson didn't want people to know it had been a tough battle because he was anxious to present himself as the greatest boxer who had ever lived. He wanted to create the impression that he could easily dismantle the best fighters in the world. Instead, he succeeded only in giving the press a way of descrediting *him*. The media picked up on the theme that Burns was a second-rate boxer, deciding it was as good a way as any to explain how a black man had managed to become world heavyweight champion in the first place.

Jack London, the famed novelist and strident white supremacist, led the anti-Burns charge. Writing for the *New York Herald*, he made Burns out to be the biggest loser who ever stepped into a prize ring. His story, which may still rank as the single most irresponsible piece of sports journalism in history, reads as follows:

The fight? There was no fight. No Armenian massacre could compare to the hopeless slaughter that took place in the Sydney Stadium. The fight, if fight it could be called, was like that between a pygmy and a colossus. It had all the seeming of a playful Ethiopian at loggerheads with a small white man — of a grown man cuffing a naughty child — of a monologue by Johnson who made a noise with his fist like a lullaby, tucking Burns into a crib — of a funeral, with Burns for the late deceased, Johnson for the undertaker, grave-digger and sexton, all in one.

There was no fraction of a second in all the fourteen rounds that could be called Burns's. So far as damage is concerned, Burns never landed a blow. He never fazed the black man. It was not Burns's fault, however. He tried every moment throughout the fight, except when he was groggy. It was hopeless, preposterous, heroic. He was a glutton for punishment as he bored in all the time, but a dewdrop had more chance in hell than he had with the Giant Ethiopian. Goliath had defeated David, that much was clear.

Johnson play-acted all the time, and he played with Burns from the opening gong to the finish of the fight. Burns was a toy in his hands. For Johnson it was a kindergarten romp.

"Hit me here, Tahmy," he would say, exposing the right side of his unprotected stomach, and when Burns struck, Johnson would neither wince nor cover up. Instead he would receive the blow with a happy, careless smile directed at the spectators, turn the left side of his unprotected stomach and say, "Now there, Tahmy," and while Burns would hit as directed, Johnson would continue to grin and chuckle and smile his golden smile.

One criticism and only one can be passed on Johnson. In the 13th round he made the mistake of his life. He should have put Burns out. He could have put him out. It would have been child's play. Instead of which he smiled and deliberately let Burns live until the gong sounded, and in the opening of the 14th round the police stopped the fight and Johnson lost the credit for a knock-out.

But one thing now remains. Jim Jeffries must emerge from his alfalfa farm and remove the golden smile from Jack Johnson's face. Jeff, it's up to you! The White Man must be rescued.

A few weeks later, when Burns ran into London, the bigoted writer apologized, then burst into tears, admitting he'd greatly exaggerated what had happened in the ring.

"Thanks, but the damage has been done," Burns replied.[2]

Indeed it had been. London, the author of such classic books as *The Call of the Wild* and *The Sea-Wolf*, was one of the most respected writers of his generation. If he said Burns was a bum, people believed it. Newspapers across the English-speaking world reprinted London's story. And those that didn't run it printed editorials claiming Jim Jeffries was still the real champion because he hadn't been defeated in the ring. The fabled "Boilermaker" was no longer the "retired champion," he was the "undefeated champion." Tommy Burns was dismissed in one newspaper as "the keeper-custodian of the heavyweight boxing title." Another said that instead of being "the real wearer of the crown, Burns was only a pretender." In London, the *Sportsman* said Burns didn't have the class of past champions. The *Daily Mail* declared he'd only won the crown because the heavyweight division had fallen to a low ebb in 1906. The *New York Times* declared Burns had an "extremely shady record."

It was easy enough, in the pre-television era, to lie about events at Rushcutter's Bay, but explaining away how Burns had managed to defeat two world champions and the title holders of four continents presented reporters with a major challenge. They got around it by destroying the reputations of those fighters as well. "Burns could never be called a first-class heavyweight, and the fact that several years ago he could not stop such pugs as Marvin Hart and O'Brien in 20 rounds created a lasting impression to this effect," one New York writer asserted. This was poppycock. Hart and O'Brien were hardly "pugs." Both would eventually be inducted into the International Boxing Hall of Fame. And in 1950 O'Brien would be named the greatest light-heavy-weight pugilist of the half century.

The *Cincinnati Inquirer*, meanwhile, trotted out boxer Mike Schreck, who claimed Burns had been a cowardly champion and had ducked "big men" like him. Even in Canada there was criticism. The Toronto *Globe* reported it had heard "rumours" that Burns had won most of his fights by bribing his opponents into taking dives. It failed to offer a shred of evidence that such was actually the case.

Once they had made the false case against Burns, the media went after Johnson. A New York paper editorialized, "Until Jack Johnson whipped Burns, the Negro did not command much respect in the fighting world, and even with that victory to his credit Johnson then could not convince many of the best judges that he possessed real class." Another newspaper greeted the black man's win by declaring, "Never before in the history of the prize ring has such a crisis arisen as that which faces the followers of the game tonight." In a front page editorial, the prestigious *New York Times* said Johnson's ascension to the throne had caused "a feeling of curiously acute dissatisfaction," even among non-boxing fans. "Consequently there is excuse for those of us who happen to be white to be a bit cast down over the result of the antipodean battle and to await with a trace of impatience the appear-ance of a champion who will put Mr. Johnson in what we cannot for the life of us help thinking is a more seemly position for one who wears his burnished livery."

Former boxing champions blasted Burns for breaking the colour line they'd upheld for so long. "Shame on the money-mad champion!" John L. Sullivan thundered. "Shame on the man who upsets good American precedents because there are dollars, dollars, dollars in it."[3] Sullivan also questioned the Canadian's skill level. Forgetting he had publicly forecasted a Burns victory beforehand, he said, "The fight came out very much as I had predicted. In my opinion Burns never was the champion prizefighter of the world."[4]

Jim Jeffries also conveniently forgot he had predicted Burns would emerge victorious. "I thought Johnson would win unless they had his legs and hands tied," he told one interviewer. "Burns had no right to fight Johnson for the heavyweight championship. I never looked for any other result, and I did not expect the fight to go so far. I never considered Burns a heavyweight champion. He always looked like a big, well-developed middleweight to me. He was too small for that husky coon. I think that Burns was a very poor representative of the American heavyweight. He licked a lot of easy ones, but the first time he went against a good fighter he lost, didn't he?" Jeffries added smugly, "I do not like to see the highest honour in pugilism rest in the hands of a black man, but it is not my fault that it does, and it is not up to me to wrest the championship belt from the Negro. I advised Burns, as well as other young fighters, to draw the colour line and not take on Johnson or Langford, and thus endanger the championship. But now that Burns has lost the title to a Negro, it's too late to draw the colour line on him, and some white man must win the title away from Johnson. But that white man will not be me. I am through with the fighting game for all time."[5]

Gentleman Jim Corbett, who was now 42, said if Jeffries wouldn't fight Johnson, he might take on the black man in order to restore the honour of the white race. "I simply feel bad to see a coloured man the champion," he said. "If I get my plans arranged I'll re-enter the ring. I'll fight Johnson, not because I want to fight a black man, but to wrest the title back." After that, he'd "try and arrange it so that by no possible future move any black man could ever regain it, for the colour line would be drawn then by all honourable white boxers once and for all."[6] In other words, Tommy Burns was dishonourable because, unlike previous champions, he hadn't run for cover at the sight of black fighters.

Only the *Detroit Free Press* seemed to realize the attacks on Burns were misguided. "Burns is being blamed, not for losing his title, but for letting a Negro have a chance to take it," sports editor Joe Jackson noted. But his rational voice was lost in the anti-Burns din. Some writers even blamed the Canadian for the violence that followed Johnson's victory. In several southern states the Ku Klux Klan greeted the news of the black man's triumph by lynching African-Americans. There were riots in Harlem, and on the streets of New Orleans a number of knifings were reported. Anxious to keep order, several governors talked openly about banning boxing altogether.

Burns remained dignified throughout this ordeal. Immediately after the fight he told reporters, "I did the best I could and fought hard. Johnson was too big and his reach was too great."[7] With that, he took his leave and went to the racetrack for the afternoon. Later, most reporters would tell the world Burns had nearly been beaten to death, that only the police intervention had saved his life. But one writer admitted, "Burns is in good condition except for discolouration about the eyes and a badly swollen jaw. At first it was feared that the Negro's heavy swings had broken the white man's jaw, but it now turns out it was only badly bruised."

In the days ahead Burns would complain about the police decision to stop the fight, but at no time did he ever question the result. In fact, he heaped praise on the new champion, conceding he had "badly underestimated Johnson's boxing skills, his tremendous strength and unquestionable cunning. The situation demanded that I move rapidly around the ring, boxing carefully, at all times. It actually was my only chance to cope with the larger man, but I had elected to tear into him and outfight him. From the start of the second round it was simply the story of a small man who never gave ground gaming it out against a great fighter. The big fellow dealt out terrific punishment as the tussle progressed."[8]

Yet again Burns was proving to be gracious in defeat. This was a difficult task, as his title had meant everything to him. But he considered himself a gentleman and wanted others to see him the same way.

Although most newspapers printed Jack London's version of events, a few were more honest. Some reporters even judged the first six rounds to be dead even. When the police stopped the fight, Australian newspaperman W. F. Corbett told his readers, Burns did not appear to be finished. His observation, however, was not picked up by other publications.

So how one-sided was the fight? The contest was captured on film, of course, but only about 13 minutes of footage remains in existence today. The early rounds are missing, along with the ending. In all, just over 4 of the 14 rounds are available for study. They don't show Burns being savagely beaten. Although Johnson is clearly in control of the action, the Canadian can be seen jogging back to his corner at the end of each round. There's no doubt that Johnson won fair and square. He did, after all, score four knockdowns during the course of the fight. But the claims that he totally dominated the action appear to be far from the truth.

Of course none of that mattered to the press in 1908. Racist reporters told the world Johnson had beaten a pathethic excuse for a champion, and generations of future authors would pick up on the theme without bothering to check the facts. But a handful of modern scribes have been perceptive enough to see through the lies that were foisted on the public so long ago. In his 1998 book, *Boxing Day*, author Jeff Wells wrote, "Modern boxing writers would have given some points to Burns, even if the scorecard was lopsided. But, of course, this did not suit the purposes of Jack London, who was looking for a new cause. A fair match-up would not have allowed him to rally the forces of white supremacy; there had to be a perceived threat. The beating of Burns had to be portrayed as complete — and primeval — for the white race to get aggravated."[9] In his book *Goin' the Distance*, author Murray Greig questioned, "Why, if the Canadian failed to land a meaningful punch, was he still on his feet and fighting back when the police stepped in? There is also the puzzling fact that it was Johnson, not Burns, who needed medical attention after the fight."[10]

Authors S. F. Wise and Douglas Fisher have lent support to the theory that Burns was belittled unfairly by reporters out to descredit Johnson. "Recent boxing historians agree that [Burns's] reputation has been downplayed undeservedly," they wrote in their book *Canada's Sporting Heroes*. "Johnson was not liked by the American boxing public. Black fighters were unpopular and Johnson's relationships with white women did nothing to improve his reputation. If Johnson was not a good boxer — the argument went — the man he defeated must be worse. Reports sent back from Australia were lurid and biased, one of the worst coming from the novelist Jack London. Sober second thought has admitted that Johnson was an exceptional champion, and no one needed be ashamed of losing to the first black heavyweight champion."[11]

Even legendary boxing historian Nat Fleischer, who once wrote that Burns "missed greatness by a wide margin," was willing to admit the Canadian had been unfairly smeared for breaking the colour line.

Because he lost the title to a black man, Fleischer said, Burns was blamed for precipitating "a period of unrest and discontent that ended only with the defeat of Johnson" seven years later.[12] Eventually, Johnson's reputation would be restored. But except for a few laudatory paragraphs in a handful of books, Burns's good name has never been repaired.

Becoming British Empire Champion

Regardless of how badly he had been hurt physically, Burns was emotionally crushed by the loss of his title. He asked for a rematch, but Johnson refused to give it. Shortly after being released from hospital the new champion sailed for North America. Burns, humiliated by the bad press he'd received in the U.S. and Canada, decided to stay on in Australia indefinitely. He couldn't bear to go home and face his family and friends. Despondent, he decided to quit boxing. To prove he was serious, he gave up training and even threw his gloves away. A homesick Jewel, meanwhile, returned to the States without him. She had been ill for days prior to the fight and was happy to leave Australia. After almost a year on the road she wanted to go home.

For the next 14 months Tommy stayed in Australia by himself. During that time he did little more than eat, drink and gamble. He visited the racetrack almost daily, eventually losing every cent he'd made in the Johnson fight. As a result, he was running low on cash. He still had more than $100,000 in a Los Angeles bank account, but he had the good sense not to wire for any of it. Instead, he decided to fight newly crowned British Empire champion Billy Lang a second time. The fight, which took place before 17,000 fans on April 7, 1910, in Sydney, was nothing like the first meeting between the two men. Burns was a pudgy 183 pounds, the heaviest he had ever been inside the ring. The taller Lang, meanwhile, was a trim 188 pounds. Nevertheless, Burns managed to squeak out a 20-round decision on points.

Unfortunately, the title of British Empire champion did nothing to restore his tarnished reputation. Under the headline "Burns gone back, was never first class," the *London Free Press* noted the Canadian had failed to score a knockout. It added he had received "what appears to

have been a questionable decision." Burns didn't seem very
impressed with the win himself.
He didn't bother to defend the
title, and relinquished it in 1911.

Burns was back in Los Angeles by the summer of 1910, but
he didn't intend to stay there
for long. Looking for a change
of scenery, he decided to take
up residence in Canada for the
first time since he'd left Sarnia
in 1900. He had never become
an American citizen, which meant
he could return home without
any difficulty. But he had no in-

Burns as a Calgary businessman.

tention of living in small-town Ontario. Instead, he and Jewel settled
in Calgary, which was a booming city with a population of 55,000
people. The place was brimming with optimism. The year Burns arrived
the *Calgary Herald* predicted "a future of marvellous and ever increas-
ing prosperity reaching out 10 years hence." Burns agreed with that
assessment and opened his own clothing store. He enjoyed being
surrounded by fine garments but quickly found the job of running a
business boring. During the first year of operation the store recorded
$100,000 worth of sales, but because Tommy paid so little attention to
the business side of things, he still ended up losing money on the
venture.

Disappointed, he sold the store, bought a sandstone mansion in
Calgary's Elwood Park, overlooking the Elbow River, and got into real
estate. His timing couldn't have been better. Historian Pierre Berton
has recounted how, at that time in Calgary, "men stood in the pouring
rain right through the night for a chance to buy" lots at inflated prices.[13]
In such a climate Burns was able to buy and sell several properties at a
good profit.

Jewel, who finally had her husband home for prolonged periods,
gave birth to four girls — Margaret, Patricia, and the twins, Mary and

Helen — between 1911 and 1917. Most men of the era preferred boys, but Burns doted on his daughters, generally leaving the question of discipline up to their mother. Finally, he was becoming a regular family man. It was beginning to look like his life as a globe-trotting adventurer was finally over.

Jack Johnson destroys Jeffries

Burns was reminded of the excitement he'd left behind when he travelled to Reno, Nevada, to watch Jack Johnson defend his title against Jim Jeffries on July 4, 1910. Johnson hadn't enjoyed his championship very much since winning the title. After taking the crown he'd expected everything to be different, that he'd be treated like a human being. Instead, he returned to North America to find nothing had changed. The night he arrived at Victoria, British Columbia, he was refused a room in a posh hotel. His first title defense came a few days later in Vancouver, against an unemployed actor named Victor McLaglen. Johnson scored an easy win and McLaglen quit boxing for good. The world would never have heard of him again, except that he finally found an acting job and went on to win an Academy Award for best actor in the 1935 film *The Informer*.

Following that victory, Johnson fought a "no decision" bout against Philadelphia Jack O'Brien, then reeled off three wins in a row, including one against middleweight champion Stan Ketchell. Still, like Burns before him, Johnson couldn't get any respect. Newspapers all over the country continued to insist Jim Jeffries was the real champion.

Finally, after being nagged for two years, Jeffries agreed to come out of retirement and whip Johnson. The fight attracted even more publicity than the Burns-Johnson battle had generated. The *New York Times* set the tone for the coverage early, declaring, "If the black man wins, thousands and thousands of his ignorant brothers will misinterpret his victory as justifying claims to much more than mere physical equality with their white neighbours." The *Chicago Tribune* echoed those sentiments, telling readers, "As essentially African, Johnson feels no deeper than the moment, sees no farther than his nose and is incapable of anticipation. That same cheerful indifference to coming events has marked others of his race even while they were standing in the very shadow of the gallows. Their stolid unconcern baffled all who beheld it. They were to be hanged, they knew, but having no fancy, no imagination, they could not anticipate it."

William Jennings Bryan, who would later become an American Secretary of State, wired Jeffries to wish him good luck. "God will forgive anything Jeffries does to that nigger in this fight. Jeff, God is with you."[14]

Just prior to fight time, Jeffries issued a public statement in which he assured people he was ready for action. "That portion of the white race that has been looking to me to defend its athletic superiority may feel assured that I am fit to do my very best."[15]

As Johnson came into the ring, a band struck up a popular tune of the era called "All Coons Look Alike to Me." All the former champions were there, including Corbett, Sullivan, Fitzsimmons, Hart and Burns. Jeffries asked Sullivan for advice. The old champion replied, "Jim, all I know is that God Almighty hates a quitter."[16] Had Jeffries asked Burns what to do, he might have been spared what was coming. The Canadian could have told him to fight defensively, to cover up and hold as much as possible. But Jeffries didn't even acknowledge his presence. No one, it seemed, respected Tommy Burns any more.

When the bell rang for round one Jeffries came charging out of his corner, determined to press the action, just as Burns had done in Australia. And just like the Canadian, he was in trouble from the start. Johnson broke his nose, shredded his lips and opened cuts over both his eyes. Then, in the fifteenth round, the champion knocked Jeffries down three times. The third time he hit the canvas, the Boilermaker was unable to get up before the count of 10.

The fight was followed by riots all over the United States. In New Orleans, a black man walked into a restaurant and said, "Gimme eggs, beat and scrambled, like Jim Jeffries."[17] The waiter responded by shooting him on the spot. Before the night was over, seven others would die, including three blacks that were shot dead in Uvaldia, Georgia. In Pueblo, California, 30 were killed or injured in a riot. The next night blacks struck back. A white railroad conductor was shot in Little Rock, Arkansas, and a police officer was killed in Mounds, Illinois. These incidents only sparked more violence. In one particularly terrible incident a group of whites fired into a crowd, killing a nine-year-old African-American girl. In some cities, order was restored only when troops were called in. The *New York Times* blamed it all on Johnson. His victory, it said, was, "a calamity to this country far worse than the San Francisco earthquake." There were renewed calls for an end to boxing. The *New York Herald* protested, "Prizefighting has not become a 'reductio ad absurdum' when the best fighter comes from the lowest and least developed race." In England, the *London Telegram* announced, "The days of the ring are over, not only because the fight was a disgusting affair, but because it inflamed and further agitated the colour problem."

One would think that Johnson's easy win over Jeffries would have helped restore Burns's reputation, but such was not the case. Reporters made excuses for Jeffries, pointing out he was past his prime and rusty after years of inactivity when he fought Johnson. Despite the drubbing he took in Nevada, Jeffries would still be accorded the status of an "all-time great" by generations of writers. Burns, who made almost twice as many successful title defenses as the Boilermaker, continues to be dismissed by most boxing writers as a lemon to this very day.

Burns returns to the ring

Anxious to repair his damaged reputation, Burns decided to return to boxing. He must have known there was no way he could ever hope to regain his title. In some ways he resembled an ageing bullfighter, returning to the ring because he couldn't live without the acclaim of the crowd. This time he proposed to fight Sam Langford, who was widely viewed as the number-one contender for Johnson's title, in the fall of 1910. Once again he was demonstrating he wasn't afraid to cross the colour line. He was also showing his fearlessness — Langford was a powerful puncher who had been dubbed "the Bonecrusher" by reporters. The fight was all set to go but fell through after Tommy injured his knee in a lacrosse game. The promoter tried to rush him back into action, but he wisely refused to be hurried. In a letter to a friend, he showed great respect for the black fighter. "I know Langford is a tough fellow and I am not going to take any chances of being caught out of condition," he wrote.[18]

When his leg finally healed the fight was on again. But it was cancelled for good when Burns injured a leg and arm in a train wreck outside Seattle just 10 days before Christmas. "December is my Jonah month," he moaned. "I had built my hope and laid my plans for fighting my way back to the top. I was to have met Langford and, after disposing of him I would then have been eligible to meet Johnson. But in one fatal minute last December my dream of regaining the title was rudely shattered."[19]

Burns, left, meets Arthur Pelkey.

Still limping four months after the accident, Burns launched a lawsuit against the railroad, claiming $50,000 in damages. The action got nowhere, so he began toying with the possibility of touring Australia with his own lacrosse team. But the idea was abandoned and he turned his attention back to boxing, knocking out a hulking, 220-pound heavyweight named Bill Rickard in a fight staged in Saskatoon, Saskatchewan, on August 8, 1912.

Searching for a Great White Hope

For a time it looked as if Burns was back in the saddle, but he was a lost soul. Unable to decide what he wanted to do next, he didn't put the gloves on again for another 20 months. This time, he battled Arthur Pelkey, a big Chatham, Ontario, boxer, to a draw in a fight staged in Calgary on April 2, 1913.

Burns talked about fighting another top contender named Luther McCarty, then cancelled the bout, deciding instead to become a boxing promoter. At the time, Jack London was promoting a worldwide search for a white man who could beat Jack Johnson. Shameful as it was, Burns realized there was big money to be made and got in on the action. Despite strong objections from the local clergy, he built a 10,000-seat arena on the outskirts of Calgary and began staging tournaments designed to find a "Great White Hope." At one such tournament, Burns watched McCarty in action against Iron Man Joe Grim. Incredibly, McCarty knocked Grim out, becoming the first boxer ever to turn the trick. Impressed, Burns told the victor he had the potential to become world champ. Within a few days he had become McCarty's manager.

A few years later McCarty was declared "white heavyweight champion" and was almost ready to take on Johnson for the world crown. But before signing for a match with the champ, he decided to engage in one more fight. This time, his opponent would be Arthur Pelkey. Burns shamelessly hyped the fight, declaring the winner would soon strip Jack Johnson of his title. And the fast talk worked. A crowd of seven thousand turned out at Calgary's Manchester Arena. It was the biggest boxing crowd in Canadian history. Sadly, what they were about to see was one of the most tragic episodes in the annals of Canadian sport.

There was something eerie about the match from the beginning. Burns, whose faith in God was becoming more important to him every day, invited a preacher to say prayers prior to the start of the action. Rev. William Walker told the audience, "Here are two fine young men. They are in perfect physical condition, ready for their big test. And it should remind all of us always to be ready to meet our Maker when the time comes."[20]

Early in the first round, Pelkey hit McCarty with what looked like a light punch. Inexplicably, McCarty collapsed in a heap. At that very moment, a ray of sunshine burst through an overhead window and landed on McCarty's ashen face. Seconds later, he was pronouced dead.

Both Pelkey and Burns were charged with manslaughter. It was the second time in his career that Burns had been arrested for what happened in the ring. The charges against him were quickly dropped, but people were so angry at his attempts to promote boxing that someone burned down the Manchester arena.

"Whoever started the fire knew his business," Burns told the *Calgary Herald*. "He started it on the proper side so that the wind would take the blaze over the great dry roof of the building. In my opinion it was a clear case of arson."

The inquest into McCarty's death, which followed two days later, cleared both Burns and Pelkey. An autopsy revealed the boxer had suffered a broken neck, which he probably sustained after being thrown from a horse a day or two before the fight. The injury had caused internal bleeding, which was slowly killing him even as he climbed into the ring.

Burns went to great lengths to ensure people knew he wasn't responsible for the tragedy. In a letter to *The Ring Magazine*, he wrote,

The coroner's verdict was that he died of a broken neck. It was a case of a man dying in a fight in which he never was hit. I do not believe there is another like it in boxing history.

I had a talk with McCarty the morning of the fight. He turned toward me and could not pivot his head. He had to move his entire body. I asked Luther what was wrong, and he replied, 'Tommy, I was sleeping near an open window last night and got myself a stiff neck. It's nothing serious.'

Well, poor Luther didn't realize how serious it was ... I am writing this to set boxing history straight, so that McCarty's death will stop being listed as a ring fatality. Luther would have died had he remained in bed.

Burns's conscience may have been eased by the coroner's verdict, but Pelkey's wasn't. Although he was found not guilty of manslaughter, he was haunted for the rest of his life by what had happened. Every time he went to sleep he had terrible nightmares in which he would see McCarty collapse and die. Burns continued to manage his career, but it was no use. Afraid to hit another man for fear that he might kill him, Pelkey lost his next 13 fights, all by way of knockout. After that he retired for good. When he died, in 1921, he was only 37 years old.

There was a final, ironic postscript to this sad tale. Burns had the unenviable task of shipping McCarty's body back to the United States. McCarty's mother was dead and his widow, from whom he had been separated, did not want the remains. Finally, Burns found McCarty's father — a Cherokee medicine man named White Eagle. Burns had been promoting a half-native as the next Great White Hope.

For Burns the end of his involvement with professional boxing was almost at hand. He defeated a journeyman fighter named Battling Brant in Taft, California, on January 26, 1914, but the press, still furious about his decision to allow a black man to fight for the title, gave him little credit. One critic wrote,

'Tommy Burns has come back,' the newspapers shout, because the Rockefeller of the ring beat up some person known as Brant. Some sarcastic person calls him 'Battling Brant' at that, but the chances are that Battling Brant is a coal heaver that Tommy picked up somewhere to practise on. Mr. Burns is looking for the Kale all the time.

The criticism would continue for years to come. Ten years after Rushcutter's Bay, one newspaper declared, "Johnson's ascendancy to the heavyweight championship threw the fistic game into chaos and it never fully recovered. Tommy Burns was primarily to blame for this, because he consented to a meeting with Johnson in Australia."

Within a few months of the Brant fight, Burns would have more important things on his mind than his boxing career. In August the First World War broke out, and Canada asked for volunteers. Although he was now 33 years old, married and the father of four children, Burns joined the Canadian army. Some questioned his patriotism, noting his parents were born in Germany. Behind his back, other soldiers referred to him as "Herr Brusso" or "Von Burns." He asked for a posting overseas, but the government had the good sense not to send him into combat. Although his reputation had been tarnished since Rushcutter's Bay, he was still a world-famous figure, and it would have dealt a blow to public morale had he been killed in action. Instead, he was given the rank of sergeant-major and made a physical-fitness instructor. For the next four years Burns helped train Canadian soldiers for the rigours of the Western Front. On a number of occasions he taught as many as one thousand men at a time. Late in the war, he agreed to a bout with Tex Foster, in which all proceeds would be donated to wounded veterans.

The fight, staged on September 19, 1918, in Prince Rupert, British Columbia, lasted only four rounds before Burns scored the 48th victory and 39th knockout of his career.

Tragic end to a marriage

Throughout all these events, Burns's marriage was falling apart. In the fall of 1918 newspapers reported Burns had filed for divorce, accusing Jewel of mental cruelty. Reporters treated this tragedy as a joke, declaring that while Burns had proven himself to be unafraid of Jack Johnson and the German Kaiser, he was running scared from his wife. In his unpublished memoirs, Burns says the two went their separate ways because of Jewel's "hysterical behaviour." Whether she suffered a nervous breakdown from clinical depression is not clear. Because historians have ignored the Tommy Burns story for almost a century, some aspects of his life have been lost, perhaps forever. Whatever went wrong, it should be remembered that only Tommy's side of the story is available. Jewel left behind no written record of what it was like for such a refined, gentle lady to live with this pugnacious, flamboyant character. But the fact that Burns was given control of their children in an age when women were almost automatically awarded custody is a clear indication that something was terribly wrong with Jewel.

Looking for a change of scenery, he put his daughters in a Vancouver convent and went to England shortly after the war ended in November 1918. Setting up his own pub in Newcastle, near the Scottish border, Burns settled into a comfortable life of semi-retirement. He let others run the day-to-day operations of his business, dropping in only occasionally to mix with the patrons. For the first time in his life he seemed to be a self-confident, contented individual. Then, one day in the spring of 1920, Burns went to a gymnasium to watch British heavyweight champion Joe Beckett in training. Beckett, who stood 6'2" and weighed 220 pounds, was a giant compared to the Canadian. He was also 13 years younger. Nevertheless, Burns became convinced he could beat the Englishman and challenged him to a match. Beckett, expecting an easy win, agreed.

Proving he hadn't lost his business acumen, Burns rented London's Albert Hall and enthusiastically promoted the fight. As a result, a

A balding, overweight Burns just before his last fight at age 39.

sell-out crowd turned out for the match, which was held on July 16, 1920. There was so much money collected that, after paying Beckett $16,000 and taking care of all the expenses, Burns still had $20,000 left for himself. The purse, his last as a prizefighter, brought his lifetime ring earnings to $209,000, or the modern equivalent of $5.2 million tax free.

Unfortunately, while the bout was a financial success, it was hardly an athletic showcase. Burns dominated the early going, then ran out of steam and was forced to quit in the seventh round. The next day, one London newspaper lamented, "He was not the fighter we knew." Realizing the truth behind that statement, Burns hung up his gloves for good.

His ring record stood at an amazing 48 wins, 5 losses, 9 draws and 1 no-decision.

Shortly after his boxing career ended his marriage came to a formal end as well, but not before Jewel made one last attempt to save it. Writing in his memoirs, Burns recalled,

I received letters from my wife pleading to return to me, and making glowing promises. So I cabled the convent in Vancouver where our children were being cared for and asked that they be released to my wife, so that she could bring them to England with her. It was wonderful to see them all again. The dull ache that I had kept hidden in my heart gave way to sheer joy, and my wife and I agreed to try to live in harmony hereafter, since we had not been divorced. We got along very well for a few months, then she began associating with

Burns with walking stick.

persons of questionable character. I objected, but this brought on difficulties that neither she nor I could tolerate, with the result that legal separation followed. Thus, it was again necessary for me to place the children in a convent — this time in England.

Sadly, the worst was yet to come. One day, when Tommy was at the beach with the children, Jewel appeared suddenly, yelling and screaming. "She created a terrific scene," Burns said. "Being under obsession, she attacked me, using profane language, and succeeded in kidnapping the children." Turning to the authorities for help, he was able to get them back. "My wife was allowed to visit them, under supervision of the convent," Burns wrote. "However, a few months later the court was forced to bar her from visiting them at all, because she appeared to be unable to stop interfering with the sisters. Later she was allowed to see the children."

Burns blamed himself for not recognizing what was wrong with Jewel. "Had I at that time understood my wife's mental condition and the evil spirit who was the root of all the trouble, I would have assisted her back to health and happiness, instead of a life of distress and separation from her loved ones," he admitted.[21] Jewel, who had been sickly much of her life, died before the end of the 1920s.

Restless retirement

Although he was still only 39 years of age, Tommy Burns was essentially a man without a future after the Beckett fight. He'd been involved in boxing for two decades and didn't know anything else. Now he had to readjust to normal life, away from the big money, the roaring crowds and the reporters. As a world famous athlete he'd received the same attention accorded a movie star, a king or a president. But now, before he'd reached his fortieth birthday, he was a man whose best years were behind him.

Still, things went well for a time. His nephew, future television star Larry Keating, had invested his money for him, allowing Burns to live a lavish lifestyle in England until 1928. From there he moved to New York, where he opened a speakeasy during the height of Prohibition. But with the stock market crash of October 1929 he lost much of his wealth. By the mid-1930s, with his fortune almost exhausted, he also lost his health. All those years of hard fighting had taken their toll, leaving him with severe arthritis in both shoulders. "Doctors sent me home to die, but Tommy Burns refused to die," he told an interviewer years later. "With the power of thought I was better in two weeks."[22] Still, the pain kept coming back and, near the end of his life, he was in constant misery. Hoping to return home to Canada, he wrote to Prime Minister R. B. Bennett requesting a government job. "I have been thinking, for some time, of coming to Canada to live — in short to finish the remainder of my life there — and, if possible, I would like to get a government position," he wrote. "The elections are coming up and I believe I would be a great asset. Any position you think would suit me would be satisfactory."[23]

Clearly, Burns was homesick. He had always been proud of his Canadian citizenship, often pointing out to reporters that he was a Canuck, not a Yank. He made public statements to that effect prior to at least three of his championship fights.

Although this was a golden opportunity to bring a national hero home, Bennett, one of Canada's more colourless prime ministers, passed it up. He wrote back saying he would keep the old boxer's letter in mind. In fact, he ignored it. Burns was still widely viewed as the man who had brought discord to professional sports by agreeing to compete with black men. There was no place for such a person in the Canadian government of the 1930s.

Disappointed, Burns headed to Texas, where he sold life insurance for a time. Still aching to come home, he moved to Vancouver in 1939. But he was unable to find steady work and left a year later, settling in Bremerton, Washington, where he got a job as a security guard at a shipyard. Not long after the Second World War began he volunteered for the Canadian Army, but this time he was turned down.

As he settled into old age Burns finally found some of the happiness that had eluded him for so long. He was also in love again. This time, the object of his affections was Nellie Vanderlip, a widow whom he married just after turning 65. For a time, he seemed to be doing quite well for himself. Jim Rondeau, who knew Burns during the 1940s, said later, "He certainly did not resemble an ex-heavyweight champion of the world. He was more like an ex-middleweight. I grew up in Bremerton and remember Tommy as a stately man, very soft-spoken, friendly. He didn't even look like a fighter. His nose wasn't even bashed. Everybody at home loved him. He was well-fixed financially, was a good

Burns as a senior citizen.

businessman, and had the respect of everyone."[24] A reporter who met him around the same time called him a "mellow, kindly little man."

As a retired senior citizen he suddenly found a new mission in life. Burns, who had always been a churchgoer, became extremely religious. For years he'd been studying the world's faiths, old and new, in his quest for spiritual truth. He even took religious books with him on fishing trips into the mountains with his nephew. In a 1952 meeting with hockey legend Cyclone Taylor, who had played lacrosse against a young Noah Brusso, he explained how his search finally ended. He was in constant pain from arthritis when, "one day I got a feeling that I can't explain, and I simply turned to religion. And here I am."[25] He was ordained a minister on Christmas Day, 1948, and travelled up and down the California coast, giving sermons about the power of love. In early 1955, speaking to a black Baptist congregation in Oakland, he called for equality between the races. In a speech that was at least a decade ahead of its time, he said, "We're all God's creatures and He loves us all equally. The barriers that separate us should be knocked down. Those who say the Negro is inferior to the white man do not know the power of love. Jack Johnson taught me the coloured man is as brave, as clever and as strong as anyone. The whole world was against him but he pulled himself up by his bootstraps and became a champion. If you do the same, with God's help, you can overcome any obstacles."[26] The African-American worshippers gave him a rousing ovation that was so thunderous it shook the wooden church to its foundations. Outside, Burns told a reporter that black fighter Joe Louis was the greatest heavyweight champion in history.

Sports writer Dick Beddoes, who wrote a number of stories about Burns for the *Vancouver Sun*, recounted, "After salvation he wrote and spoke millions of pious, if sometimes confusing, words about the world of the spirit. As a moral philosopher, he had great stamina. Some of his letters ran six or eight pages long. In these, as in his platform work, the tone was consistently lofty."[31]

His niece, Audrey Adamson, says Burns was writing religious letters long before he became a minister. "He used to send my grandmother [his mother, Sofa, who died in 1913] letters, which were religious tracts, but there was never any note saying how he was or anything."[27]

Burns did more than just talk and write about love. From time to time he visited orphanages, hospitals and jails, where he did volunteer work. No task was too menial. He helped out in kitchens, emptied bedpans and even scrubbed floors. In February 1954 he returned to Canada for the first time in years to speak at a sports celebrity dinner hosted by Toronto journalists. While other head-table guests demanded hefty fees for their appearances, Burns asked only that he be allowed to leave a small religious message at each table. He denied, however, that he was seeking to convert people. "I am not interested in converts — what every man chooses to think is his own business," he said.[28]

In an interview, he said he wasn't interested in boxing any more. "I've got something better than that — and it is love for my fellow man. My main object in life is to help the sick and the suffering. I was fighting all my life, from the time I was a youngster, and I look back and see what a foolish person I was." When the reporter tried to steer the subject back to boxing, he gently but firmly told him the sport was "vicious and full of hatred. I had the power of hate when I fought Johnson. I hated him so much that I beat myself and hate nearly put me in my grave because I took a terrible beating."[29] In a letter to a friend, he wrote, "It was never meant for a person to try and knock the life out of another being — even an animal. As the scriptures say, 'He that killeth an ox is as if he slew a man.' Had I known in my younger days what I know now, I would never have become a fighter, let alone a world champion."[30]

The only person who could get him to talk about the ring was Canadian heavyweight champ Earl Walls, who was ranked seventh in the world behind champion Rocky Marciano. A picture taken at the sports dinner shows Burns giving tips to the young black fighter.

Most of those on hand were taken aback by Burns's tiny frame. "I was young and impressionable but I couldn't believe this little man had ever been heavyweight champion of the world," sports writer Jim Hunt said later.[31]

After a search that had lasted almost a lifetime, Burns had finally found peace. With the encouragement of a friend named Betty Crawford, he began writing his memoirs. He finished them in the early 1950s, but was unable to elicit much interest in it. A number of publishers rejected the autobiography, which was never printed.

In May 1955, at the age of 73, he returned to Canada for the last time. He was visiting the Vancouver home of John Westaway, leader of an evangelical group known as the Temple of Christ Healing, when his long journey finally came to an end. Burns was descending a flight of stairs when he suddenly stopped, sat down and called out Westaway's name. By the time his friend reached him, Tommy Burns was dead of a heart attack. There had been no hint beforehand of trouble. "He seemed in good health. He didn't complain about not feeling well," Westaway said.[32]

The passing of this sports icon went virtually unnoticed. The *Detroit Free Press*, which had sent reporters around the globe to cover his championship fights, didn't even report his death. His obituary was carried in major Canadian newspapers, but many of those who read it were hearing about Burns for the first time in their lives. In Vancouver, meanwhile, it was discovered that the former champion had been virtually penniless, and he went to a pauper's grave in the city's Ocean View Cemetery. There was no funeral service, and only four people attended the burial — two gravediggers and a pair of strangers who happened to be passing by. Although two of his sisters were still living, neither made the long journey from Ontario to be in attendance. Nor did his wife make the trip from California. Newspaper accounts of the period give no hint as to why they didn't come. In his will, Burns left his few possessions to his third wife, Nellie. His four daughters, who were living in England, didn't receive a cent.

Burns lay under a patch of grass in an unmarked plot for five years before Vancouver sports writer Dick Beddoes reported how ignobly the former champion's remains had been disposed of by his own country-men. One of those who read the article was hockey star Cyclone Taylor, who described the situation as "a sad, sad business. Poor Noah never did seem to find much happiness, except perhaps in the last few years, when he turned to religion in desperation."[33]

Anxious to do something, Taylor sought out three British Columbia men who had known the teenaged Noah Brusso at the turn of the century. The four of them made a visit to the cemetery where, after a long search, they located the champ's final resting place. "We found it with great difficulty," Taylor said. "Just a mound of tangled grass, with no marking. Not even a number. We pledged to start a fund to buy a proper memorial tablet."[34] True to their collective word, they were back a couple of months later. With the help of Beddoes, they had raised $300 for a bronze plaque.

Thirty-seven people, including Beddoes and Cyclone Taylor, turned out on a blustery November 20, 1961, for a plaque-laying ceremony. A cold wind was blowing in off the Pacific Ocean. Rev. Arthur Turpin, whom Beddoes described as a grey man in a black army beret, asked the mostly elderly mourners to keep their hats on. "It's pretty chilly," he said. But most, anxious to show Burns the respect that had been missing at his 1955 burial, took them off anyway.

After the marker had been gently set down, Rev. Turpin spoke a few words. "There should be cheers for the fallen, whether winning or not," he said. "Nobody can take away from Tommy Burns what he did, although people forget."

One of the mourners, an old boxing fan named Jack Elliott, was reminded of lines from the poet M. J. McMahon:

> *Forgotten by 10,000 throats*
> *That thundered his acclaim*
> *Forgotten by his friends and foes*
> *Who cheered his very name*

Reverend Turpin called for the playing of "The Last Post" in recognition of Burns's service in the First World War.

"The last bugle note of *The Last Post* hung for an instant in the raw breeze, and then was gone," Beddoes wrote later. "Men put on their hats, shivering."[35]

Beddoes knelt down and placed a bouquet of flowers on the old boxer's grave.

Reverend Turpin, looking on, said slowly and deliberately, "The lonely warrior can rest in peace at last."[36]

Shortchanged by History

Was Tommy Burns a champ or a chump?

That question has been raised from time to time ever since the battle at Rushcutter's Bay. The general consensus through the years has been that the Canadian fighter was one of the worst heavyweight champions in history; possibly even the worst ever. In his 1974 book, *The Encyclopedia of World Boxing Champions Since 1882*, author John McCallum writes, "While there is plenty of room for argument as to who was the greatest heavyweight champion up to the retirement of Gene Tunney in 1928, there's very little doubt that Burns was the worst."[1] British sports writer Bert Blewett, writing as recently as 1996, described Burns as "one of boxing's more forgettable champions."[2] Scores of writers have branded him as a poor champion who compiled a phoney record against a pack of weaklings.

But was he? Or was he rather the victim of a smear campaign carried out by Jack London and his bigoted contemporaries?

In order to answer that question, we must look at the records of all the heavyweight champions who have reigned since the gloved era began with John L. Sullivan. That's no easy task — with so many governing bodies in boxing today, there are often two or three different "world champions" at any one time. To get around the problem, many boxing experts have learned to ignore the preposterous rulings of the various sanctioning groups. Instead, they recognize only the lineal champions, or "the man who beat the man," from Sullivan's era to the present.

During all of that time, from 1882 to 2000, only 35 men have held the lineal championship. Most of them, it should be added, were undisputed champions. Needless to say, they're members of a very exclusive club that includes in its ranks some of the most famous athletes who ever lived. Names such as Muhammad Ali, Joe Louis, Rocky Marciano, Gene Tunney, Mike Tyson, Jack Dempsey, Jack Johnson, Gentleman Jim Corbett and John L. Sullivan are still remembered by millions.

Burns, on the other hand, has been all but forgotten. That's puzzling, considering how his record compares to those of the other 34 champs. For Tommy Burns is at or near the top of just about any heavyweight record you could care to name. He's fifth, for example, in the number of successful title defenses, behind only Ali, Louis, Larry Holmes and Tyson. He defeated more challengers in the two years and 10 months he held the crown than Sullivan, Corbett, Fitzsimmons, Jeffries and Hart put together. And those five gentlemen were on the throne for a combined total of 24 years. In terms of knockout victories by a champion defending his title, Burns trails only Ali and Louis. And the Canadian still holds the record for most consecutive knockouts by a reigning champion. On top of that, his KO of Irishman Jem Roche was the fastest recorded by a heavyweight king. When it comes to first-round KO's by a champion, he's in second place with four, behind only Louis. Over his entire career, Burns's knockout percentage stood at .600. The great Gene Tunney, by way of comparison, had a KO percentage of only .537. Even the immortal Jack Dempsey, who is generally considered one of the hardest hitting boxers who ever lived, had a knockout percentage of only .605.

One of the few boxing writers ever to give Burns his due was John Lardner. Writing in *Newsweek* in 1956, he stated, "Tommy Burns has come down in tradition as one of the minor heavyweight champions, but it's likely he was better than anyone who has held the title since Gene Tunney, with the exception of Joe Louis, and perhaps, Rocky Marciano. Burns was not big, but he was strong, fast, and he could hit."

If we are to accept Lardner's expert opinion, it means Burns was better than heavyweight champions Max Schmeling, Jack Sharkey, Primo Carnera, Max Baer, James Braddock, Ezzard Charles, Jersey Joe Walcott and possibly even the fabled Rocky Marciano.

If we take a closer look at these men it becomes obvious that, with the exception of Marciano, none of them could hold a candle to Burns.

Burns in a classic fighting pose.

Schmeling won the title on a foul after being hit by a low blow from Sharkey. After that, he made just one successful defense before he was dethroned. What's more, the big German boxer lost twice as many career fights as Burns. As for Sharkey, he lost his title the first time he defended it and ended up with 13 career losses to go with just 38 wins. Carnera was big but basically unskilled. He made only two successful defenses before being defeated. And historians suspect many of his ring victories were recorded in fixed fights. Baer was yet another weak champion who lost his crown during his first defense. Indeed, he lost virtually all of his important fights and finished with three times as many defeats as Burns suffered during his career. Braddock was even worse. He also failed to make a single successful title defense and his overall won-lost record was a dreadful 46–23. Ezzard Charles wasn't much better, losing three of seven title fights. As for Walcott, he only won the crown on his fifth try. It's true he won 50 fights, but he suffered 18 defeats, a huge number for someone claiming to be an elite boxer.

By any objective standard Lardner was right — Burns was better than at least seven champions who reigned from 1928 to 1956. However, Lardner's assertion that Burns may have been better than Rocky Marciano is less convincing. The Brockton Blockbuster would likely have won any duel between the two. He was probably the best body puncher who ever lived. Besides that, he was incredibly tough. He proved that in his September 23, 1952, fight with Jersey Joe Walcott. Walcott battered him around the ring for 12 rounds, splitting his nose almost in half with one terrible smash. But Marciano refused to quit. In the thirteenth round he caught Walcott with a devastating right hand that knocked him out. The simple fact is that Marciano *always* won. Today, almost half a century after he retired, he remains the only undefeated heavyweight champion in history, with a perfect 49–0 won-lost record.

Lardner's comments, as interesting as they may be, address only the period from 1928 to 1956. What of the champions who reigned before that time? To suggest Burns was the worst champ from the beginning of the modern era in 1882 until the arrival of Gene Tunney is frankly ridiculous. For one thing, he defeated Marvin Hart for the title, which would suggest he was a better champion than the big Kentuckian. For another, he was a much better fighter than the fabled John L. Sullivan.

Sullivan is listed in virtually every boxing history as an all-time great. But in fact, he wasn't a skilled prizefighter at all. Most of his career was spent knocking out raw amateurs, many of whom had never been in a professional boxing ring in their lives. After becoming heavyweight champion he defended his title just three times, winning only one of those fights. He drew a second and lost the third. And it should not be forgotten that he ducked the excellent black fighters of his era, including such noted boxers as Peter Jackson and George Godfrey. He was a crude, straight-ahead fighter who was better suited to bar-room brawling than prizefighting. More than that, he was a ring bully who didn't know what to do when he came up against a stylish opponent. Tommy Burns boxed circles around dozens of such men. Had the two men met in their primes, the scientific, fleet-footed Canadian would likely have cut the big man to pieces. As Australian boxing historian Jeff Wells has noted, had Sullivan spotted little Tommy in a saloon, "He might have laughed enough to spill his beer. However, had he challenged Burns, the Boston Strongboy would soon have been rolling in the sawdust."[3]

A strong case could also be made that Burns was a better fighter than Jess Willard. Willard took the title from an ageing Jack Johnson in 1915, but he won only 23 of 35 fights. He was a hulking giant but, like Sullivan, he knew nothing about the finer points of the game. He beat Johnson only because he was younger and better able to handle the sweltering heat of Havana, Cuba, where the fight was held. Johnson was winning most of the way but eventually wilted in the 39°C temperature. Willard subsequently defended the title just twice, fighting a lacklustre no-decision match with an unknown named Frank Moran before losing to Jack Dempsey.

In any case, the addition of Sullivan, Hart and Willard to Lardner's list gives us 10 champs between 1882 and 1956 whom Burns would likely have beaten hands down.

How would Burns have done in the era from 1956 to the present? Most fight fans believe the oldtimers would fare poorly against the big, modern heavyweights and they're probably right. Today's fighters have the advantage of better training methods, superior coaching and healthier diets. But although it's hard to imagine little Tommy Burns beating many of the men who have held the lineal title since Marciano's time, there are several he could have defeated. The names Floyd Patterson, Ingeman Johannson, Leon Spinks, Michael Spinks, Buster Douglas, Michael Moorer and Shannon Briggs come immediately to mind.

Patterson was a gentleman who seemed to lack the killer instinct. Although highly talented, he lost 8 of 64 fights, including four with the title on the line. Most of his successful defenses were against easy pickings. One of his challengers was Peter Rademacher, who was appearing in his first professional fight! Johansson, who won the crown by upsetting Patterson, almost always lost when the chips were down. As an amateur he suffered the shame of being disqualified during an Olympic gold medal bout for "not trying" against American Eddie Sanders.[4] And in his three world heavyweight championship fights he lost twice. He had a powerful right hand but would have been no match for Burns when it came to infighting or the will to win. Leon Spinks defeated an ageing Muhammad Ali in 1978, then lost the crown during his first title defense and faded from the scene. His brother, Michael, won only two title fights before being destroyed by Mike Tyson. Buster Douglas won the championship by upsetting a poorly trained Tyson, then lost it eight months later in his first defense. In all, he lost 16 of 60 fights. Briggs was probably the worst of them all. He won the title after scoring a hotly disputed victory over 46-year-old George Foreman, then lost the crown while making his initial defense.

That gives us at least 17 champions whom Burns would likely have defeated in any head-to-head encounter. There are several others he might have been able to beat with just a little luck. It should not be forgotten, for instance, that Burns beat Fireman Jim Flynn when Flynn was in his prime. Several years later, an ageing Flynn knocked out Jack Dempsey in a non-title fight. That isn't to say that Burns was better than Dempsey, but it does suggest he could have held his own against the famed Manassa Mauler. Nor should we forget that Nat Fleischer, the most famous boxing writer of the twentieth century, once said Burns was a harder hitter than Tunney or Corbett and one of the best infighters ever.

The claim that Burns fought mostly lemons and second-raters is likewise nonsense. He took on most of the best fighters of his generation. Men like Hart, O'Brien, Flynn, Squires, Moir and Johnson were

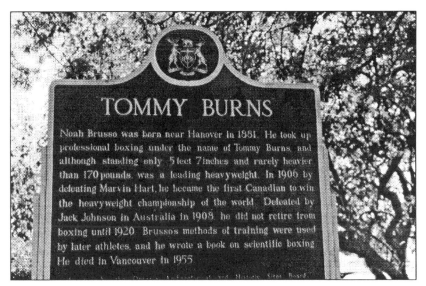

A plaque on the outskirts of Hanover, Ontario commemorates the career of Tommy Burns.

all considered dangerous challengers when Burns went up against them. Most, in fact, were favoured in the betting prior to fight time.

Instead of relying on racist writers of the early twentieth century when judging Burns, we should take a close look at his record. It is, without question, one of the best ever assembled by any boxer in any weight category. This fact has been ignored by many writers, but it has not gone unnoticed by some big-name boxers.

George Chuvalo, the famous Canadian fighter of the 1960s and 1970s, said, "For a man of his size he was quite something. From what I've seen in old film clips, he was quick and he moved quite well."[5] Mike Tyson, who has made a study of all the heavyweight champions down through the years, summed up the Canadian simply when asked his opinion: "Tommy Burns was a good fighter."[6]

But Burns should not be remembered just because he was handy with his fists. First and foremost, he should be honoured as one of the men who broke the colour line in big-time sports. Of his 62 official fights, 8 were against black boxers — two with Fred Thornton and one each with Harry Peppers, Billy Moore, Jack Butler, Billy Woods, Earl Thompson and Jack Johnson. Counting his exhibition bouts with Thompson, Moore and Woods, he went into the ring against black fighters no less than 11 times. He also took part in a large number of public sparring sessions with black heavyweight Klondike Haynes. And if fate hadn't interfered in the form of a 1911 train wreck, he would have met Sam Langford as well. In other words, when it came to defying the colour line, he was, by far, the most progressive white boxer of his era. He fought more blacks than Sullivan, Corbett and Jeffries combined. Of course, there had been the odd fight between black and white boxers before Burns came along, but never with the World Heavyweight Boxing Championship on the line. Once a black man was given the opportunity to compete for what was in those days the most prestigious sporting title on earth, it was only a matter of time before blacks would take part in all the other professional sports as well. Several white champions reinstated the colour line after Burns left the scene, but the genie was out of the bottle. Although he has received almost no credit for it, Burns helped integrate the world of professional sports. Without question, it was his greatest accomplishment.

Of course his motives were not purely altruistic, but the perceptive Billy Woods hit the nail on the head when he said what Burns did was far more important than what he said or thought. And what he did was give black athletes a chance to compete at the major-league level when virtually no one else — in or out of boxing — was doing so. He also employed and socialized with people of colour in an era when such things simply weren't done.

Besides that, he helped curb the shameless exploitation of professional athletes of all colours. Until his reign, most sports figures were paid dirt wages. Boxers, who put their health — and even their lives — on the line every time they entered the ring, were paid only a few dollars at a time. Burns helped reverse that practise by demanding — and getting — big purses. The $30,000 he made at Rushcutter's Bay was an unheard-of figure for the time. But just 13 years later Jack Dempsey got $1 million for a single fight. Today, many professional athletes in all the major sports are wealthy, and they can thank Tommy Burns for helping to make it possible. He was, without doubt, one of the architects of big-money athletics.

If all that wasn't enough, Burns also helped revolutionize training methods for professional athletes. Until he appeared on the scene,

The author at the Burns commemorative plaque in Hanover, Ontario.

training was exceptionally tedious and primitive. After he started winning on a regular basis, athletes everywhere copied his innovative techniques, forsaking long walks for swimming, climbing and more gym work. Some of them are still in use today.

As we enter the new millennium, prizefighting appears to be in decline. Championship bouts are still watched by millions, but boxing no longer captures the public imagination the way it once did. More and more people see it as a senseless, brutal pastime in which violence is glorified and brain cells are destroyed. But that doesn't change the fact that Tommy Burns was one of the most important sports figures of his time. Surely, after ignoring him for almost a century, Canadians can finally recognize his personal bravery and athletic skill, regardless of how they view the sport at which he excelled.

Photo Credits

Boxing Record of
Tommy Burns

The following is a list of all 70 of Tommy Burns's bouts and their outcomes. Abbreviations used:

KO — Knockout victory
TKO — Technical knockout
W — won on points
L — lost on points
ND — No decision
D — Draw

Date	Opponent	Result/no. rounds	Remarks
1900			
Dec.	Fred Thornton	KO 5	
1901			
Jan. 2	Billy Walsh	KO 2	
Jan. 3	Archie Steele	KO 1	
Jan. 4	Ed Sholtreau	KO 1	
Jan. 5	Billy Walsh	KO 6	
1902			
Jan. 16	Fred Thornton	KO 5	
Mar. 3	Harry Peppers	KO 2	

Mar. 5	George Steele	KO 2
May 16	Ed Sholtreau	W 10
Jun. 27	Dick Smith	KO 2
Jul. 9	Dick Smith	W 10
Sept. 19	Jack O'Donnell	KO 8
Oct. 24	Billy Moore	Exhibition bout
Nov. 6	Reddy Phillips	KO 9
Dec. 8	Jim Corbett	Exhibition bout

1903

Jan. 16	Mike Schreck	L 10
Feb. 13	Jim O'Brien	W 10
Mar. 25	Dick Smith	KO 2
Mar. 25	Reddy Phillips	KO 3
Apr. 18	Earl Thompson	KO 3
Sept. 25	Jimmy Duggan	KO 9
Oct. 12	Jack Hammond	KO 3
Oct. 25	Billy Moore	D 10
Nov. 8	Jack Butler	KO 2
Nov. 25	Jack O'Donnell	KO 11
Dec. 31	Tom McCune	W 10

1904

Jan. 28	Ben O'Grady	KO 3
Feb. 26	George Shrosbee	KO 5
Feb. 27	Mike Schreck	D 6
Mar. 18	Tony Caponi	D 6
Apr. 9	Tony Caponi	W 6
Jul.	Joe Wardinski	KO 1
Aug.	Klondike Mike Mahoney	L 3
Aug. 20	William Cyclone Kelly	KO 4
Sept. 16	Billy Woods	D 15
Oct. 7	Jack O'Brien	L 6

1905

Jan. 31	Indian Joe Schildt	KO 6
Mar. 7	Jack Twin Sullivan	D 20
May 3	Dave Barry	W 20
Jun. 7	Hugo Kelly	D 10
Jul. 28	Hugo Kelly	D 20
Aug. 31	Dave Barry	KO 20
Oct. 17	Jack Twin Sullivan	L 20

1906

Feb. 23	Marvin Hart	W 20; won world heavyweight title
Mar. 28	Jim O'Brien	KO 1
Mar. 28	Jim Walker	KO 1
Oct. 2	Jim Flynn	KO 15
Nov. 28	Jack O'Brien	D 20

1907

Jan. 10	Joe Grim	W 3
May 7	Billy Woods	Exhibition bout
May 8	Jack O'Brien	W 20
Jul. 4	Bill Squires	KO 1
Dec. 2	Gunner Moir	KO 10
Dec. 16	Charlie Wilson	Exhibition bout

1908

Feb. 10	Jack Palmer	KO 4
Mar. 17	Jem Roche	KO 1
Apr. 14	Johnny Douglas	Exhibition bout
Apr. 18	Jewey Smith	KO 5
Jun. 13	Bill Squires	KO 8
Aug. 24	Bill Squires	KO 13
Sept. 2	Billy Lang	KO 6
Nov.	Snowy Baker	Exhibition, 4
Dec. 26	Jack Johnson	L 14; lost world heavyweight title

1910

Apr. 7	Billy Lang	W 20
May 2	Larry Foley	Exhibition bout

1912

Aug. 8	Bill Rickard	KO 6

1913

Apr. 2	Arthur Pelkey	ND 6

1914

Jan. 26	Battling Brant	KO 4

1918

Sept. 19	Tex Foster	KO 4

1920

Jul. 16	Joe Beckett	TKO loss

Sources

Ali, Muhammad, with Richard Durham. *The Greatest: My Own Story*. New York: Random House, 1975.

Batchelor, Denzil. *Jack Johnson and His Times*. London: Phoenix Sports Books, 1956.

Batten, Jack. *Champions: Great Figures in Canadian Sport*. Toronto: New Press, 1971.

Berton, Pierre. *Klondike: The Last Great Gold Rush, 1896–1899*. Toronto: McClelland & Stewart Inc., 1972.

Berton, Pierre. *The Promised Land. Settling the West. 1896–1914*. Toronto: McClelland & Stewart Inc., 1988.

Birmingham, Stephen. *California Rich*. New York: Simon and Schuster, 1980.

Blewett, Bert. *The A to Z of World Boxing*. London: Robson Books, 1996.

Bohum, Lynch. *Knuckles and Gloves*. London: W. Collins, 1992.

Bowen, Ezra. *This Fabulous Century 1900–1910*. Volume 1. New York: Time-Life Books, 1970.

Brooke-Ball, Peter. *The Boxing Album: An Illustrated History*. London: Acropolis Books, 1995.

Burns, Tommy. *Scientific Boxing and Self-Defence*. London: Health and Science, 1908.

Burrill, Bob. *Who's Who In Boxing*. New Rochelel, New York: Arlington House, 1974.

Campbell, Cork, editor. *Normanby Reflections: A History of Normanby Township*. Compiled and published by the Normandy history committee, 1989.

Coates, Ken S. and William R. Morrison. *Land of the Midnight Sun: A History of the Yukon*. Edmonton: Hurtig Publishers, 1988.

Corri, Eugene. *Gloves and the Man: The Romance of the Ring*. London: Hutchinson and Co. (Publishers) Ltd.

De Coy, Robert H. *The Big Black Fire*. Los Angeles: Holland House Publishing Co., 1969.

Denison, Merrill. *Klondike Mike: An Alaskan Odyssey*. New York: William Morrow Co. Publishers, 1943.

Durant, John. *The Heavyweight Champions*. New York: Hasting House Publishers, 1964.

Farr, Finis. *Chicago: A Personal History of America's Most American City*. New Rochelle, New York: Arlington House, 1973.

Fleischer, Nat. *Fifty Years at Ringside*. New York: Greenwood Press Publishers, 1969.

Fleischer, Nat. *The Heavyweight Championship: An Informal History of Heavy-weight Boxing from 1917 to the Present Day.* New York: G.P. Putnam's Sons, 1949.

Gilmore, Al-Tony. *Bad Nigger! The National Impact of Jack Johnson.* Port Washington, New York: National University Publications. Kennikat Press, 1975.

Glazer, Sidney, *Detroit: A Study in Urban Development.* New York: Bookman Associates Inc., 1965.

Greig, Murray. *Goin' the Distance: Canada's Boxing Heritage.* Toronto: MacMillan Canada, 1996.

Grombach, John V. *The Saga of the Fist: The 9,000 Year Story of Boxing in Text and Pictures.* South Brunswick and New York: A.S. Barnes and Co., 1977.

Hall, Rodney. *Journey Through Australia.* London: John Murray Publishers Ltd., 1988.

Hamilton, Walter R. *The Yukon Story.* Vancouver: Mitchell Press Ltd., 1964.

Houston, Graham. *Superfights.* New York: Bounty. 1975.

Holli, Melvin, G., editor. *Detroit.* New Viewpoints. New York. 1976.

Jakowbek, Robert. *Jack Johnson Heavyweight Champion.* New York/Philadelphia. Chelsea House Publishers, 1990.

Johnson, Jack. *In the Ring and Out.* London: Proteus Publishing Ltd., 1977.

Johnston, Alexander. *Ten and Out! The Complete Story of the Prize Ring in America.* New York: Ives Washburn Publishers, 1947.

Liebling, A.J. *A Neutral Corner. Boxing Essays.* San Francisco: North Point Press, 1990.

May, Ernest R. and the editors of Time-Life Books. *The Life History of the United States. Vol. 9: 1901–1917. The Progressive Era.* New York: Time-Life Books, 1964.

McCallum, John D. *The Encyclopedia of World Boxing Champions.* Radnor, Pennsylvania: Chilton Book Co., 1975.

Mullan, Harry. *The Ultimate Encyclopedia of Boxing: The Definite Guide to World Boxing.* London: Carlton Books Ltd., 1996.

Myler, Patrick. *Gentleman Jim Corbett: The Truth Behind a Boxing Legend.* London: Robson Books, 1998.

Newman, Peter C. *Portrait of a Promised Land: Canada — 1892.* Toronto: A Madison Press Book produced for McCelland & Stewart Inc. and Penguin Books Canada, 1992.

Oates, Joyce Carol. *On Boxing.* Hopewell, New Jersey: The Ecco Press, 1994.

Plimpton, George. *Shadow Box.* New York: G. P. Putnam's Sons, 1977.

Reid, Brian. *Our Little Army in the Field. The Canadians in South Africa. 1899–1902.* St. Catharines, Ontario: Vanwell Publishing Ltd., 1996.

Remnick, David. *King of the World.* New York: Random House, 1998.

Roberts, Randy. *Papa Jack: Jack Johnson and the Era of the White Hopes.* New York: The Free Press (a division of Macmillan Inc.), 1993.

Roxborough, Henry. *Great Days in Canadian Sport.* Toronto: Ryerson Press, 1957.

Suster, Gerald. *Champions of the Ring: The Lives and Times of Boxing's Heavy-weight Heroes.* London: Robson Books, 1992.

Webb, Michael. *Happy Birthday Hollywood! One Hundred Years of Magic 1887–1987*. Hollywood, California: Published by the Motion Picture Television Fund, 1987.

Wells, Jeff. *Boxing Day: The Fight that Changed the World*. Sydney: Harper Collins Publishers Pty Limited, 1998.

Whitehead, Eric. *Cyclone Taylor: A Hockey Legend*. Toronto: Doubleday Canada Ltd., 1977.

Wise, S.F. and Douglas Fisher. *Canada's Sporting Heroes*. Don Mills, Ontario: General Publishing Co. Ltd., 1974.

Newspapers/Magazines

Canada

Globe/Globe and Mail, Toronto Star, Toronto Sun, London Free Press, Vancouver Sun, Vancouver World, Calgary Herald, Edmonton Journal, Winnipeg Tribune, Montreal Star, Halifax Herald, Hanover Post, Galt Weekly Reporter, Woodstock Sentinel Review, Sarnia Observer, Maclean's, The Canadian Sportsman

United States

Detroit Free Press, Detroit Times, Detroit News, Lansing Journal,Chicago Tribune, Chicago Inter-Ocean, Newsweek, San Francisco Examiner, Cincinnati Inquirer, Seattle Times, New York Sun, New York Times, New York Police Gazette, New York Herald, St. Louis Post-Dispatch, The Ring, KO Magazine, World Boxing, Boxing Illustrated, Boxing Digest, Boxing 91

Ireland

Irish Times, Irish Independent

United Kingdom

London Times, The London Sportsman, London Express, The Daily Mail, The Sporting News

Australia

Fairplay, The Lone Hand, Sydney Illustrated Sporting and Dramatic News, The Australian Star, The Sydney Referee

Notes

Introduction

1. Associated Press, March 5, 1882.
2. Robert De Coy, *The Big Black Fire* (Los Angeles: Holland House, 1969), 27.
3. Patrick Myler, *Gentleman Jim Corbett* (London: Robson, 1998), 178.
4. Jeff Wells, *Boxing Day* (Sydney: Harper Collins, 1998), 109.
5. Red Wilson, interview.
6. Gerald Suster, *Champions of the Ring* (London: Robson, 1992), 43.

Chapter One

1. Ted Huehn, interview.
2. Peter Newman, *Portrait of a Promised Land* (Toronto: McClelland & Stewart, 1992), 142.
3. *Cambridge Times*, Sept. 4, 1996.
4. *London Free Press*, Dec. 5, 1907.
5. *Globe and Mail* magazine, July 3, 1971.
6. *Globe and Mail* magazine, July 3, 1971.
7. Phyllis Huddart, interview.
8. *Cambridge Times*, Sept. 4, 1996.
9. Red Wilson, interview.
10. Joyce Carol Oates, *On Boxing* (Hopewell: The Echo Press, 1994), 28.
11. Red Wilson, interview.
12. Audrey Adamson, interview.
13. *Cambridge Times*, Sept. 4, 1996.
14. *London Free Press*, Feb. 6, 1907.
15. *Cambridge Times*, Sept. 4, 1996.
16. *Cambridge Times*, Sept. 4, 1996.
17. *Globe*, Dec. 7, 1907.
18. Undated *Sarnia Observer* column, Red Wilson collection.
19. Red Wilson, interview.
20. Sydney Glazer, *Detroit* (New York: Bookman, 1965), 77.

21. Henry Roxborough, *Great Days in Canadian Sport* (Toronto: Ryerson, 1967), 69.
22. Al Rosaasen, interview.
23. *London Free Press*, Dec. 15, 1905.
24. Roxborough, 70.
25. Murray Greig, *Goin' the Distance* (Toronto: MacMillan, 1996), 17.
26. Red Wilson, interview.
27. *Globe and Mail* magazine, July 3, 1971.
28. *Globe and Mail*, July 3, 1971.
29. Greig, 11.

Chapter Two

1. Red Wilson, interview.
2. Robert Jakowbek, *Jack Johnson Heavyweight Champion* (New York: Chelsea House), 32.
3. Muhammad Ali, *The Greatest* (New York: Random House, 1975), 324.
4. Ali, 325.
5. Brian Reid, *Our Little Army in the Field* (St. Catharines: Vanwell, 1996), 6.
6. Red Wilson, interview.
7. Lynch Bohum, *Knuckles and Gloves* (London: Collins, 1992), 151.
8. Randy Roberts, *Papa Jack* (New York: The Free Press, 1993), 64.
9. Joe Louis, interview.
10. Audrey Adamson, interview.
11. Al Rosaasen, interview.
12. *Globe and Mail*, July 3, 1971.
13. Ali, 98.
14. Al Rosaasen, interview.
15. Red Wilson, interview.
16. David Remnick, *King of the World* (New York: Random House, 1998), 24.
17. Red Wilson, interview.
18. Red Wilson, interview.
19. Tommy Burns, *Scientific Boxing and Self-Defence* (London: Health and Science, 1908), 116.
20. Burns, 116.
21. Burns, 116.
22. Oates, 73.
23. Red Wilson, interview.

Chapter Three

1. Audrey Adamson, interview.
2. *The Lone Hand*, Dec., 1908.
3. Audrey Adamson, interview.

4. *Globe and Mail*, July 3, 1971.

5. Fred Phipps, interview.

6. Ezra Bowen, *This Fabulous Century* (New York: Time-Life, 1964), 34.

7. Eugene Corri, *Gloves and the Man* (London: Hutchinson), 32.

8. Red Wilson, interview.

9. Al Rosaasen, interview.

10. *London Free Press*, April 22, 1907.

11. Burns, 166.

12. Newman, 142

Chapter Four

1. Burns, 164.

2. Red Wilson, interview.

3. Red Wilson, interview.

4. Bert Blewett, *The A to Z of World Boxing* (London: Robson Books, 1996), 240.

5. Finis Farr, *Chicago* (New Rochelle: Arlington House, 1973), 282.

6. Farr, 297.

7. Red Wilson, interview.

8. Pierre Berton, *The Klondike* (Toronto: McCelland & Stewart), 367.

9. Berton, 367.

10. Al Rosaasen, interview.

11. William Denison, *Klondike Mike* (New York: Morrow, 1943), 298.

12. Al Rosassen, interview.

13. Denison, 298.

14. Al Rosassen, interview.

15. Denison, 298.

16. Denison, picture page.

17. Denison, 298.

18. Al Rosassen, interview.

Chapter Five

1. Wells, 85.

2. Audrey Adamson, interview.

3. Stephen Birmingham, *California Rich* (New York: Simon and Schuster, 1980), 107.

4. Michael Webb, *Happy Birthday Hollywood* (Hollywood: Motion Picture Television Fund, 1987), 25.

5. Birmingham, 107.

6. Burns, 96.

7. *The Lone Hand*, Dec. 1908.

8. Burns, 96.

9. Red Wilson, interview.

10. Joe Louis, interview.

11. Red Wilson, interview.

12. A.J. Liebling, *A Neutral Corner* (San Francisco: North Point Press, 1990), 30.

13. Roxborough, 71.

14. *Boxing* 91 magazine, January, 1991, 21.

Chapter Six

1. Harry Mullen, *The Ultimate Encyclopedia of Boxing* (London: Carlton, 1996), 85.

2. *Globe and Mail,* Aug. 5, 1997.

3. *Globe and Mail,* Aug. 5, 1997.

4. *London Free Press,* Sept. 15, 1906.

5. Greig, 16.

6. Jakowbek, 43.

7. Jakowbek, 39.

8. Jakowbek, 39.

9. *Boxing Illustrated,* 1960.

10. Red Wilson, interview.

11. Nat Fleischer, *The Heavyweight Championship* (New York: Putnam, 1949), 138.

12. *Boxing* 91, January 1991, 20.

13. *London Free Press,* Feb. 20, 1906.

14. Red Wilson, interview.

15. *London Free Press,* Nov. 20, 1905.

16. Undated *Mclean's* magazine article in Burns file, Canadian Sports Hall of Fame.

17. *London Free Press,* Nov. 20, 1905.

18. *Detroit Free Press,* Feb. 23, 1906.

19. *Detroit Free Press,* Feb. 23, 1906.

20. Red Wilson, interview.

21. Greig, 17.

22. *Globe and Mail,* July 3, 1971.

23. *Boxing* 91, January 1991.

24. Eric Whitehead, *Cyclone Taylor* (Toronto: Doubleday, 1997), 47.

25. Whitehead, 47.

26. *Globe,* March 1, 1906.

27. *Globe,* Feb. 1906.

28. Unidentified clipping, Burns file, Hanover Public Library.

29. Red Wilson, interview.

Chapter Seven

1. *Globe,* Dec. 3, 1907.

2. *Sunday Sun,* Dec. 24, 1989.

3. *Winnipeg Tribune,* Dec. 10, 1910.

4. Ernest May, *The Life History of the United States* (New York: Time-Life, 1964), 62.

5. Bowen, 244.

6. *Winnipeg Tribune*, March 19, 1910.

7. *Detroit Free Press*, Dec. 2, 1906.

8. Red Wilson, interview.

9. S.F. Wise, Douglas Fisher, *Canada's Sporting Heroes* (Don Mills: General, 1974), 139.

10. Wells, 70.

11. Corri, 30.

12. *Globe*, Nov. 1906.

13. *Globe*, Dec. 1, 1906.

14. *London Free Press*, Nov. 29, 1906.

15. *London Free Press*, Nov. 29, 1906.

16. *The Ring*, Dec. 1990.

17. George Plimpton, *Shadow Box* (New York: Putnam, 1977), 185.

18. *The Ring*, Dec. 1990.

19. *The Ring*, Dec. 1990.

20. *The Ring*, Dec. 1990.

21. Plimpton, 185.

22. Denzil Batchelor, *Jack Johnson and His Times* (London: Phoenix, 1956), 56.

23. Red Wilson, interview.

24. Red Wilson, interview.

25. Batchelor, 57.

26. Batchelor, 57.

27. *London Free Press*, May 10, 1907.

28. *Boxing* 91, Jan. 1991, 65.

29. *Globe*, May 10, 1907.

30. *London Free Press*, May 15, 1907.

31. *London Free Press*, Feb. 5, 1907.

Chapter Eight

1. *London Free Press*, April 25, 1907

2. *Detroit Free Press*, July, 1907.

3. *London Free Press*, July, 1907.

4. *London Free Press*, Jan. 15, 1907.

5. *London Free Press*, April, 1907.

6. Unidentified newspaper clipping, Burns file, Hanover Public Library.

7. Greig, 19.

8. *London Free Press*, June 7, 1907.

9. *London Free Press*, July 5, 1907.

10. *London Free Press*, Sept. 13, 1907.

11. Burns, 26.

12. Greig, 21.

13. Robert De Coy, *The Big Black Fire* (Los Angeles: Holland House, 1969), 22.

14. De Coy, 25.

15. Bohum, 149.

16. *Globe*, Jan. 23, 1908.

17. *Cambridge Times*, Sept. 4, 1996.

18. *Cambridge Times*, Sept. 4, 1996.

19. *London Free Press*, Sept. 12, 1907.

20. *Globe*, Jan. 7, 1908.

Chapter Nine

1. *London Free Press*, Nov. 15, 1907.

2. *Grand Rapids Free Press*, November 1907.

3. Roberts, 51.

4. Roberts, 51.

5. *Irish Independent*, March 3, 1908.

6. *London Free Press*, Nov. 15, 1907.

7. *Detroit Free Press*, Nov. 1907.

8. *London Free Press*, April 24, 1908.

9. *London Free Press*, Nov. 15, 1907.

10. Corri, 30.

11. Graham Houston, *Superfights* (New York: Bounty, 1975), 71.

12. *Globe*, Dec. 3, 1907.

13. *Globe*, Dec. 1907.

14. *Globe*, Dec. 4, 1907.

15. *Globe*, Dec. 10, 1907.

16. *Vancouver World*, Dec. 27, 1910.

17. *Globe*, April 1908.

18. *Globe*, Dec. 17, 1907.

19. Burns, 34.

20. Batchelor, 61.

21. *Globe*, Dec. 5, 1907.

22. *Globe*, May 11, 1908.

23. *Globe*, April 1908.

24. *London Free Press*, April 22, 1908.

25. De Coy, 72.

26. Whitehead, 92.

27. *Globe*, May 11, 1908.

28. De Coy, 66.

29. *London Free Press*, May 30, 1908.

30. *Irish Independent*, March 11, 1908.

31. *Irish Independent*, March 10, 1908.

32. *Globe*, February 11, 1908.

33. *Irish Independent*, March 16, 1908.

34. *Globe*, March 14, 1908.

35. Greig, 20.

36. Roxborough, 74.

37. *Globe*, March 18, 1907.

38. *Globe and Mail*, July 3, 1971.

39. Batchelor, 61.

40. Red Wilson interview.

41. Corri, 172.

Chapter Ten

1. Wells, 83.

2. Roberts, 55.

3. Roberts, 55.

4. *Winnipeg Tribune*, Sept. 24, 1910.

5. *Globe*, Oct. 5, 1908.

6. Wells, 106.

7. *Globe*, Oct. 5, 1908.

8. Rodney Hall, *Journey through Australia* (London: Murray, 1988), 176.

9. Jack Johnson, *In the Ring and Out* (London: Proteus. 1977), 126.

10. Roberts, 56.

11. Johnson, 128.

12. *Globe and Mail*, July 3, 1971.

13. Corri, 31.

14. *The Lone Hand*, Dec. 1908.

15. *Chicago Tribune*, Sept. 23, 1908.

16. *Globe*, Nov. 3, 1908.

17. *Globe*, Nov. 6, 1908.

18. *Sydney Referee*, Dec. 1908.

19. *London Free Press*, Dec. 24, 1908.

20. Batchelor, 68.

21. *Globe and Mail*, July 3, 1971.

22. Batchelor, 69.

23. *Globe and Mail*, July 3, 1971.

24. Batchelor, 71.

25. Roberts, 62.

26. Batchelor, 71.

27. Batchelor, 72.

28. *Globe*, Dec. 26, 1908.

29. Wells, 166.

30. *Globe and Mail*, July 3, 1971.

Chapter Eleven

1. *Globe*, Dec. 27, 1908.

2. Greig, 30.

3. Al-Tony Gilmore, *Bad Nigger!* (Port Washington: Kennikat Press, 1975), 71.

4. *Globe*, Dec., 1908.

5. *Globe*, Dec. 26, 1909.

6. *London Free Press*, Jan. 4, 1909.

7. *Globe*, Dec. 26, 1908.

8. Wise/Fisher, 138.

9. Wells, 167.

10. Wells, 189.

11. Wise/Fisher, 137.

12. Fleischer, 137.

13. Pierre Berton, *The Promised Land* (Toronto: McCelland and Stewart, 1998), 334.

14. De Coy, 114.

15. De Coy, 113.

16. De Coy, 111.

17. De Coy, 125.

18. *Halifax Herald*, Nov. 15, 1910.

19. *Winnipeg Tribune*, March 23, 1911.

20. *Calgary Herald*, May 25, 1913.

21. *Globe and Mail*, July 3, 1971.

22. *London Free Press*, Feb. 18, 1954.

23. Burns file, Canadian Sports Hall of Fame.

24. John McCallum, *The Encyclopedia of World Boxing Champions* (Radnor: Chilton, 1973), 16.

25. Whitehead, 195.

26. Red Wilson, interview.

27. *Cambridge Times*, Sept. 4, 1996.

28. *Globe and Mail*, July 3, 1971.

29. *Globe and Mail*, July 3, 1971.

30. Whitehead, 195.

31. *Sunday Sun*, Dec. 24, 1989.

32. *Hanover Post*, May 1955.

33. Whitehead, 196.

34. Whitehead, 196.

35. *Cambridge Times*, Sept. 7, 1996.

36. *Cambridge Times*, Sept. 7, 1996.

37. Red Wilson, interview.

Chapter Twelve

1. McCallum, 16.

2. Blewett, 149.

3. Wells, 61.

4. Mullen, 36.

5. *Toronto Sun*, Jan. 17, 1996.

6. Suster, 43.

Index